Praise for *The Best Game Ever:*

"Bowden, a skilled journalist . . . has written *The Best Game Ever* as a labor of love. . . . His explanations of shifts in the teams' offensive and defensive strategies are lucid, and he knows enough about the extreme physical and mental demands the game exacts to convey a strong sense of the players' exhaustion and determination as the contest ground toward its conclusion. . . . *The Best Game Ever* is sure to become an instant sacred text."

—Jonathan Yardley, *The Washington Post*

"Mr. Bowden succeeds in making a contest from a half-century ago seem fresh, in part because he has a keen sense for the anecdotal. . . . [His] best trick, though, is that he gets out of the way of a great story and a great game."　—Steve Wulf, *The Wall Street Journal*

"A tremendously detailed play-by-play account of the game that helps the reader reconstruct what many people said then and still say now—it was the greatest game ever played."

—Profootballweekly.com

"Bowden dives into the trenches of the 1958 NFL Championship game, where New York and Baltimore waged an overtime battle that wowed TV audiences and ensured the future of pro football. . . . He astutely contrasts Frank Gifford's glamorous Giants with the blue-collar Colts of Johnny Unitas."　—*Entertainment Weekly*

"A sharp look at the 1958 National Football League Championship game . . . [Bowden] wisely focuses on a few individuals—Johnny Unitas, Raymond Berry, Weeb Ewbank, Art Donovan of the Colts; Frank Gifford, Sam Huff, Vince Lombardi, and Tom Landry of the Giants—to explain the game's singular link to the NFL's past and future. The author deftly examines the larger historical context shaping this coming-of-age moment, which propelled professional football to its current position as America's favorite sport. . . . A delight for anyone interested in the history of the NFL."

—*Kirkus Reviews*

W9-BPP-166

"Bowden handles [the story] deftly, using a spare writing style to illuminate the historic tussle." —*Newsday*

"The secret to great nonfiction is to build suspense around events to which your readers already know the outcome. . . . And it's in this key area that Mark Bowden largely succeeds in *The Best Game Ever* . . . [We] were enamored by the countless little details recounted by Bowden that added rich texture to *The Best Game Ever*." —ColdHardFootballFacts.com

"Bowden does a marvelous job focusing on the most memorable anecdotes and characters. Resisting the temptation to throw everything but the water cooler into the post-game analytical mix, Bowden delivers a relatively modest and understated account. His smartest move is to highlight the enigmatic Berry and the means by which he molded himself into one of the first great receivers in the history of the league. I've been to too many NFL games in Oakland and Candlestick to share that ESPN–mandated reverence for the pro game, but I walked away from this book a much bigger fan of Berry and Bowden." —*The Oregonian*

"A great buy . . . [*The Best Game Ever*] is not just aimed at the fans of a certain age that actually remember the game; Bowden shows its relevancy toward the development of the modern game of football." —Bleacherreport.com

"Bowden weaves the text seamlessly from the events of the game to the players to the coaches to the plays and the strategy behind the game. Showing how everything came together, he recaptures the excitement of the occasion and brings the story alive on the page." —Diane Scharper, *The Baltimore Sun*

"A fascinating character study of some of the game's most interesting players, and a history lesson about the place of sports in post-war America . . . In the wrong hands, such an undertaking could have turned into the stuff of high school history textbooks, but Bowden is the perfect writer for this job."—NFL.Fanhouse.com

"Befitting a skilled reporter, Bowden uncovers new material to enliven his retelling. His interviews with several Colts and Giants players, as well as with the Colts' then-assistant coach Charley Winner, yield new insights. In particular, receiver Raymond Berry's detailed game notes from the day itself are invaluable, as are excerpts from the transcript of the NBC radio broadcast by Joe Boland. . . . This book is a fine account of one of the most significant games in sports history."   —*Library Journal*

"Entertaining and informative narration . . . [Bowden] frames the picture with a wide lens, but then focuses on the roles and lives of a few key players."   —*Publishers Weekly*

"With the same precision he used to dissect a firefight in Mogadishu, Bowden anatomizes the 1958 NFL Championship between the Baltimore Colts and the New York Giants, which featured a death-defying comeback by the Colts and was also one of America's first 'truly communal live national events.'" —*Time*

"[Bowden's] latest account feels definitive, not needing future retellings. . . . This is a familiar story, well told."
        —*The Philadelphia Inquirer*

"Tight and tidy . . . As we become more familiar with the participants in this drama, there is a shock of recognition on seemingly every page. It is remarkable learning what these men, who all played in one game, went on to do with their lives, both on and off the football field. . . . Reading through Mr. Bowden's reconstruction of the game, one does get the sense that this game was, if not the best ever, at least one of the most intriguing."
        —Peter Hausler, *The Wall Street Journal*

THE BEST
GAME EVER

Also by Mark Bowden:

Doctor Dealer

Bringing the Heat

Black Hawk Down

Killing Pablo

Finders Keepers

Road Work

Guests of the Ayatollah

THE BEST
GAME EVER

Giants vs. Colts, 1958,
and the Birth of the Modern NFL

MARK BOWDEN

Grove Press
New York

The Ogden Nash poem, "The Introduction to 'My Colts,'" copyright ©
1968 by Ogden Nash. Reprinted by permission of Curtis Brown, Ltd.

"*Distant Reply*" firt appeared in the *Atlantic* magazine, October 2008.

Published simultaneously in Canada
Printed in the United States of America

FIRST EDITION

ISBN-13: 978-0-8021-4412-6

Grove Press
an imprint of Grove/Atlantic, Inc.
841 Broadway
New York, NY 10003

Distributed by Publishers Group West

www.groveatlantic.com

09 10 11 12 13   10 9 8 7 6 5 4 3 2 1

For David Halberstam

THE BEST
GAME EVER

Bert Bell, NFL commissioner 1946–1959. (Courtesy of *The Sporting News*/Zuma Press)

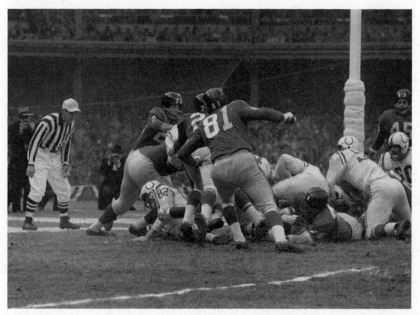

Giants third-quarter goal-line stand. (Courtesy of Hy Peskin/*Sports Illustrated*)

New York assistant coach Tom Landry (with ball) and the Giants' defense, Nov. 6, 1958. (Courtesy of AP)

Baltimore head coach, Weeb Ewbank, briefs his team on the day before the big game, Dec. 27, 1958. (Courtesy of AP)

1

Football Noir

It was freezing in Yankee Stadium. A balmy Sunday afternoon had faded into night, three days after Christmas, 1958. When the football game had started, nearly two hours earlier, the mildness of the day had surprised the players, particularly the New York Giants. They had played twice here in the preceding two weeks against the Cleveland Browns in bitter cold, first in a blizzard, and then in such a deep freeze that the field felt like marble. There were still wet patches here and there, but the turf was mostly dry and soft. Anticipating another frigid contest, the grounds crew had given the field a protective coating of brown mulch that contained manure, which warmed as it decomposed and gave off a pungent odor, flavoring the fabled sports arena with the aroma of a cow pasture. Every scramble kicked up clouds of fragrant dust.

But as the game moved into its third quarter and the sun dropped behind high stadium walls, winter was back. High above the grandstand, with its graceful white-picket-fence frieze, banks of arc lights lit the field brightly. The 64,185 paying customers (considerably fewer than a full house) peered out at the contest from frigid blackness. The Giants wore their dark blue helmets with the single red stripe and blue wool jerseys with white numbers, and the Baltimore Colts, with the familiar horseshoe emblem on their white helmets, were in badly soiled whites with blue numbers and trim. This was the colorful spectacle for those present, but for the far bigger part of its audience, the most celebrated game in football history would be remembered primarily in black and white.

Spooky black and white. An estimated forty-five million people, the largest crowd to ever witness a football game, saw spectral players battling in shades of white and gray against a stark black backdrop. National Football League rules had forbidden local television stations from broadcasting the championship game, but many determined New Yorkers, particularly those living north of the Empire State Building, happily discovered that they could pick up the signal only slightly impaired from over the southwest horizon, beaming from Channel 3 in Philadelphia. The country was transfixed. President Eisenhower had a clear signal on his farm in Gettysburg, Pennsylvania, where he was watching while playing bridge with friends, including William E. Robinson, the president of Coca-Cola. Brooks Robinson, the second-year third baseman for the Baltimore Orioles, was watching at Fort Hood, Texas, where he was doing his off-season National Guard duty. Ernie Accorsi who would later become general manager of the Cleveland Browns, the team that had fallen twice in the two previous weeks to the Giants, was in a clubhouse on a golf course in Palm Beach, Florida, where he had decided to forego finishing his round in order to watch. Pete Rozelle, a public relations man for the Los Angeles Rams who had recently been promoted to general manager, watched from his team's offices, a little sore that the Rams wouldn't spring to fly him out to see the championship game live. Auto mechanic Ed Chaney, Jr. was watching from Henny Mack's Pub, his favorite bar in Glen Burnie, Maryland, along with a few dozen other rabid Colts fans. Chaney had to work that evening, but had set aside this afternoon for the game. At the home of the famous doggerel poet and Colts fan Ogden Nash in suburban Baltimore, the entire Nash family was gathered in the living room. At a novitiate in Baltimore, burdened with a mean-spirited local ecclesiastical admonition against watching the game on TV, the obedient but clever Mother Superior draped a blanket over the set—there was no rule against *listening*.

Many of the viewers just beginning to tune in were not regular watchers of pro football, and they were seeing something starkly different than the traditional college games played on sunny autumn afternoons. This was more like mortal combat from some dark underworld. As in some medieval rite, the players on both sidelines were draped in long capes. A master cinematographer could not have lit the scene more dramatically.

In the shadow of the stands, men wore long wool overcoats and gloves. Many wrapped wool scarves over their heads, covering their ears, and scrunched fedoras on top of the scarves. They smoked cigarettes or cigars, and when they cheered or spoke their faces would momentarily cloud in smoke and steam. Beneath the red, white, and blue bunting draped from the second tier, the stands smelled of tobacco and beer and occasionally a whiff of whiskey or rum or the pungent stab of a struck match. Nineteen-year-old William Gildea, who would grow up to be a sportswriter for the *Washington Post*, was there with his father, sitting high over one of the end zones. They had been going to Colts games together since the first one the team had played in 1947, and had taken the train from Baltimore to New York the day before.

Behind the end zone on the eastern side of the stadium, out where the left-field bullpen was during baseball season, stood Neil Leifer with his Yashica Mat twin lens reflex camera. It was Neil's sixteenth birthday, and he was spending it the way he had spent every Sunday afternoon that season. He had joined a camera club at the Henry Street Settlement House, to where the camera and film he carried had been donated. The club had taught him to shoot, develop, and print his own pictures, and he had discovered a potential market for them with the magazines and wire services around town. Neil knew their deadlines and he had shopped his work after every home game. So far he hadn't had any luck, but this was a big game. He had to be on the field for the shots he wanted, but the club wasn't handing out sideline passes to teenagers with borrowed cameras. Neil was tenacious, though. He had learned that before every game, busloads of disabled veterans arrived at the loading ramps outside Yankee

Stadium's outfield walls. There was no place for men in wheel-chairs up in the stands, but the Giants allowed them to watch from their chairs against the outfield wall behind the end zone. They even provided blankets and hot coffee. When the buses started arriving from the various veterans hospitals in the hour before kickoff, there was always a need for able-bodied vol-unteers to push them into the stadium. Neil knew that the sta-dium guards and cops, in return for his help, would let him stick around. Sometimes they would even let him creep up the sidelines, although usually the accredited photographers would kick up a fuss and he would have to come back. The market for still shots from the game was small, and the pro shooters didn't welcome competition, even from a sixteen-year-old on his birthday.

The surly culture of beery male boorishness that would come to typify football crowds had not yet taken hold, so there were many women in the stands. They, too, wrapped scarves around their heads and across their faces, and huddled under blankets. Joanne Kemp, the young wife of Giants back-up quar-terback Jack Kemp, was there, pregnant with their first child, Jeff, who would grow up to be an NFL quarterback. Marcia Hersh was huddled under a blanket with her mother. She was sixteen, and had come up from Baltimore on the bus with a big group of Colts rooters who were now in the upper deck over the fifty-yard line. Her father, Abe, who owned a furniture store, was so excited that he screamed himself hoarse. Years later Marcia would remember his eyes glowing with excitement as he had rasped to her, "History is being made!"

It was hard not to sense it.

Consider the men on the field. Many were already famous; others were just starting their careers. Among the Giants were Roosevelt Brown, Rosey Grier, Frank Gifford, Sam Huff, Emlen Tunnell, Mel Triplett, and Andy Robustelli. Kicking for New York was Pat Summerall, who would become, as would Gifford, among the most famous TV faces and voices of pro football. Roaming that Giants sideline were future Hall-of-Fame receiver Don Maynard, and Jack Kemp, the eventual AFL quarterbacking star, future congressman, U.S. Secretary of Housing and Urban Development, and vice presidential candidate. For the Colts, there were Johnny Unitas, Raymond Berry, Jim Mutscheller, Lenny Moore, Alan Ameche, Art Donovan, Jim Parker, Ordell Braase, Bill Pellington, and Gino Marchetti. And the men on the sidelines were every bit as notable, with three who would become icons of the pro game. On the Giants' side of the field, coaching the offense was Vince Lombardi, who was just a few years away from building his dynasty in Green Bay, and coaching the defense, Tom Landry, who would shape the Dallas Cowboys into another NFL power. Coaching the Colts was Weeb Ewbank, who in his career would steer two different pro franchises to championships. It was the greatest concentration of football talent ever assembled for a single game. On the field and roaming the sidelines, including Giants owners Wellington and Jack Mara, were seventeen future members of the NFL Hall of Fame.

In 1958, the great postwar boom was still in full stride, but some new and discordant notes had sounded. A year earlier the Soviet Union had orbited *Sputnik*, a technological stunt that disturbed the smug certitude of American power and demonstrated that the Russian foe could deliver its nukes anywhere on the globe. The vast Kansas night sky where President Eisenhower had grown up looked a little bit less friendly. There was talk of a "missile gap." The National Aeronautics and Space Administration was created that year.

The Ed Sullivan Show was the most popular hour of television. The tube was still full of cozy half-hour programs that depicted idyllic families enjoying the country's new suburban lifestyle, programs like *The Adventures of Ozzie and Harriet* and *Leave It to Beaver,* but the strong cultural fabric of self-satisfied consumerism, traditionalism, and sentimentality was starting to unravel. *Playboy* magazine was a huge hit, Andy Warhol was working as an illustrator in Manhattan, and the country had watched with horror in its living rooms as racist mobs taunted nine black teenagers trying to integrate a high school in Little Rock, Arkansas. Senator John F. Kennedy, who had already begun campaigning in earnest for the White House, was a frequent spectator at Giants games in Yankee Stadium. A guerrilla organization called the Viet Cong had begun to battle the anticommunist government of South Vietnam.

Just over the horizon was a decade of restless social, political, and cultural upheaval, but none of that was obvious yet. Americans had never been more affluent, and had never had more leisure. And pro football, which was about to catch hold, would just shoulder on through all this coming change, growing ever more popular and ever more rich. The audience and the league were on the cusp of an explosion that would quickly turn this era of pro football into a piece of a simpler past.

It would be this game that would provide the spark.

Early in the third quarter, the Giants had their backs to the wall, just as they had all season. They were an established NFL power in America's greatest city, with a lineup of star athletes expected to dominate the league for years to come, but this year had been a gutty, bitter struggle. They had the best defense in the league statistically (the Colts were rated second), but an inconsistent offense. Baltimore's offense was the league's best. So New York could ill afford to fall far behind, and they were on the verge of doing just that, to a young team of castoffs from a small city that had never participated in a national championship in any sport. Baltimore was a blue collar train stop between Philadelphia and Washington, steel mills and dock works and a grimy inner harbor slick with oily urban slough. But the comparative wealth and glamour of New York City meant nothing on the gridiron, where the Giants had started the second half behind by eleven points, 14-3, and were now backed up to their own five-yard line.

They had purchased this toehold with a tenacious goal-line stand. The Colts had begun the second half by driving the length of the field with ease in just five plays. The cunning play calling and precision passes of Baltimore's sensational quarterback, Johnny Unitas, who had been named the league's most valuable player the preceding year, confused the Giants' vaunted defense again and again, but with their backs to the goal line, facing the prospect of falling hopelessly behind, the defenders had a slight advantage. Unitas's receivers had less room to maneuver. Lindon Crow, the Giants' wily cornerback, no longer had to contend with his constant worry that Colts speedster Lenny Moore would turn upfield and leave him behind, and the other cornerback, Carl Karilivacz, knew the Colts' shifty left end Raymond Berry would not have time for anything fancy. The battle was simplified; it was muscle on muscle. And with the New York crowd amping up its glee with each failed Colts attempt to push across the goal line, the Giants had held.

The Colts had decided to go for it on fourth down. A team that cannot push in from the one-yard line in four tries begins to feel overmatched. His linemen blowing and spent after the third effort, Unitas had elected trickery. He called an option pass around the right end for fullback Alan Ameche, who raced for the right corner of the goal line with Giants defenders in hot pursuit. The play called for one of Ameche's three blockers, tight end Jim Mutscheller, to slip off his block and step into the end zone, at which point Ameche would surprise his pursuers by tossing a short touchdown pass. It had worked precisely as drawn up—Mutscheller was standing unattended in the end zone just five yards away—but in the din at that corner of the field, Ameche had misheard the call. The option pass, which Baltimore had not run at all that season, was called "648," as opposed to "48," the standard right sweep. Ameche assumed Mutscheller would hold his block on linebacker Cliff Livingston as he bulled his way in for the score. Instead, when the tight end let Livingston go, the delighted linebacker had a free shot at the running back. As Mutscheller stood watching in the end zone, waiting for the toss, Livingston dropped Ameche hard on the five-yard line.

It set up one of the most dramatic turning points in football history. How best to recapture the moment? The television broadcast of the game is lost to history. Most New Yorkers were following the old-fashioned way, on the radio. The tinny roar of the crowd, the cigarette and appliance commercials, the jingles and slogans—"Call for Phillip Morris!" and "There's a lot to like in a Marlboro / Filter, flavor, flip-top box!"—the distant sound of a marching band, all of it framing a smooth river of play-by-play from NBC's Joe Boland, the sounds were as familiar as a fire in the hearth and the smell of Sunday dinner. Boland had a perfect radio voice, warm, lightly southern, slightly nasal, and unfailingly upbeat, and he delivered a narration so mannered and professionally modulated that it was a kind of song:

> — *The New York Giants defense is great! They hold them off! Baltimore leading fourteen to three had a chance to get some icing on the cake as they marched steadily down to the New York one-and-a-half-foot line, and there the New York defense manifested itself! Bill, wasn't that a dandy?*

Boland's broadcast partner was Cleveland Browns announcer Bill McColgan, who in his rush to comment revealed his unfamiliarity with the Colts. He confused the actual runner on the futile fourth-down play, Ameche, with the Colts' other running back L.G. Dupre, and, ignorant of the play-call mix-up, lauded Livingston for making the play:

— It sure was, it looked for a moment as if Dupre was going to get around that right end but Livingston was wise to the call and he was in there and made a fine defense play to stop it. So now the Giants' offense will have a first and ten on their own five.

The goal-line stand lifted the hearts and voices of the New York crowd, and it gave the Giants a reprieve. The crowd noise, which had prevented Ameche from hearing the play call, now surged again. New York's canny veteran quarterback, the taciturn old marine Charlie Conerly, whose ruggedly handsome features would become famous as the Marlboro Man, trotted out, shedding his blue cape and wading into the chill. He had the whole field stretched out before him, and a Colts defense that had not shown much give.

Looking on from the owner's box in the sheltered mezzanine with his son and daughter, no doubt praying for a Giants comeback, was Bert Bell, the league's rotund, benevolent, and long-suffering dictator. Bell had been nursing the sport along for more than a decade, drawing up each season's complicated schedule by hand on the dining room table of his house in the Philadelphia suburbs. He had persuaded the tight-knit club of cut-throat team owners to accept numerous compromises for their mutual benefit, and the reforms had paid off. Total attendance was the highest it had ever been in the league's thirty-eight years, closing in on three million, and nearly all twelve of the league's teams were in the black—only four had been making money when Bell had taken over the league in 1946. A big round man with a broad, fleshy face and a double chin, he was gruff, gravel voiced, earnest, and well-liked by owners, coaches, and players. He ran the league like one big college team, meeting with the players before every season and handing out his phone number, encouraging them to call him directly in Philadelphia if they had any problems. Many did so, and Bell took their complaints and suggestions seriously.

He was self-made, in a peculiar sense, because by any social measure Bell was aggressively downwardly mobile. He had been born de Benneville (note the small "d") Bell, son of a blueblood Philadelphia Main Line family. His father was a former Pennsylvania attorney general and his brother was one of that state's Supreme Court justices. Young de Benneville himself attended a private prep school and the Ivy League University of Pennsylvania (where his father was a trustee), but along this gilded path he had discovered the gridiron, embraced its blue-collar ethic, and never looked back. He became "Bert," adopted a tough-guy, blue-collar manner, and somehow acquired an accent that was more Brooklyn than Brahmin, dropping his "g"s and abandoning learned syntax—as *New York Times* man Al Hirshberg put it, "He talks like a dock walloper."

Bell played football in college and, after several misspent postgraduate years squandering his family's money— accumulating drinking and gambling debts totaling $50,000 —he straightened out, married, gave up drink, and found a home in the professional game. The former gambler now kept a close eye on the oddsmakers, keen for the slightest hint of meddling with honest competition, and to fend off would-be fixers he hired former FBI agents to police every team. He weathered competition from an upstart rival league, the All-American Football Conference, and corralled it with a merger—the Baltimore franchise emerged from that maneuver. He instituted "free substitution" to improve the quality of play, and crafted draft rules that allowed the teams with the worst records to have first picks of the emerging college football stars each season. If a team owner complained about Bell's frequent and often summary rulings, the commissioner was fond of invoking with stern finality, "Article I, section 14, paragraph B." He knew full well that nobody knew the league's bylaws better than he did. The passage read, in part, "The commissioner is authorized to cancel a contract for any action detrimental to the welfare of the National Football League," a relatively narrow prerogative, but rules are meant to be interpreted, and the commissioner of football interpreted them broadly and enthusiastically. He wielded "I-14-B" like a cudgel, and found that so long as the league prospered, nobody complained.

He had no rooting interest in this Colts-Giants contest, except that it stay close. Despite Bell's accomplishments, pro football still lived in the long shadow of baseball. No matter how good the games were, the NFL was still just a diversion during the long cold months of baseball's annual hiatus. The Giants played in Yankee Stadium. The nation was attuned to the rhythms of the summer game, which dwarfed football in ticket receipts and national attention.

Newspaper coverage of football was often relegated to the inside pages, and then, suddenly, there wasn't even that—in mid-December, 1958, New York's newspapers were shut down for more than two weeks by a strike. The lack of newsprint bally-hoo had contributed to poor ticket sales in the past week—there were alarming pockets of empty seats—but that wasn't the only problem. It wasn't the first time the championship game had failed to attract a full house, and Bell knew that if you couldn't do it in New York it was not a healthy sign.

Still, there was TV. This was the ninth time the NFL Championship game had been on national television, and each year the audience had grown. The number of Americans with sets was exploding, from a mere twelve thousand in 1946 to four million just four years later. When World War II ended, just a half of 1 percent of American homes had TV sets; by 1962, just four years after this game was played, 90 percent would. Television was working profound changes in American politics, marketing, journalism, and entertainment, and part of this concerned the way people watched sports. Pro football had begun to attract a larger and larger number of viewers on Sunday afternoons. An estimated 37 percent of those who turned on their sets in that time slot were watching the NFL. Television was perfect for action, particularly the suspense of live action. That's how it had struck Orrin E. Dunlap Jr. of the *New York Times* after the first-ever televised game in 1939, a college matchup between Fordham University and Waynesburg College. Dunlap wrote, "With a camera on a dolly at the forty-yard line, the coach himself has nothing on the televiewer in the armchair at home. Both are on the sidelines. . . . Football by television invites audience participation . . . the contest is in the living room; the spectator is edged up close. His eye is right in the game."

He might have written eyes and *ears*, because televised football also added a helpful running commentary that explained the game to those who had never played. Baseball seemed made for radio, because it afforded the best broadcasters the opportunity to gift wrap the game in words, fill a slow-paced contest with description, anecdote, and analysis, and react to its flashes of action with colorful homespun expressions—"Well I'll be a suck-egg mule!" would say that Mississippi poet of the diamond Red Barber. If radio and baseball went together perfectly, football seemed made for television. Its bunched and scripted action fit neatly in the frame of the set, while skillful cameramen and broadcasters helped viewers follow the ball as plays unfolded. Later would come stop-action and slow-motion replay.

Today's kickoff at two o'clock meant that the game's finish might spill into early evening, into the promised land of prime time, the sweet spot of TV programming, when more ears and eyes were focused on the same thing than in the entire history of humankind. If the game were close, and exciting, it might creep into this national hearth, when the multitudes switched on their TVs for Sunday night viewing, the most valuable time slot of the week. If even a small portion of those who tuned in liked what they saw, Bell knew interest could soar. A blowout, one of those games that peaked early and then ground to a predictable finish, would have the opposite effect. It could be a disaster.

But this game would be no disaster. It was about to ignite.

There is a phenomenon known to every sport, but particularly to football, where the sustained high decibel roar of tens of thousands of fans, sheer condensed will, can assume a force like wind, can nudge (or at least appear to nudge) events on the field in the desired direction. This had already happened on the botched Ameche option play, and now it was about to happen again. The first two Giants plays from scrimmage gained eight yards, but the next try, on third down with two yards to go, would become one of the most famous fluke plays in football history, one of those remarkable combinations of skill and sheer luck that make the game so much fun to watch. It was not only going to answer Bert Bell's prayers by upending the course of this game, it was going to change the history of pro football.

In the full-throated din, Conerly took the snap and back-pedaled. The Colts' relentless front four—Marchetti, Donovan, Big Daddy Lipscomb, and Don Joyce—rapidly collapsed the Giants' pass protection, but just before he was hit, the quarterback lofted an off-balance prayer of a pass over the outstretched hands of the rushers, toward the middle of the field, where Giants flanker Kyle Rote was angling across from his position on the far left side. Rote was matched stride-for-stride with the Colts' cerebral cornerback Milt Davis, who was playing on a right foot he had broken just two weeks earlier. It was so swollen that Davis was wearing tennis shoes, and so shot up with Novocain that it felt like a wooden peg. Rote had him by a numbed step.

— *Rote is open! He's got it! Shakes loose one man, shakes loose another. . . .*

Lunging from behind, Davis, the first would-be tackler, slid off Rote, who turned upfield in full stride. The crowd screamed with excitement; there had not been many big plays in the game for New York, and Rote was running free. Angling across was the Colts' bow-legged weak safety Carl Taseff, the second would-be tackler (this was happening in seconds), who dove at the ballcarrier. Rote neatly sidestepped, sending Taseff flying past empty-handed, but the dodge slowed him, and now two more Colts defenders closed in, cornerback Raymond Brown and strong safety Andy Nelson. It was Nelson who caught him, lunging, and before dragging him down from behind managed to slap the football free.

The play wasn't over.

— *The ball is loose! And it's picked up by New York!*

Alex Webster, the big-chinned Giants halfback, had lined up at the start of the play as a flanker on the other side of the field from Rote, and like all disciplined players was trailing the play even though he was, for all intents, out of it. But when Nelson knocked the ball free, it tumbled forward, five yards, ten yards. Webster shouldered aside Brown and scooped it up in stride. He kept on running, nothing but an empty forty yards between him and a touchdown. But the Colts' players were also disciplined. Taseff had jumped to his feet after forcing Rote's dodge. The cornerback again gave chase. He was faster than Webster, but the halfback had a head start. It was a dramatic footrace, Taseff angling closer and closer, Webster sprinting for the corner of the field to buy an extra step or two. The crowd cheered frantically. At the final moment, just yards from the goal line, Taseff dove in desperation at the big halfback's legs and sent him flying. Webster landed hard past the goal line but out of bounds. It looked like the top half of his body had stayed in bounds as it flew over the goal line, and amid the raucous celebration of Giants fans, Boland prematurely awarded the touchdown.

— And I think on one of the world's most amazing plays, New York has scored here. No, wait a minute. No, the ball is going to be put down on about the one-yard line! It's ruled that he was tackled there. I thought he'd gone in for the score, but he had been hit and then crawled over. The ball is spotted on the one-yard line. . . . Eighty-six yards overall. Conerly to Rote, fumble to Webster, Webster to the one-yard line with a first and goal to go for New York.

It didn't matter. Two plays later the Giants scored, and the extra point by Summerall made the score Colts, 14, Giants, 10. Just minutes earlier it had looked like the Colts were going to pull away for good, and for Bell it would have been easy to imagine millions of TV sets being switched off, or millions of channels being changed, as the attention of the vast home audience drifted. But not now.

Given the game's inherent appeal and its neat fit with TV, pro football was bound to click at some point with the American public. This was the moment. Just like that, with one goofy eighty-six-yard play, the championship's outcome was again uncertain. The commissioner of football could breathe easy.

The real battle had just begun. As late afternoon eased into darkness and prime time, America was going to get not just a good football game, but the best anyone had ever seen.

Colts wide receiver Raymond Berry, 1958. (Courtesy of *Sport* magazine)

Baltimore head coach,
Weeb Ewbank (far left), and
his assistant Charley Winner (far right),
1962. (Courtesy of Ted Patterson)

Johnny Unitas, Raymond Berry, 1958. (Courtesy of *Sport* magazine)

From left to right: Weeb Ewbank, Johnny Unitas, George Shaw, Dec. 25, 1958.
(Courtesy of AP)

2

Raymond

The tall, skinny young man in glasses who moved next door to Al Brennan had some peculiar exercise habits. Every morning in the fall and winter, like clockwork, he would emerge from his house in Lutherville, Maryland, dressed in a gray sweat suit and carrying a cinderblock with a rope tied around it. He would stand at the top of the stairs that led from the sidewalk, set the cinderblock on a lower step, tie the other end of the rope around his thigh, and start lifting his leg and setting it back down. After a set number of repetitions, he would untie the block and fasten it to the other leg and do the same. Every morning, the same routine.

Brennan had only this glimpse of his neighbor's unique methods. If he had followed him through winter and into spring and then into the blazing hot summers of Paris, Texas, where he had grown up the son of the local football coach, he would have seen his young neighbor perform the same exercise on the steps of the empty grandstand at Wise Field, and then walk out to the center of the sun-baked gridiron, where he would set a piece of paper down on the grass, and for several hours race off carrying a football in one direction or the other, stop, return, catch his breath for a few moments, consult the paper, assume a set position, and then sprint off again. Sometimes he would angle off to the left for a short distance, and sometimes he would angle off to the right. Sometimes he would stop and turn back for a few steps, or perform a shuffle, what looked like a little dance step, in the middle of his sprints, and abruptly change direction. Sometimes he would run only ten yards and sometimes the length of the field before he came back. There didn't seem to be any pattern to it, so it would have been hard for anyone to guess, but he was playing an entire football game at the end position in pantomime.

He had chosen the film of a particular game, usually one that featured a lot of passing, observing each route run by the receiver, timing each play and interval between plays with a stopwatch, and then in tiny, meticulous handwriting, sketching the patterns and noting the sequences. Every play, whether the receiver was thrown the ball or not, every huddle, every time out, every stretch spent on the bench between offensive series. He noted the time spent in each phase, routes and recovery times, and consulting his hand-written script out on the grass, acted out the entire game, whistle to whistle. Out on the playing field of his hometown in the dead of summer there was no one to observe his obsessive devotion, no teammate, no neighbor, no coach. There was no one he was trying to impress. It was pure desire. No, not just desire. The young man in gray sweats and glasses was *desperate*.

His name was Raymond Berry, and he was a football player unlike any his new coaches in Baltimore had ever seen. A lowly twentieth-round pick in the summer of 1955, he was not expected to be around for long when he reported to his first training camp in Westminster, Maryland. It was the job of Charley Winner, the Colts' ends coach, to check him in.

"Hey, Ray, welcome to training camp. We're glad to have you."

"My name is Raymond," he told Winner.

And that was that. There would be a specific moment in the fourth quarter of the famous 1958 championship game on which the outcome would turn, but to fully appreciate it, you first need to appreciate Raymond. At a time when most players had full-time jobs off the field he was, at age twenty-two, a complete, full-time football player. He worked at it night and day. NFL and college teams had long employed film to break down the formations and tendencies of their opponents and to plan strategies, and they used it as a teaching tool for their players, but the players themselves generally viewed such classroom sessions as a chore, and a bore. Not Raymond. He bought himself a sixteen-millimeter projector and when his day of practice and mandated classroom work was done, when his teammates were out drinking beer, he would go home and study film on his own. His coaches used it to study formations and tendencies for whole teams; Raymond focused in on his position alone. He scrutinized the men who would be defending against him, cornerbacks mostly, but also linebackers and safeties. He sought out film of successful NFL receivers, and studied their routes and their moves, making page after page of notes in his tidy handwriting.

He was different in other ways, too. While other young athletes spent their bonus money or paychecks on cars or booze or women, Raymond spent his on things like contact lenses, at that time an expensive novelty, or on a specially fitted tooth guard to cushion impacts that might cause concussion—a precaution many of the rough men in the game would have considered borderline unmanly. It didn't stop there. No detail was too small to absorb Raymond. He found the canvas fabric of his practice football pants too heavy and binding, particularly when they grew damp with sweat. The team's fancier game pants had a shiny white fabric on the front, and on the back were made of a lightweight material that stretched and breathed. Raymond wrote a letter to the company that manufactured the game pants and asked if they would make him some practice ones out of the stretchy material. They complied. To keep his special pants from getting lost in the team's daily piles of laundry, Raymond would hand wash his own gear after practice, in the sink, and hang them up in his locker to dry.

Imagine how professional football players viewed a new teammate who insisted on wearing custom-made practice pants, on doing his own laundry, and on being called by his full and formal first name. These were rough men, men with broken teeth and crooked noses. They regarded tolerance for pain and an appetite for violence as prerequisites for the game. Scars, broken molars, black eyes, scrapes, bruises, broken bones, these were badges of honor. Most were hard-drinking, fun-loving rowdies, many of them veterans of World War II and Korea. To these men, there was something antithetical about Raymond's approach, his attention to uniform and protective gear, his excessive study and obsessive, eccentric preparation. Real men showed up hurt, or with a hangover, and they didn't out*think* their opponent, they kicked his ass. Mouth guards and doing your own laundry? Raymond was also *fussy*. His locker was like a museum display case, with everything perfectly in place. He was jealous and protective of his things. One day teammate Art Donovan, a loud, comedic defensive lineman called "Fatso," who epitomized the old school, borrowed Raymond's hairbrush and, knowing his teammate's ways, made a point of returning it to its proper place on his locker shelf. So he was surprised when the receiver confronted him.

"Why did you use my brush?" Raymond asked, accusingly.

Donovan didn't even try to lie.

"How did you know?" he answered.

"When you put it back, it wasn't lined up on the shelf the way I had it."

Impressed wasn't the right word for how that made Donovan feel about Raymond. He was impressed, sure, but the feeling also leaned slightly in the direction of appalled. Maybe the right word is *wonder*. You give a guy like that a little more room.

Raymond had been drafted before pro football teams had extensive scouting organizations, and before there were film libraries on college prospects. He was taken in the winter of

1954 as a "futures" pick, which was a throwaway category, down in the lower echelons of the draft where teams grabbed players in a *what-the-hell* frame of mind. He still had another year of eligibility for college ball. An entire college season went by, and still no one from the Colts' organization had bothered to travel to Southern Methodist University to scout their new possession. They never laid eyes on him before he showed up at training camp. Even Raymond was unsure how he came to be chosen. But when his name had popped up in the draft, it had changed his life. He had never even started a game at SMU, and because he already had enough credits to graduate, he had pretty much decided to quit football and go back home and look for a real job. Then his college teammates, in recognition of his inspirational work habits more than his accomplishments on the field, unexpectedly voted him cocaptain. These two things, the draft and the vote, had so honored and inspired him that he decided to stick around for that final season. Maybe it was possible for a man like him to have a future in the game.

The story of Raymond Berry is more than the story of an overlooked, talent-deprived young athlete who by dint of sheer effort, will, and dedication, turns himself into a star. There are players who fit that description on every team. It is a cliché. Raymond's story goes beyond that. His personality and his obsessions changed not only his own life, but those of his teammates and the Colts' organization, and ultimately the history of pro football.

He had always been an extraordinarily organized and self-possessed young man, tall and lean, with narrow, wide-set eyes, wavy brown hair worn longer on the top than the sides, and a thin smile that unfolded at a slight angle that made you wonder what else he meant by it. He looked more like a grocery store clerk than a football player. He was quiet, but not shy. His dad was known to one and all back in Paris as "Ray," which is why young Raymond insisted on the full pronunciation of his name. He was his own man. He was *poised*, as though he had pondered everything a little harder than anyone else. This made him generally impervious to what other people thought or preferred, and made him, among other things, uncoachable—or, more accurately, *in no need* of coaching. More than any player Winner would ever meet, Raymond was his own coach. The way you handled him was to leave him alone. He could be present and also not present, lost in his own thoughts, which ran along very disciplined lines. Off the field, he carried slips of paper in his shirt pocket on which he made lists of reminders and observations.

Football was a game played for the most part with speed, brute strength, and natural athleticism. Star running backs simply knew how to elude tacklers; great receivers and pass rushers relied on speed, strength, and instinct to shed defenders and blockers. Great players were typically at a loss when sportswriters wanted to know exactly how they accomplished something remarkable on the field. They would give this look: *How pathetic to even ask.* The very idea that something as fluid and beautiful and natural as an athletic move in the heat of a game could be explained! It was meant to be admired. Athletic ability was uncomplicated; it just was. It was the opposite of thought. Indeed, there were those who held that thinking itself was the enemy, it slowed you down, it muddied the ideal of a pure act. In the split second of opportunity, if you had to *decide*, you were dead.

Not Raymond. He was the opposite of this kind of player. His teammates considered him a nut. Sportswriters found that he could talk your ear off not just about why and how and when he had made a particular move, but about how, why, where, and when he had dreamed it up and planned it. He had sketched it out at some point, broken it down into its component parts and *named* them, rehearsed it a thousand times in his head and then a thousand more times on the field, and held it in reserve to employ at precisely the right moment. To a degree considered hilarious and sometimes tiresome, Raymond was entirely cerebral in his approach to the game, or, more precisely, to his position, because he knew he was suited for only one job at the pro level. He was deconstructing and reinventing the position of wide receiver.

The idea of splitting a player out to one side to concentrate exclusively on running pass routes was relatively new. It had only been nine years since Los Angeles Rams coach Clark Shaughnessy, one of the game's greatest innovators, had created the position by placing Elroy "Crazy Legs" Hirsch seven yards wide of the line of scrimmage. Hirsch had become famous running the ball for the universities of Wisconsin and Michigan, and his nickname heralded both his speed and the surprising moves he made in the open field, but by the time Shaughnessy got him he had injured his leg and lost a step. In part to spare Hirsch the bruising contact at the center of the field, his new pro coach split him wide of the scrum. He was free from that position to sprint unmolested into the other team's backfield, a dangerous target for Rams quarterbacks Bob Waterfield and the rookie Norm Van Brocklin. Shaughnessy split another receiver wide on the other end of the line and he, along with the tight end, opened up a passing attack unlike any the league had ever seen—the Rams breezed through their regular season that year before losing the championship game to the superb defense of the Philadelphia Eagles, who were aided by a cold rainstorm that dampened the air show.

Football had long been afraid of the forward pass. It was unveiled in 1906 by St. Louis University and it led their team to an undefeated season. It was considered so powerful a weapon that an assortment of rules were put in place to limit it. The quarterback was allowed to throw only from a spot five yards directly behind where the ball was snapped, and his throw had to travel at least five yards to either side of that position. This was to prevent quick passes up the middle, which were thought unstoppable. The rule briefly turned the gridiron into a checkerboard—lines were drawn not just from side to side every five yards, but from end to end, so that referees could more easily determine if a thrown ball met the five-yard rule. Incomplete passes were turnovers, and an uncaught ball thrown across the goal line was a touchback. As a result, teams used the weapon sparingly.

But crowds loved it, especially the bomb, which could move a team from one end of the field to the other in one brilliant arcing throw. Passes opened the game up to a much more freewheeling, exciting brand of play. Before the throwing game, football was more like a rugby scrum, and when evenly matched teams played, it could resemble a prolonged wrestling match. The checkerboard pattern vanished four years later when college and pro teams loosened the passing restrictions, allowing the quarterback to throw the ball anywhere over the line of scrimmage. Some years later the rule requiring the thrower to be directly behind center was also scrapped, so quarterbacks could roam anywhere behind the line of scrimmage looking for open receivers. Thus was born the rollout, and the option— plays where the ball carrier (like Ameche in the 1958 championship game) ran laterally with the option of either throwing or running. Incomplete passes became simply a loss of down.

Two other major innovations led directly to Hirsch and, ultimately, Raymond Berry.

The first was a change to the football itself. It was originally a rugby ball, much fatter, designed to be easily drop-kicked and to fit comfortably in the curve of a man's arm. To better accommodate the pass, the dimensions of the ball were changed in 1934. It became skinnier and more pointed so that it fit more easily into a man's hand, and was more aerodynamic when thrown. The change inadvertently eliminated the drop-kick, because the more tapered ball bounced so erratically that a quick, short kick might end up bouncing almost as far backward as it was booted forward. Few mourned the drop-kick, though, and talented quarterbacks hit sprinting targets half to three-quarters of the field away.

The second innovation was more significant and more controversial. In the beginning, football teams fielded the same players on offense and defense. This was part of the rugged appeal of the game. Men took the field at kickoff, and unless they were too injured to continue, played until the final whistle. Substitutions were strictly limited. But as strategies for moving the ball became more complex, evolving from the single-wing formation to double-wing, and then the T-formation and the forward pass, coaches were more and more tempted by specialty players. A smaller, quicker man who could evade defenders and catch the ball with great skill would find his size a serious detriment when forced to play defense, to shrug off blockers and make tackles. There were three-hundred-pound men who could seal off an offensive backfield like a brick wall, but who lacked the stamina to play every down, and the speed and agility to rush the passer on defense.

Slender, speedy, agile men did not *look* like football players. Hulking, big-bellied linemen didn't even look like athletes. But with free substitution all types found their place on the field. The change meant trading a vital piece of the game's mystique for an improvement in the quality of play. The upstart All-American Football Conference adopted free substitution when it was formed in 1946, and began playing games with separate offensive and defensive squads. When that league merged with the NFL in 1950, free substitution was also adopted, all but ending the age of the two-way player. There were still a few athletes remarkable enough to play both ways—the last was the Eagles Chuck Bednarik, who played both center and linebacker until retiring in 1962—but the fifties ushered in pro football's age of the specialist.

Which meant that the key to success was no longer all-around athletic ability. It would take some time for this notion to penetrate down to the high school and college ranks, however, where coaches still defined talent mostly by an assessment of size and speed. When the position of wide receiver was invented, Raymond Berry was sixteen years old. He saw a movie about Crazy Legs Hirsch and decided, in the way Raymond decided things, to become a football player. His father was head coach of the Paris High School football team. Raymond wanted to play, but he was too skinny, and too slow. He had a bad back. He was near-sighted, and because he couldn't wear glasses on the field, competed in a fog. His feet were so big that his nickname was "Skis." Ray Berry put his son on the roster, but Raymond didn't make the starting team until he was a senior. Ray Berry was the kind of coach who liked intelligent football players, so much so that he didn't strictly abide by the tradition of letting the quarterback call the plays in the huddle. He picked the smartest kid on the field, whether he was a lineman or a running back or a tight end. Raymond called the plays in his senior year. By then he was the best football player Paris High School had ever seen, one who really understood the game, and one who had an unmistakable genius for catching a football.

Along with those big feet came big hands, really big hands, and Raymond could jump. He wasn't very fast, but became a standout on the high school track team as a long jumper and high jumper. He had always been told he was too slow to play football, but discovered that it wasn't necessarily how fast you were, it was how you used your speed. He could fool a defender into thinking he was slower than he really was, and then startle him with a burst at a critical moment that left the defender behind. When he couldn't outrun a defender, Raymond figured he could outsmart him, out-position him, and outjump him, and with those big hands, he could catch better than anyone he knew. Boy, could he catch. He was what football coaches called "a big target." All a quarterback had to do was put the ball in Raymond's vicinity, and most of the time, no matter how closely defended he was—because Raymond wasn't capable of running away from most defenders—he came down with the ball.

It was the kind of skill that could only be demonstrated in action, however, and in football, more than in any other sport, your chance to see action depended entirely on a coach's evaluation of your skill. It was what Joseph Heller in a few years would dub a Catch-22. Raymond had skills that could only be seen in competition, but he couldn't compete unless the coach thought he was skilled enough to play. When it came time to run the forty-yard dash or to compete in passing drills, he was rarely the best-looking player on the field. So his career proceeded catch by catch. No college wanted him after high school, so Raymond spent one year at Schreiner Junior College in Kerrville, Texas, before convincing Rusty Russell, the longtime head coach at SMU, to give him a shot, as much in deference to Ray Berry—college coaches needed high school coaches to steer them talent the way pro coaches needed college ones—as to the young man's potential.

"I'll give you a one semester trial scholarship," said Russell. "You transfer from the junior college to here. You're not eligible to play because of the transfer, so you'll work against our varsity squad every day, and I'll watch you this fall."

It was a chance just to practice with the team, to be a member of what Russell called his "T-team." They wore red shirts. The coaches would program the T-team with offensive plays run by whatever team SMU faced next, and Raymond would run that team's pass patterns against the varsity defense. Throwing passes for the T-team was SMU's star quarterback, Fred Benners, and together he and Raymond started to light up the practice field. Raymond earned his scholarship, but his skill was considered so specialized that he was used only on occasion. He caught only five passes as a sophomore, and just eleven as a junior. At the end of that season he had still never started in a college game, which was why his selection by the Colts came as such a surprise. Without sophisticated scouting networks, pro teams relied on word of mouth from coaches and sportswriters. Some of those eleven catches in his junior year had been spectacular. A *Dallas Morning News* reporter named Charlie Burton had noted Raymond's skills, and may have put in a word for him. And Benners, Raymond's T-team quarterback, was drafted by the New York Giants in 1952. An injury ended his career after his rookie season, but he had friends in the pro game and might have talked up his old practice-field receiver. Raymond never did find out exactly.

As a "futures" pick, Raymond still had one more year of college ball to play. He caught sixteen more passes in his senior year. There were no other pro teams even remotely interested when he boarded a plane to Baltimore, then a bus for the forty-minute drive out to the Colts' training camp in Westminster that summer.

The team was a new franchise, having returned from a hiatus just two years earlier (they had been a part of the AAFC in the late forties, but were disbanded after just one season when the two leagues merged). They were doormats, having won only six games in the two previous seasons, and while they lacked talent everywhere, Raymond noticed to his delight that they were particularly thin at his position.

He made the team, one of twelve rookies the Colts kept that year, but Raymond knew that it was not much of an accomplishment. The team won only five games in 1955 under its new head coach, Weeb Ewbank, and he had hardly distinguished himself. He had caught only thirteen passes, none of them for a touchdown, and he knew why. He was overmatched by pro defenders. In college, he had run only simple, predetermined routes, hooks, posts, crossing routes. All he had to know was his assignment on a given play. If it worked as planned, he would find himself in an uncovered spot and sometimes catch the ball. In the pros, there were no uncovered spots. Pro defenders played mostly man-to-man, which meant that once the ball was snapped, Berry had a superbly trained athlete in his ear. They bumped him, pushed him, tripped him (when the refs weren't looking), threw him off stride, and then slapped the ball out of the air or intercepted it if it got close. He could not catch a pass unless he could shake off that man, and he lacked the quickness and speed to get away from most of them. The only reason he caught thirteen passes in his first year, just over one catch per game, was that the art of defending against a wide receiver was relatively new, too.

The record didn't show how much the team had actually improved in that first season under its new head coach. Its Heisman Trophy–winning rookie running back, Alan Ameche, crashed through the line and ran seventy-nine yards for a touchdown the first time he was handed the ball. He went on to lead the NFL in rushing and was voted Rookie of the Year. The team's other first-round pick that year was a "bonus" pick; in some years clubs were allowed to draw numbers out of a hat and were awarded an extra pick in whatever round they chose. The Colts had won a first-round bonus, and had used it to draft University of Oregon quarterback George Shaw, who stepped right into the starting role and had a great first season. Shaw was at that point the team's most obvious draft success. The speedy little quarterback was the cornerstone of the franchise Ewbank had boldly promised to lead to an NFL championship in just five years. There were other good rookies that season, running back L.G. "Long Gone" Dupre, and linemen Alex Sandusky and George Preas, who along with veteran defensive stars like Gino Marchetti, Art Donovan, Don Joyce, and Bill Pellington were coming together as a contending football team. They all knew they were getting good. But no one was more aware than Raymond how badly his rookie season had lagged. Any hope he had of staying with this improving club faded in the off-season when the Colts signed two new receivers, both of them former all-Americans. Raymond felt he was in the center of the bull's-eye.

Unless he got better fast, he was going to lose the thing that he loved most. So as his teammates went home to enjoy the long, relaxing off-season, Raymond went to work. Using his father's sixteen-millimeter film projector, he set about breaking down and studying the position of receiver like no one ever had. The Colts provided him with all the game film he wanted. He asked for games that featured the best receivers in the NFL; Harlan Hill, Max McGee, and others, and slowed down the projector to dissect their moves. He began to develop his own repertory, naming each juke and fake after the players he admired. He picked the brains of collegiate receivers. From Howard Schnellenberger, a star tight end at the University of Kentucky who would go on to a long career as a football coach, he learned the double fake.

"See, Raymond, the first fake is always in the direction that you eventually intend to go," he explained. He practiced the zig-zag moves in pantomime at Wise Field. Then he began experimenting with triple fakes.

He also got himself in terrific shape. At the time, the prevailing notions about diet and fitness were decidedly unscientific. Players played and lived hard. Most of them smoked— cigarette advertising powered the radio and TV broadcasts of their games. In deference to the general notion that cigarettes detracted from a strict training regimen, they would hide the cigarettes when they appeared in public, or when there were cameras around, but it was typical for players to calm themselves down before games by smoking, or reach for a cigarette at half-time.

The big men kept weight on by drinking and stuffing themselves. Some were prodigious overeaters. Art Donovan, whose weight would sometimes approach three hundred pounds, was particularly fond of fatty meats—hot dogs and bologna were his favorites—washed down with Schlitz beer. He worked late as a liquor salesman after practice and was in the habit of gorging himself just before going to bed every night. On the road, he would sit at the edge of his hotel bed, hours after the team dinner, with a pile of bologna sandwiches or hot dogs or hamburgers, wrap a towel around his shoulders, and stuff himself, washing it down with beer, and then flop over backward on the bed and fall asleep, snoring clamorously. Don Joyce, a big defensive end who had been a boxing champion—his nickname on the team was "Champ"—rarely slept. He ingested uppers, pills he got from long-haul truckers, that he bragged enabled him to stay up all night drinking beer, and that turned him into a demon on the field. Joyce would stop eating and drinking completely every Wednesday night, and starve himself for the team's weekly weigh-in on Friday—players were fined ten dollars per pound for being over- or underweight. Joyce would camp in a sauna and have trainers throw buckets of cold water on him every fifteen minutes. Come Friday, he always made his 265 pound limit. He would treat himself to a feast immediately afterward. All of this was tolerated, even encouraged. Exercise was regarded with suspicion. Football players in the off-season were discouraged from engaging in any activity that might develop the "wrong" muscles. Running, swimming, and lifting weights were discouraged. The teams recommended instead golf, tennis, and handball. Many also designed regimens of calisthenics, but rare was the player with the mental discipline to stick with such rigorous and intensely boring routines.

Raymond was one of those rare ones, but he was also inclined to ignore conventional wisdom. He was neither a smoker nor a drinker, and he watched his weight carefully. Motivated by what he would later call "absolute terror," he started lifting and running. He set about remaking himself.

Football coaches always talked about being in "game shape." Players, they said, could do calisthenics all they wanted, but the only thing that could get you in shape to play football was to play. That's why Raymond got out his stopwatch and began simulating entire games by himself. He began in March. The first few times he tried it, he was exhausted by the end of the first half. So he would work out hard for a full week and then try again. Gradually, his stamina improved. By early summer, he could play an entire game without feeling winded. He knew his athletic ability might not measure up to the men he would be competing against in July and August at Westminster, that was something he could not control. But he could make sure he was in better shape than anyone else. And when the grueling two-a-day drills started, his obsessive training methods paid off. Given their lackadaisical off-season programs, most of his teammates paid a heavy price in July. Getting in shape was training camp's primary purpose. It was a dreaded ordeal of heat, soreness, vomiting, and exhaustion. It was not unusual for the big men to pass out. By getting himself into playing shape *before* camp, Raymond was going against the grain in 1956, and it paid amazing dividends. The workouts were a breeze. He had never felt anything like it.

"Raymond, your shirt's not even wet," one of his teammates remarked after a morning workout.

Despite his new strength and stamina, Berry was suffering a crisis in confidence. His fear of getting cut, knowing that the slightest mistake might undo all of his hard work, ate away at him. When he dropped a pass thrown to him in the team's first preseason game, he found himself hoping that the quarterback would not throw him the ball, which was like a death wish for a receiver. He fought the fear of failure. It spurred him to work even harder, and practice longer.

One of the things that Raymond had absorbed watching all that film in the off-season, was that the great receivers weren't successful just because they had slick moves, elusive speed, and sure hands. All of them had what appeared to be an almost mystical connection with a quarterback. Green Bay's Max McGee, for instance, would run a route that delivered him to an open spot on the field at the same moment the ball arrived, which meant that his quarterback had thrown the ball *before* he was actually open. Quarterback and receiver had their timing down so precisely that they knew not just where McGee was going, but how long it took him to get there. But who was going to work with Raymond like that? Quarterbacks on pro teams tended to be highly paid prima donnas. They were aloof, and often had more of a relationship with the coaches than their teammates. They were, in effect, coaches on the field, because at that time they called all the offensive plays, which meant their decisions determined who would carry the ball or catch it most often. Ambitious running backs and receivers vied for the attention of the quarterback. So how was a struggling receiver, unlikely to even make the team, going to cultivate that kind of relationship with George Shaw, one of the hottest young stars in the game? How would Raymond get him to listen to his new insights into the passing game, and into the importance of synchronicity between quarterback and receiver?

He couldn't. But there was a new quarterback at training camp that year, a skinny, bow-legged, slightly stoop-shouldered young man with abnormally long limbs, enormous hands, a blond flattop, a big crooked-toothed smile, and an utterly unflappable manner who had about as much of a chance of making the team as Raymond. He was a tough kid from a working-class ghetto in Pittsburgh whom the Colts had picked up from a semi-pro sandlot league after he was cut by the Pittsburgh Steelers. In Shaw, Baltimore already had the most promising young quarterback in the league, but they were trying out a few arms for the role of backup. This kid had cost them little more than the bus fare from western Pennsylvania.

His name was John, but pretty soon the sportswriters would insist on calling him Johnny.

Johnny Unitas in his
rookie season, 1956.
(Courtesy of Frank Gitschier)

Paul Brown, 1947. (Courtesy of AP)

Lenny Moore (Courtesy of the Baltimore Colts)

Top right: Art Donovan
Bottom right: Gene Lipscomb
(Courtesy of the Baltimore Colts)

Johnny Unitas, 1958 NFL Championship game.
(Courtesy of Hy Peskin/*Sports Illustrated*)

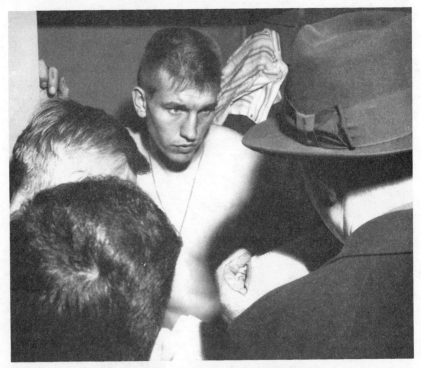

Johnny Unitas, 1958. (Diamond Images/Getty Images)

3

Johnny U

Raymond got his first look at the new arm when he reported to training camp in the summer of 1956. The dorms and gymnasium at the Westminster complex were high on a hill overlooking the practice field. The rookies had already been in camp for several days when the veterans began to arrive but Raymond hardly felt like a veteran. He had made the team the year before because Weeb Ewbank had been desperate for a flanker, and he'd felt overmatched in every game. Now, with the receivers Weeb had signed in the off-season, Raymond felt like he was just one bad practice or preseason game away from a ticket home. He stood on the hill and watched wistfully as the rookies went through the end of their afternoon practice, wondering if he had arrived at the last stop of his football career.

"That's the free-agent quarterback," one of his teammates said, pointing to the tall, slightly stoop-shouldered passer. "Unitas."

John Unitas had grown up in a Pittsburgh neighborhood called Mount Washington, in a yellow house that afforded a sweeping view of the smoggy downtown that looked north across the Monongahela River. It was a Catholic, working-class district. John's father had run a coal delivery business until he died of pneumonia at age thirty-eight, leaving his wife, Helen, with four children. At the time, John was five, the third oldest. Before he was a teenager he had followed his older brother Leonard into the family business, shoveling coal after school—three tons would pay him one dollar and fifty cents. It was hard labor, working in clouds of coal dust, and men didn't live long doing it. John's great uncle was afflicted with "miner's disease," or black lung.

That hard way of life was the well-worn path for men in the Unitas family, and when John didn't exhibit any special affinity for school, it seemed all the more inevitable. But even with class work and jobs after school, boys in John's neighborhood found time to play, and here he excelled. Sturdy and smart and gifted with a degree of natural coordination that belied his gangly frame, he stood out in all of the games. He had an intuitive feel for strategy, for being one step ahead of his opponent. Football is the sport that grabbed him most. He wasn't much of a reader, but he had discovered a book in the school library about the legendary Notre Dame coach, Knute Rockne. John checked it out again and again. When a substitute teacher passed the time one day by asking the children one by one what they wanted to be when they grew up, the boy with the buck teeth and tangle of blond hair told her, "I'm going to play professional football."

At the time, it was an unusual ambition. Baseball was the national pastime, the fates of the major league teams each season were followed as faithfully as the rebounding stock market or the march of Hitler's armies in Europe. The big stars of the game were paid huge salaries and were national celebrities and a boy ambitious for riches and glory would have looked there. Football was still primarily a college game, and it would have been more likely for a Pittsburgh boy like John to aspire to playing for one of the Big Ten schools in his part of the country—Purdue or Indiana—or perhaps Rockne's Notre Dame, the favorite team of every Catholic schoolboy in America. Pro football had none of the luster of the college games.

The pro game had been around for most of the twentieth century, with towns and cities in the Midwest fielding teams that drew small crowds of devoted local fans. The players were strictly part-timers, working men picking up a quick weekend paycheck—usually less than one hundred dollars—for knocking each other silly. In 1920 the country's most famous all-around athlete, Jim Thorpe, who was near the end of his remarkable career as an Olympic champion, professional baseball, football, and basketball player, presided over a meeting in Canton, Ohio, where fourteen teams agreed to unite under the umbrella of the American Professional Football Association, which two years later was renamed the National Football League. In the years before the war, dozens of teams were formed and folded. Those that survived did so because they were owned by singularly devoted football men, whose love for the game was coupled with an unshakable conviction that it would one day rival pro baseball for the hearts and wallets of American sports fans. Most would live to see their vision rewarded. This core club of owners consisted of Chicago's George Halas (the Bears) and Charley Bidwill (the Cardinals), Pittsburgh's Art Rooney (his Pirates became the Steelers in 1940), Green Bay's Earl "Curly" Lambeau (the Packers), New York's Tim Mara (the Giants), Washington's George Preston Marshall (the Redskins), and Philadelphia's Bert Bell (the Eagles).

"The tight band of owners fought like brothers," wrote Michael MacCambridge in his comprehensive history of pro football, *America's Game*, "but persevered in the face of several rival start-ups, the indifference of the American public, the condemnation of many in college football, and the failures of several of their partners. Those who remained were cautious, inherently suspicious of change, and not eager to test their horizons."

Pro players were regarded as roughnecks and mercenaries. The idea of playing for hire was still considered ignoble; college athletes, amateurs who played for the glory of their alma mater, were the authentic football heroes. Thorpe himself, the most famous athlete associated with the pro game, had been stripped of his Olympic medals because he had compromised the purity of his amateur status by playing a few games as a schoolboy for a minor league baseball team. Pro football was the haunt of brawlers, boozers, and big-time gamblers. In 1946, when John was turning thirteen and about to enter St. Justin's High School, news stories broke about an attempt to fix the NFL Championship game between the Giants and the Chicago

Bears. Giants running back Merle Hapes and quarterback Frank Filchock, members of the losing team, were suspected of taking bribes to throw the game. They were both suspended indefinitely. The new All-America Football Conference was challenging the struggling NFL, but the only teams in either league that were profitable were the championship ones. A grade-school boy with his heart set on making a living by playing pro football was motivated by only one thing, love of the game.

John would go on to play quarterback for St. Justin's, one of the smaller Catholic high schools in Pittsburgh. He was already so bow-legged that his run looked more like a scuttle, but he was fast, and he could throw the ball further and more accurately than anyone the Pittsburgh scholastic leagues had ever seen. The football seemed small in his oversized right hand, which gave him a big advantage. Most grown men needed both hands to keep the ball from flying out of their grasp prematurely if they tried to fake a toss in one direction and then throw in another, but even as a teen John could perform what looked like a real pass, holding on to the ball with one hand, which really *sold* the fake. He would send linebackers and defensive backs diving in one direction, then neatly pivot and throw it the other way. It was a little thing, but in the heat of the action, it was nearly always effective. John's knowledge of the game grew and grew. Like all the players in those years, he played both offense and defense, and when he called plays—and his high school coach had John calling all of the plays—he seemed to know exactly what his opponents were thinking. St. Justin's was overmatched against the bigger schools, but at the end of his senior year in 1951 when the All-Catholic team was picked, John Unitas was its first-string quarterback.

As John was maturing into a college prospect, winning a scholarship to the University of Louisville, America was going through a growth spurt of its own. Millions of American men had returned home from World War II and marched straight into a period of unprecedented prosperity. There were jobs aplenty, bigger salaries, and more leisure time, which meant the average working man had more money to spend and more time to spend it on fun. Television was becoming a fixture in American living rooms, and there were new living rooms under construction everywhere. Suburbs were sprouting up around every major city. Couples who had delayed marriage and children until after the war got to work, triggering a baby boom. That and the new affluence would prompt sweeping social change in the coming decade and beyond. One part of this new America would be an explosion in the attraction of spectator sports. Games had long been popular, but they were about to start generating wealth beyond even the most ambitious imagination, particularly in football. There was a unique confluence of trends. A vast market was forming for pro games just as the technology was being perfected to package and deliver them to every home. And at the same time the game itself was evolving. It was getting better.

The tangle of big men grappling around a line of scrimmage had long held a brute appeal, but as the game's experimentation with the forward pass and free substitution progressed, football was growing more aesthetically interesting and complex. With the invention of the flanker position, the quarterback no longer just called a signal indicating who would be given the ball and which direction he would run; he now worked from a broader palette of possibilities. There were routes assigned to receivers and holes assigned to running backs, and depending on whether the ball was thrown or handed off, the players could be either decoys, blockers, or ball handlers. Blocking patterns differed on pass plays and running plays, and within those shifts clever coaches designed stunts to confuse defenders. On the other side of the ball, teams had to decide whether to defend against the pass by dividing the secondary into zones, or assigning defenders to stay with the flankers and runners, man to man. Should the linebackers hang back to watch the play develop? Drop back to help guard against the pass? Charge into the backfield after the quarterback? The added layer of alternatives altered the timing of plays—some routes took longer to run than others. Should the quarterback take a three-step or five-step drop? Should the tailback retreat to help protect the thrower? Plunge into the line, pretending he had just been handed the ball? Slip off a block and swing out into the flat to become a third receiver himself? The game was growing bewilderingly complex, and awaited its first master tactician. His name was Paul Brown.

In the words of MacCambridge, Brown was a man who had spent his adult life "viewing football not as a sport but a field of study, worthy of the fine and close attention of academic inquiry." As a high school coach, he led his team to eighty victories and only eight defeats. He took over the top coaching job at Ohio State shortly before the war, and when his talent all disappeared into the service, Brown followed it, doing his bit at Naval Station Great Lakes outside Chicago, where he turned the base's football team into a terror. When he was named head coach of the newly formed AAFC Cleveland club at war's end, he came with such a big reputation that the city's fans voted to name the team after him. The Cleveland Browns would dominate pro football for a decade, more than any team before or since.

Brown did it not just with masterful strategy, but with a ruthlessly efficient system of assessing and acquiring talent, and a level of organization and discipline entirely new to the game. It was not enough for prospective players to be talented athletes, they had to pass Brown's intelligence and psychological tests. Other teams had three assistant coaches; Brown had five. And they no longer held seasonal jobs; they worked long hours year-round. He stunned his players by regimenting every aspect of their lives. They were given playbooks with descriptions and diagrams of every play, and after studying them in classrooms, were forced to spend hours at night copying them out by hand in their own notebooks, which were collected and graded.

"Some players learned by hearing it," explained Charley Winner, who worked as a scout for Cleveland during those years and later helped implement Brown's system in Baltimore. "Other players learn by watching you draw it up on a blackboard. Others players learn by seeing it, so we show them the film. Others learn by walking through it on the practice field. Others learn

by drawing it out themselves by hand. We covered all the learning methods, so when we were through, by God, they knew it."

Before Brown, football practice was loose. By the time players reached the pros, they were thought to have mastered the
game and the coach's job was to keep them in shape and help
devise a plan of attack against opposing teams. Theories of
physical training were eccentric, and varied widely from team
to team. Most operated on the principle that the only way to
rightly prepare to play football was to play football, so scrimmages were the rule. You warmed up, scrimmaged, and then
fooled around until it was time to go home. In the days before
a game, concerned about keeping players rested and healthy,
coaches rarely demanded much. Winner remembered scouting
a practice session of the hapless Dallas Texans, a short-lived
expansion franchise that would later move to Baltimore and
become the Colts, and reporting to his Cleveland bosses that
the team did nothing more than play "volleyball" with a football, using the goal post as a net. For Brown, classroom study
and practice sessions were where you won football games, every
bit as much as on the gridiron. He ran tightly scripted practices,
breaking down the game plan and focusing players on the specific tasks they would be expected to perform in the game.
Coaches orchestrated with whistles and stopwatches, moving the
players briskly from one assigned exercise to the next. There was
relatively little scrimmaging. Other teams scouted their opponents, and Brown did that, too, but he also scouted himself. He
assigned his assistant Blanton Collier to prepare a detailed analysis of his own team, watching film and breaking down every play

and player from the previous season. Brown termed the process his "flaw-finder." Such study and regimentation was for him an organic part of "playing" football. You did your homework, you made your plans, and you made certain each player knew exactly what was expected of him on every play. It all came together when the ref blew the whistle Sunday afternoon.

Led by Otto Graham, the prototype of the modern quarterback, and fullback Marion Motley, Cleveland effectively ascended to a new level of the game. They lost only twice in their first season, on their way to winning the AAFC championship, and they lost only twice more in the next three years, claiming the trophy thrice more. Absorbed into the NFL in 1950, the Browns were regarded as the best team from a lesser league until they rolled right through the more established competition, too, losing only twice on the way to a fifth straight championship. Other NFL teams stopped sneering at that point and started imitating, but Cleveland made it to the championship game in each of the next four seasons, and won again in 1954 and 1955. Otto Graham retired after that season, by which time the rest of the league finally caught up to Brown, although his team would remain a powerhouse for years to come. It was late in this dominating run that the owner of the newly formed Baltimore Colts hired away one of Brown's assistants, Weeb Ewbank.

Weeb was a faithful disciple of the Cleveland system, which he had helped run for five years, but he was no Paul Brown. Brown was a stern, aloof figure on the football field: tall, lean, ascetic, and commanding. Alongside him, Weeb was more like Sancho Panza: short, stocky, and energetic, full of brio. He had a broad face with a lower half that was a third longer than the top, which under his crew cut gave him a low forehead and an extraordinarily wide, round jaw. In most photographs of Weeb his mouth is open.

His unusual name came from childhood; Wilbur had been too hard for his little brother to pronounce, and it had become Weeb so far back that most people would never even know his real first name, which might have been the point. In his youth, he had been a good athlete. At Miami University of Ohio, he had played quarterback during football season, on the same team as Paul Brown, and during the summer he played semipro baseball under an assumed name in order to preserve his status as an amateur. His true vocation, however, was coaching, and he had started at a high school in Oxford, Ohio, where he took over the school's baseball, basketball, and football teams. He reconnected with Brown during the war, helping to coach the Navy team at Great Lakes, and after a few successful postwar years coaching football at Brown University and Washington University in St. Louis, Brown had hired him on in Cleveland.

As dissimilar as they seemed in appearance and personality, they were both serious students of the game, great believers in study and preparation, and they were alike in something else. Lacking the size and talent to play at the highest levels of the game themselves, both coaches reveled in their complete control over the destinies of the bigger, more physically talented men they coached. More than in any other sport, coaches can make or break football players, and some relish that power more than others. Both Brown and Ewbank had a mean streak, a tendency to belittle players, sometimes cruelly. Brown called it "needling."

Ray Renfro, who would go on to become one of the best receivers in Cleveland history, remembered Brown seeking him out on the sidelines early in his career, after he had dropped a pass. Brown sneered at him, "You always choke." The insult stung, and stayed with Renfro long after his playing days were over.

At its best, this could be seen as a motivational technique. All pro players who make mistakes in games face the ignominy of having their errors replayed during film sessions in slow motion at team meetings the following week, but Browns and Colts players knew the embarrassment would come spiced with pointed official derision. Players cut from the team were often sent packing with gratuitous insult and scorn. The upside of this meanness was the way it made those who remained on the roster feel special, part of an elite, exclusive club. Pet players, the team's enduring stars, formed lasting bonds of affection with Weeb, but the tendency to needle also alienated some exceptional players, those who, for whatever reason, found themselves in the doghouse and who resented the coach's acid tongue.

Baltimore's fun-loving, devil-may-care running back Alan "The Horse" Ameche rubbed the coach the wrong way early in his career, most likely because his broader interests—he was an opera lover and a shrewd businessman who would later make millions in the fast-food business—made him appear less focused and dependent on football than his teammates. He seemed incapable of showing up for meetings on time, and was often fined for failing to get his ankles taped before games with the rest of the players. He had a tanklike body and a jovial, boisterous, and sometimes crude nature. Ameche was famous for loosing horrific farts in classrooms, sometimes so bad that everyone would have to clear out for a few minutes. He would curl up with laughter. Weeb would scowl. He got the idea that his big fullback, a fierce competitor on the field, for some reason needed to be goaded into playing hard. "You didn't have to do that to Ameche," Unitas would say years later. Despite the running back's remarkable performances—he was elected to the Pro Bowl four times—he was a constant butt of Weeb's ridicule. He retired after only six seasons, still hale and hearty, largely because he disliked playing for the coach.

It was an ugly side to the winning method Weeb had learned in Cleveland, one that some of even the old coach's most loyal players feel he might have done better without. Raymond would reflect years later that Weeb might have corrected it himself if he had been called on it by the players closest to him, but none of them, Raymond included, had the gumption in those years to do so.

Despite this tendency, Weeb at first lacked the sure hand of his mentor in Cleveland when it came to head coaching. In his first year, Weeb asked his players to help him make the final cuts at the end of training camp. The team was assembled in the Pikesville Armory, where they began working out when training camp was over. The six players still considered potentially expendable were asked to leave a team meeting and wait in the hallway outside. The coach then asked the shocked remaining players to vote on which of the six should be allowed to fill the two remaining spots on the roster. At first no one in the room wanted to speak. Most players felt a certain solidarity with their teammates and were reluctant to torpedo the dreams of those they had been working alongside for weeks. Wasn't this supposed to be the coach's job? Finally, Bert Rechichar, a defensive back and kicker, spoke up.

"That damn Enke ain't gonna help us any," he said, referring to quarterback hopeful Fred Enke, Jr., who after seven years in the NFL was about to head home to a lifetime of cotton farming. "Let's get rid of him," said Rechichar.

"Okay," said Weeb, "that's one. Who else?"

Somebody suggested that they cut Jim Mutscheller, a prospective rookie tight end, because he had "Army legs." The Notre Dame graduate had just returned from a tour of duty in Korea, and it was assumed—in keeping with the odd notions of that era about exercise—that hauling a knapsack on long hikes made one unsuited for the short bursts of speed demanded by football.

The discussion continued. Most of the players were horrified. Finally the veterans asserted themselves and refused to do the coach's dirty work for him. Weeb never tried that approach again. For the rest of his life, even after he had developed a deep affection for the coach, lineman Artie Donovan would always refer to him as "That weasel bastard." The players who had contributed suggestions would never fully shake their reputation for being turncoats.

The coach kept Mutscheller, "Army legs" and all, and would be glad for the rest of his life that he did.

✳   ✳   ✳

In the years Weeb was apprenticing in Cleveland, pro football was making its way back to Baltimore by a circuitous route. The Colts were one of the three AAFC teams absorbed into the NFL when they merged, but despite the enthusiastic efforts of Baltimore Mayor Tommy D'Alesandro, Jr., who also brought the city the Orioles, its major league baseball franchise, the club struggled so badly on the field and at the box office that its owners sold it back to the league in 1951. For two years the franchise drifted. In New York it became the football Yankees, and was then moved to Dallas, where interest was so low that midway through its first season the club went bankrupt. The players and coaches were put up in a hotel in Hershey, Pennsylvania, for the remainder of that season, and played all of their remaining games on the road.

Determined to keep the franchise alive, and pestered by Mayor D'Alesandro to give Baltimore another chance, Commissioner Bell turned to a wealthy Baltimorean named Carroll Rosenbloom, who had played on a University of Pennsylvania team Bell had helped coach in 1927. Rosenbloom had made a fortune in the war manufacturing khaki uniforms. Bell talked his former player into teaming with several Baltimore partners to buy the club, and then challenged D'Aleasandro to sell fifteen thousand season tickets in six weeks to demonstrate a fan base in the city. The ticket packages sold in just four. When the new Colts won only three games in their first season, Rosenbloom bought out his partners to become sole owner, and eased out head coach Keith Molesworth, promoting him to club vice president. Then he started searching for someone who could build a winner.

Weeb got the job partly by virtue of a timely plug from Charley Winner, who had played for him in college. Winner had flown seventeen missions in a B-17 in the war, and spent six months in a German POW camp before returning home and playing for Weeb at Washington University. In those years he met and married one of the coach's daughters. He was coaching at Case Western University and scouting for the Browns in 1953 when he found himself on the same plane with Don Kellett, the Colts' general manager. Both men were on the way back from scouting talent at the annual Blue-Gray Game, a college all-star game. Winner struck up a conversation with Kellett, knowing the Baltimore club was looking for a new coach. He wasn't above a little subterfuge on behalf of his ex-coach and father-in-law.

He got Kellett talking about the coaching search, and, knowing the Baltimore executive knew nothing of his marital connection to Weeb, asked, "Did you ever consider this guy Ewbank?"

"Yeah, we wanted him but Paul Brown said he didn't want to be head coach," said Kellett.

"That's not true," said Winner.

Winner knew Brown to be jealous of his assistants, and that his father-in-law had lost several college head-coaching opportunities because Cleveland wouldn't release him from his contract. The NFL had rules about such things, however, and Winner knew that if the Colts wanted to talk to Weeb, Brown couldn't stop it.

He told Kellett that he thought Ewbank would be very interested. Every team in the pro league was trying to emulate

Brown's system, so a line on one of Cleveland's assistants was valuable.

"Give me his home number," said Kellett. By the next season both Weeb and his son-in-law had jobs in Baltimore. Winner was younger than some of the veteran Baltimore players he coached that year, but would go on to spend almost forty years on NFL sidelines, including two stints as a head coach. With the Colts, he became his father-in-law's right-hand man.

Weeb arrived in Baltimore with a bang. He boldly promised an NFL championship in just five seasons. Putting the Cleveland grading system in place, he began assessing players on a scale numbered zero through five. Zero meant a missed assignment. If you knew what to do and didn't do it, that was a one. If you got a lot of ones, that meant you knew what to do, you just weren't good enough to do it. If you got a two, it meant you knew what to do and you did an average job. Three meant you knew what to do and did it well. Once in a while a player would do something truly remarkable and earn a four. Fives were exceedingly rare. Players would earn a five maybe once or twice in a season. Those who scored zeroes and ones were soon pursuing other lines of work, and in time Weeb weeded out players who scored a lot of twos. He prized mean, aggressive players and awarded extra credit for the useful application of violence.

This kind of incentive sometimes startled opposing players, who were used to an unwritten code of conduct between professionals. San Francisco 49ers fullback Joe Perry was running a standard decoy pattern on a running play in 1954, well away from the action, when he was clubbed to the ground by a Colts tackle named Tom Finnin.

"Hey, Finny, what the hell are you doing?" he complained.

Finnin shrugged.

"I get points for that," he said.

Weeb worked hard to simplify the vocabulary of Brown's playbook, which like many things that evolve over years had become needlessly complicated. He was always working to improve on it, to invent new twists for successful plays. Like his old boss, at heart Weeb was a teacher, and he could be obsessive about it. Winner recalled that at his father-in-law's it was hard to make even a small comment at the dinner table without provoking a little homily from the coach. One of his receivers in those early years, Royce Womble, remembered catching a pass in a game and running it into the end zone, only to have Weeb corner him on the sidelines to offer further instruction.

The coach said, "Womble, the next time you run that pattern, try making this move just as you're coming out of your turn," executing a little dance step to demonstrate.

Womble just stared at him.

"Hell, Weeb," he said, "You can't get any more than six points!"

John Unitas had the best and most eager arm on the practice field that summer of 1956. He knew it was likely to be his last chance to latch on to a pro job after his year on the sandlots in Pittsburgh.

"We're looking for a backup quarterback for George Shaw," Kellett had told him in what would later become the most storied eighty-cent phone call in football history. John looked up a Colts roster and saw that the only quarterback they had backing Shaw was a rookie, so he thought he might have a chance. Still, he told the friend who drove with him out to the Colts' training camp, "This may be a total waste of time."

John was convinced Pittsburgh had never given him a fair shot. He had been such a standout at the University of Louisville that he became the school's starting quarterback in his freshman year, when he weighed only 141 pounds. After his stellar first season there, the university decided to de-emphasize sports, and fifteen of the team's players lost their scholarships. John had to play both offense and defense for a team short on talent, and despite quarterbacking performances that became legend at the school, the Cardinals teams he led mostly lost. Then an injury sidelined him for most of his all-important senior season. The team won only one game, and its benched starting quarterback was not a highly sought-after prospect by the pros. His hometown team drafted him in the ninth round, and cut him before the season started.

If John had one goal at that first Colts training camp, it was to make sure the Baltimore coaches got a good, long look at what he could do, an ambition that would meet its perfect complement in Raymond Berry's sophomore-year desperation. The receiver arrived that summer looking for a quarterback whom he could enlist for his personal practice sessions, someone to work on timing with him long after the rest of the players had left the field.

Staying after practice for extra work was unheard of, a bewildering habit chalked up to the receiver's well-known eccentricity. Artie "Fatso" Donovan wondered aloud about how strange it would be to play with a team full of Raymonds.

"The coach would have to punish them by cutting practice short!" he said.

Most of the players staggered off the field after the second daily practice session, particularly big men like Donovan, who usually had to drop many off-season pounds. As with everything else, Fatso made a joke out of his weight. He would arrive at the communal weigh-in room, strip off every stitch of his clothing, and then, before stepping on the sale, make a show of delicately removing his false teeth. Donovan made most things fun, but there was no way to ease the torture of training camp. The brutal summer practices were worsened by Weeb's old-school approach to hydration. It was considered a sign of weakness for a player to take a drink of water during practice, even when the August heat and humidity soared toward three digits. Offensive tackle Jim Parker for years kept a photograph of himself on the bench at Westminster sipping from a cup, and he would tell everyone, "That's me with a five-hundred-dollar lemonade." It was a sweltering day, and the mammoth Parker got so thirsty he told his son to fetch him a drink in defiance of the coach's ban. He had to pay a $500 fine, but swore for the rest of his life that it had been worth every penny.

Competition was fierce, and veteran players employed any trick they could to hang on to their jobs. Smaller men trying to qualify for jobs on the line had the opposite problem of Fatso's.

Like most players, center Buzz Nutter lost weight rapidly once camp started, something he could ill-afford. He was undersized for his position, and overate all through the off-season to pack on pounds, only to watch them melt away in the weeks of two-a-day drills. At one camp, when he was just 215 pounds, ten pounds under the weight his contract called for, and perilously underweight for his job, Nutter borrowed one of Donovan's tentlike T-shirts and put five-pound barbell weights under each armpit. He made the cut.

For those who had no trouble in the weight room or on the field, there were other hazards. Offensive guard Alex Sandusky, Nutter, and an impressive young end from Pepperdine University, a full-blooded Indian named Jack Bighead, went drinking on their first night off training camp in 1954. Bighead had been drafted by the Dallas Texans and picked up by Baltimore when that franchise folded. He was lighting up the field in scrimmages, far outperforming the scouting reports, and challenging the team's established receivers. A veteran end offered to give the three a ride into Baltimore, and promised to pick them up at ten o'clock to return them to Westminster. The three took the ride, went out on the town, and then showed up on time at the pickup spot, a little lightheaded with beer. Their ride didn't show. It didn't take long for them to realize they had been had. The senior player was trying to sabotage Bighead: they would all have been cut for failing to show up at practice the next morning. Pooling the money they had left, they found a kindly cab driver (and newly minted Colts fan) who for their twelve dollars was willing to run them out to Westminster, an hour drive west. A friendly assistant coach let them back into the dorm and Weeb never found out. They never forgot that making a pro roster meant forcing another man out of his job.

Raymond found that the new quarterback was happy to stay after practice. Unitas wasn't just obliging, he was eager. He was willing to throw for as long as Raymond wanted to catch. This was a quarterback who never worried about wearing out his arm, the way most did. He had a smooth, almost exaggerated way of uncoiling his throws, right down to the way he snapped his wrist as he released the ball so that his long fingers were splayed downward. The motion seemed effortless. It was also not lost on either Raymond or John that toiling away together for hours after practice was the kind of devotion that scored points with the coach. Weeb encouraged it quietly, making sure that the players had nothing scheduled for a few hours after the last field session. Sometimes Raymond would see him watching them from a distance.

The coaches were all amazed by John's arm. No one could yet foresee how great their bargain quarterback would become, but it was clear from the start that the Steelers had made a big mistake. Were they blind? They had cut him without giving him a chance to play. It was true that he didn't look like much of an athlete. He was hollow-chested and his gangly frame had matured into an ungainly stoop so that he ran like an old man, with a crooked scuttle. The first few times he took off with the ball in game, opponents were so startled by his awkward intensity that it took them a few seconds to react. After watching him scoot for a thirty-four-yard gain, Ed Modzelewski of the Browns described it as "a crazy man running through a burning building; would you want to get in his way?" Unlike George Shaw, the kid wasn't going to pose much of a threat with his legs. But he could throw the ball like nobody else. One of the most difficult passes in football was a fifteen-yard "out" pattern, thrown at such an angle that the ball had to travel twice that far. Most throwers put a little arc on the ball, trying to drop it in the right place. John's ball came flat and hard, and with such accuracy that it might have been on a wire. It arrived with such zip that it stung his receivers' hands.

"I can work with Unitas," Weeb told Raymond early that summer. "I can work with him."

Passer and receiver became fast friends. John understood Raymond's perfectionism, and the advantage of close coordination and timing in the passing game. Don Shula, one of the team's defensive backs at practice that summer (he would be traded to the Washington Redskins that year and would return later to succeed Weeb as Baltimore's coach), played against both Unitas and Shaw in practices that summer. Shula told John's biographer Tom Callahan that he was one of the first to notice that the extra work between John and Raymond was paying off. When Shaw was throwing to Raymond, he had no trouble defending, but when Unitas was throwing, he could not. It wasn't just Shula's imagination. He had to defend against Raymond in a real game the following season, and the receiver caught twelve of John's passes (one shy of his rookie season total) for 224 yards and two touchdowns.

Lenny Moore was the team's first-round draft pick that year, a flashy, high-stepping phenom from Penn State who played with a Bible wedged beneath his right thigh pad and who wrapped white tape around his ankles and the top of his shoes, earning him the nickname "Spats." Tall, big, and fast, Moore was the best athlete anyone in Baltimore had ever seen. He was also smart and sunny and selfless, traits not often found in such sought-after talent. Weeb was eager to exploit Moore's potential both as a running back and a flanker, but the discipline of pass routes was new to Moore. When Raymond first invited the heralded rookie to stay after practice for some extra work, the suggestion was received with some astonishment. Volunteer for more practice?

"Lenny, John won't ask you to stay after practice," said Raymond. "You have to do it yourself. He has to know that after three and two-tenths seconds, *this* is where you are going to be. You've got to time it up with him. It's like music. The same beat has to be playing in all of our heads."

Moore started staying late. Shula noticed he was getting damn hard to cover, too.

Both Raymond and John made the team that year, and their bond deepened. Raymond was living as a bachelor in a walk-up apartment in a row house near Memorial Stadium, the Colts' home field. He was the only teammate John began inviting to share dinner with him, his wife Dorothy, and his children. Raymond invited John to the private film-study sessions in his apartment. On their own time, the man with a magnificent feel for football was teaming up with the Colts' resident nut.

For all of this intensity and method, Weeb's new team struggled. He had won only three games in his first season, and only a combined total of ten in his next two. He and his staff all expected to be fired after the 1956 season, the year John took over as quarterback. Carroll Rosenbloom was a charming man given to flamboyant acts of generosity with his players, but he was hard on his coaches. He would berate Weeb mercilessly after a loss. The Colts' coaching staff figured that they were all going to get the boot as their third losing season drew to a close. In the last quarter of the final game, a home game against the Redskins, down by four points, assistant coach Frank Cuminskey turned to Winner high in their box over the field and said, in disgust, "Charley, we're gone and I'm leaving." He walked out. He wasn't there when Mutscheller, with his "Army legs," caught a pass from John for an exciting last-second win, bringing the team's record to five and seven.

Cumiskey was never invited back, but Weeb, to his surprise, was. Rosenbloom had it out with the coaching staff after the season, but then he met with the head coach and the team's general manager, Kellett, in Miami. Expecting to be fired, Weeb was completely candid. He felt his hands were tied by the team's stinginess. He could not offer competitive bonuses and salaries to his players, so he lost talent to other teams. He could not build the kind of draft program Brown had built in Cleveland because the team would not pay for scouts and travel expenses. Rosenbloom was surprised to hear this. He wanted his football team to win, and actually enjoyed spending his money. It was not unusual for him to make spontaneous, generous gifts to his players. When Gene "Big Daddy" Lipscomb was upset after a game to find that a large amount of cash had been stolen from his wallet in the locker room, Rosenbloom just peeled off an amount in excess of Lipscomb's loss and handed it over. At the beginning of each season, Rosenbloom met with the players, apart from the coaches, swore them to secrecy, and then violated league rules by offering them substantial under-the-table incentives for victories. He promised to match their official winnings if they captured the league championship. So Rosenbloom was perfectly willing to spend money if that was what winning required. The problem, Weeb was happy to explain, was Kellett, who was paid a percentage of the team's profits. The less of the team's money he spent, the greater the profit and the more he made. Rosenbloom and Kellett were old and close friends; they had played football together years earlier at the University of Pennsylvania, so Weeb felt sure his complaint would hasten his firing. Instead, the owner gave both men new contracts. Kellett's earnings were no longer tied to the club's profits. The owner promised more money for scouting and recruiting, and even loaned Weeb his own plane to use on weekends for scouting trips.

Weeb already had the nucleus of a good team. With linemen Marchetti, Lipscomb, and Donovan, and middle linebacker Bill Pellington, he was strong against the run, and with his new ability to recruit he shored up the team's pass defense by adding the speedy, cerebral free agent cornerback Milt Davis, and a fast, vicious safety from Memphis State University named Andy Nelson.

His offense was set. John had trundled out on the field in Chicago midway through the fifth game of the season after Shaw suffered a knee injury. The first pass he threw was intercepted and run back for a touchdown, and the Colts had ended up getting shellacked, 58-27. On the bus after that game, Mutscheller happened to sit behind the losing rookie quarterback and the *Baltimore Evening Sun* reporter Walter Taylor. He was surprised to hear John, after that awful performance in his first outing, calmly and confidently dissecting the loss. Unitas broke down his own mistakes and the team's, and described exactly how they would correct them. Mutscheller wondered, *Who is this guy?* From that first day forward, John radiated command. He steered the team to victory in his next two games, including an impressive win over Weeb's old mentor, Brown. In that game, he connected on a forty-three-yard touchdown pass to Raymond that seemed as natural and as untroubled as the routes they worked on after practice. It was a harbinger of things to come. With John throwing the ball, Raymond nearly tripled his production that season, catching thirty-seven passes.

After the last losing season the Colts would see in years, the team drafted Jim Parker, a 273-pounder who had been the nation's premier collegiate offensive lineman at Ohio State. Weeb turned Parker into a left offensive tackle, protecting the right-handed quarterback's blind side, and gave him one assignment, "Keep them off John." Parker would do his job so well that he played his way into the Hall of Fame, becoming the prototype for the massive left tackles who today are considered to be as important as quarterbacks in the NFL. With Parker, Weeb had all the pieces he would need.

But most importantly, he had John, or "Johnny," as he was now called. The young quarterback quickly became a favorite of Baltimore sportswriters, and would soon captivate the more literary scribes writing for the new national magazines like *Sports Illustrated* and *SPORT*, which catered to the growing preoccupation with professional games. There were all sorts of reasons for loving football, and John embodied one of the big ones. The fascination went beyond the sheer joy of serious competition, the brilliant athleticism on display, or the fun of rooting for the home team that swept over whole cities and regions. It went beyond wagering a few bucks on the outcome, as Carroll Rosenbloom liked to do. On a deeper level, sports creates a well-defined forum for excellence, and for character. The forum is condensed and simplified, so that the kind of traits that merit success in the wider world over a career or a lifetime are distilled into the frame of a season, or a single afternoon. Football, in particular, was an arena where courage and resilience were rigorously and publicly tested. Just as in the larger world, success was sometimes unfair, and players of poor character, judgment, and habits achieved on the basis of luck and reckless talent alone, but usually not for long. More often success came to those athletes and teams who combined extraordinary ability with selflessness, teamwork, stamina, discipline, and fortitude. When a clever athlete like Raymond Berry could overcome a lack of natural talent with intelligence and hard work, it confirmed those bedrock virtues for all.

John's story, the discarded gem rediscovered almost by accident, was too good to make up. But what made him irre-

sistible were his own qualities. He epitomized the kind of man-
hood prized by a generation formed in the war, battle-tested men
who had learned the hard way that a phony in command got
people killed. John was a man of action, not of words. He knew
that the only thing that mattered, ultimately, was success. He
seemed amused by sportswriters' insistence that he comment on
his performances—"I always figured being a little dull was part
of being a pro," he said years later. "Win or lose, I never walked
off a professional football field without thinking of something
boring to say to [*Baltimore Sun* football writer] Cameron Snyder."

He was the opposite of flashy; he hid his wit inside a gruff,
taciturn shell, and he looked goofy wearing black high-top cleats
on the end of those skinny, bandy legs. He didn't look good, he
didn't sound good, he just *was* good, and he knew it. He was a
natural leader, and not just because he called the plays. Long
before he had begun to demonstrate his excellence with wins
and completion percentages, his teammates trusted him completely. According to Tom Callahan, when the team's equipment manager wondered out loud in the locker room one day
in the middle of that losing 1956 season, when Shaw was coming back, the veteran Marchetti told him, "Shaw ain't coming
back." That respect radiated outward from the Colts' offensive
huddle. The men who relied on him trusted him. John knew
that it didn't come from write-ups in the press, the size of his
salary, or even the opinion of his coach. It did not come from
his talent or from his eventual celebrity. It came from his judgment and his character. There was not a flashy or celebratory
bone in his body, just as there was no outward sign of defeat.

On the sidelines after he had thrown a touchdown or an interception, his demeanor was the same. He was utterly unaffected by the attention focused on him as he grew increasingly noticed and successful. He was simply a man at work.

He saved that game against the Redskins, the one that ended the 1956 season with a play that Cumiskey never saw, a perfect example of what he brought to the field. Every coach believes that his system is foolproof, that if he could just find the right players to execute his perfectly designed plays, they would succeed every time. Ever since that abject loss against the Bears, when John had made his pro debut, Weeb had been feeding his offensive system to him a little at a time. But it was clear very quickly that John didn't just execute Weeb's system, he *played* with it. It was the difference between a music student playing the right notes and a master owning the material.

Real success on the gridiron is messier and harder than the diagrams in a playbook. It resides in the immediate reality of the field, a sense of the game that only comes from being immersed in the action, in the moment, like the knowledge that the middle linebacker has been leaning to his right, or that the attacking right defensive end has just twisted his knee but has resisted letting his coaches know, or that the cornerback has been set up to bite on an outside fake. In that sense, John was the master of *now*. Like a talented boxer in the ring, he had such a good sense of his opponent that when things were clicking he would play with a defense, setting them up patiently for a killer right hook, using sometimes a whole offensive series to prepare what he planned to do next; waiting, waiting, waiting until the perfect moment to throw the knockout punch. Throughout the game he would solicit ideas from his teammates: receivers, running backs, and linemen. "What have you got for me?" he would ask. "What do you need?" "What do you want to run?"

Raymond would grab the quarterback before the team huddled and deliver intelligence, telling him this or that pattern would probably work, or that he had patiently set up a particular fake. John would take it in, survey the defense, and come up with his own idea of what would work *at that moment.* Weeb scripted the first three plays of every game, and after that he would occasionally send one in with a substitute, but other than that he deferred to his new field general.

John clearly knew what he was doing. In his huddle there was respectful silence. You didn't presume to tell him what play to call, you planted a seed and waited for it to sprout. In the case of the winning pass in that Redskins game, it grew out of John's observation that the cornerback was quicker than the Colts' tight end Jim Mutscheller, so much quicker that he had grown cocky. He was covering him five yards too deep, figuring he could break back quickly enough to disrupt the play. John guessed that in his zeal to prevent a last-minute touchdown, the cornerback would be playing it safe, leaning deep longer than it was wise to lean deep. With just fifteen seconds left in the game, on a dark late afternoon in Baltimore, down 17-13, the quarterback didn't bother with Weeb's playbook. He gave his linemen their blocking assignments and then looked Mutscheller in the eye.

"Go deep, Jim," he said, "and then loop back."

It was improvisation. It was also the touchdown that saved all of their jobs, the one that opened the door to all that would follow.

Giants coaches (from left to right) Tom Landry,
Jimmy Lee Howell, and Vince Lombardi, 1956.
(Courtesy of *NY Daily News*)

Giants linebacker Sam Huff, 1958.
(Courtesy of Getty Images)

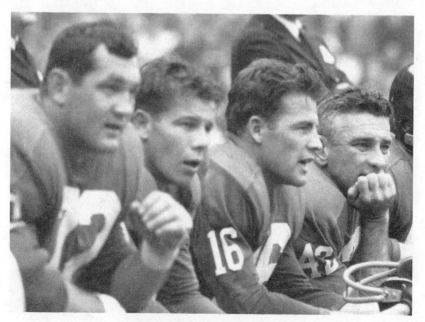

Giants bench (from left to right):
Frank Youso, Kyle Rote, Frank Gifford, and Charlie Conerly. (Courtesy of Getty Images)

Left to right: Giants secretary Wellington Mara, Yankees general manager George Weiss, NFL commissioner Bert Bell, and Giants owner Jack Mara. (Courtesy of *NY Times*)

Vince Lombardi, 1958.
(Courtesy of *Sport* magazine)

Top right: Rosey Grier
Bottom right: Jim Patton
(Photos courtesy of *Sport* magazine)

4

Huff

The Colts team that showed up in New York the day before that 1958 Championship game was, statistically speaking, the best in the league. "Johnny" Unitas had proved to be more than a great quarterback, he was a catalyst, that rare athlete who makes a whole team click. His fellow pros had voted him the league's Most Valuable Player in 1957, and he could easily have been that again the following year if not for Cleveland's Jim Brown, who had begun rewriting the NFL record books for running backs, rushing for seventeen touchdowns and more than 1,500 yards. John was still considered the best quarterback in the league. His career was just getting started, but already the Steelers' oversight looked like not just a blunder, but the single biggest personnel error in NFL history.

There was more to it than that, though, because if John had stayed in Pittsburgh he might never have developed the way he did in Baltimore. Paul Brown's revolution had matured the game from its smash-mouth, leather-helmet, grind-it-out roots to a physical contest with a challenging intellectual side.

Players like Raymond Berry, who studied film on their own and practiced obsessively, were still rare. Today such off-field work is essential, and digital technology has made it easier to do. Pro and college teams have layers of assistant coaches who wear their eyes out looking at video and tutoring position players, and just to be competitive in the NFL players have to work on their position year-round. But fifty years ago it was unlikely that John would have encountered a partner like Raymond. Their long film study sessions in the receiver's living room, studying moving images projected on a white wall, added new layers of authority to the quarterback's intuitive field judgment. The study was supplemented by hours of extra practice, with Raymond running route after route. A big part of John's success was also Raymond's. In 1957, their first full season playing together, he caught forty-seven passes for eight hundred yards and seven touchdowns, and was elected All-Pro.

Success not only confirmed the value of Raymond's approach, it deepened it. He carried a football with him everywhere, on and off the field, to accustom himself to holding it. When he wasn't involved in a scrimmage during practice, he would pick a kid out of the crowd of spectators and ask him or her to roll him the ball on the ground so he could practice pouncing on fumbles.

Raymond no longer just practiced catching the football, he broke down the various ways of doing so, depending on the position of his body, the location of the ball, and how he had to position his hands. He labeled each kind of catch. There were twelve kinds of short passes, most of which are self-explanatory—the High Look-In, High Back-to-Passer (looking at the throw first over the left shoulder, then the right), High Hook (turning and jumping for a ball thrown high), Low Ball, Scoop, Behind (the ball is thrown behind the direction of the receiver, who has to reach back for it), High and Behind, Back to Passer, One Hand, Toe Dance (keeping both feet in bounds at the edge of the field), Holler Ball (the receiver stands with his back to the thrower, who "hollers" when he throws, and the receiver has to pick up the ball in midflight), and Concentration (having a defender try to distract you while catching the ball). Raymond identified seven types of long passes—the Inside Shoulder, Outside Shoulder, Directly Overhead, Wrong Shoulder, End Line Toe Dance, Tightrope Toe Dance, and Harassment. He had John throw him three or four of every type every day, patterning the movements required to catch it, watching the ball all the way into his hands. To simplify the drills he strung netting from the goal posts to catch the balls he missed.

Weeb sometimes worried that John would wear out his arm.

"John, you've thrown enough," he told the quarterback one day, after seeing him and Raymond at work again long after practice.

"Coach, I just work here," John said. "You better tell him," pointing at the receiver.

Weeb had such respect for Raymond's methods and insights that he rarely questioned or instructed him. It was clear to the other players that Raymond enjoyed a special status, which is what John had meant by, "I just work here." In one game, the head coach sent in a substitute with a suggested play. He usually left the play-calling to John, and had been known, on occasion, to send in general encouragement and even suggestions like, "Get a first down," which would make the players in the huddle chuckle, but this time Weeb had a specific pass play in mind, a pass to Raymond. John called the play, and the end, who rarely spoke in the huddle, objected. It was rare indeed for a receiver to veto a play where the ball was to be thrown to him; they were universally inclined to beg for the ball. But Raymond said, "It's not there, John." So the quarterback called a different play, which failed. When he came off the field, Weeb was livid. He let loose a stream of obscenity, concluding with, "Why didn't you run the play I sent in?"

"Raymond said no," John told him.

"Oh," said Weeb, immediately placated. "Why didn't you say so?"

During the season, Raymond would come to John on Tuesdays with his yellow legal pad full of notes. He would stop by Weeb's office the day after the game to borrow film for the next opponent, and would spend hours on Monday studying the cornerback he would face next. Then he would tell John, "This is what I want to run on this guy this week." That's what they would work on in practice all week, nothing else. Weeb built a game plan, Raymond built a wide-receiver plan, and John digested both. Once he knew Raymond's preferred routes, he and Weeb would work out blocking assignments and play action.

Even as the receiver's dogged, analytical style worked its influence on the team, his teammates continued to consider him odd. And Raymond *was* odd, but he was also the future of their sport. The days of the hard-drinking, hard-living bruiser who showed up on Sunday with a hangover were dwindling. No one quarreled with Raymond's results. He got better every year. He caught fifty-six passes in 1958, which led the league. He was so careful and deliberate about the way he caught and handled the ball that he would fumble only once in his thirteen-year career, perhaps the most remarkable and telling of all his lifetime stats. His excellence raised John as much as the quarterback's talent raised him. They were reciprocal.

With an intimidating veteran defense and a remarkably balanced offense that could march upfield with either the run or the pass, Baltimore had coasted through that season, putting up more points than any other team. They lost only one game on their way to clinching the western division championship. That one loss, however, had come at Yankee Stadium to the Giants, 24-21. It was also the only game that year that John didn't play. He watched it on television from a hospital bed in Baltimore, nursing broken ribs and a collapsed lung, compliments of the Green Bay Packers, whose defense the week before had turned especially surly in the midst of a 56-0 rout. George Shaw, now the team's back-up quarterback, played well in the Giants' loss, but the game demonstrated, as if the Colts didn't already know, how vital Unitas was to their ascendancy. The Giants had sat on their lead through the game's closing minutes, taunting the Baltimore defense from the sidelines. Art Donovan grew so frustrated at the end that he started picking stones out of the turf and pelting the New York bench.

If there was one team that could stop the Colts, it was this one. The Giants were an established power, a team beloved in New York but in the fine tradition of American sports, mostly hated in the rest of the country. They were the golden franchise, situated in the media capital of the world, and featured many of the league's best known and best paid athletes. Its stars were written about in national sports magazines and signed lucrative advertising contracts. They had been champs in 1956, had stumbled the following year, but seemed poised for years of dominance.

The Giants' franchise was in many ways the opposite of Baltimore's, which was one of the league's newest and had a rich playboy owner whose gambling habits raised persistent if unproven rumors of meddling to cover point spreads. The Giants were one of the original NFL teams, founded by Tim Mara, a legal bookmaker, who eventually handed it over to his sons Jack and Wellington. The Maras were football aristocracy, and they ran the club like a family trust. Jack, the eldest, controlled the business side, while Wellington devoted his professional life to the game. A rock of respectability, Wellington, a slender man with a broad, muscular forehead and eyes that squinted out from two narrow slits, was a devout Catholic, the product of Loyola High School in Manhattan and the Jesuit Fordham University. Self-effacing, stoic, and unfailingly polite, he was one of the most beloved and respected figures in the league, someone who belonged by birth to the old guard, but by age to the new one. He had literally grown up with the team, carrying water to players on the field in their first games in 1925.

The old owners, including Tim Mara, had been businessmen first and football men second. The division of labor between the two younger Maras, however, enabled Wellington to be a football man first. He knew the game, he knew talent, and he knew how to get and use it. He was always looking for ways to be useful. During the 1956 championship game, he had climbed up on the roof of Yankee Stadium with a Polaroid camera, and taken snapshots of the Chicago formations. He would put the pictures in a sock weighted with a few cleats, and toss it down to the Giants' sideline, where the coaches used them for reference. He proved himself most useful, however, in acquiring and keeping talented football players. The dominant core of coaches and players he assembled in the 1950s was a professional triumph.

More than most teams, New York's had a split personality. The Maras had hired as head coach Jim Lee Howell, one of their former players. He was a blustery, towering ex-marine and pass-catching end who had the good sense to delegate most of the hands-on coaching to his two extraordinarily able young assistants, Tom Landry on defense and Vince Lombardi on offense. Nobody knew yet just how right he was to entrust his team to these two, but Howell seemed to have no doubt. He joked that his only job was to inflate the footballs and rake the stadium infield smooth before every game. He was an old-school football coach, someone whose long history in the game had imbued him with its manly culture. Football was about toughness and will, blood and guts and broken teeth, and with his background as a player and drill instructor in the marines, Howell had the leather-lunged qualifications to rally and goad, the traditional tools of the profession. Landry and Lombardi, on the other hand, were from the new, Paul Brown school of coaching. Like Weeb, they relished toughness and the controlled violence of the game, but they were also devotees of organization and careful preparation. Landry in particular was a film-study buff who approached coaching not as a job, but as a vocation. The year before Howell, Lombardi, and Landry took over, the Giants went three and nine. It took them just three seasons to reverse those numbers and win the NFL championship.

A squat, dark, driven man with a bull neck and a gap between his two front teeth, the son of an Italian butcher, Lombardi had gotten the impression when the Maras first approached him in 1954 that they wanted him as head coach. So it was with some reluctance that he accepted the lesser role, which he did in part because, on a visit to Howell's Arkansas pig farm, he was promised a free hand with the offense. The pugnacious Brooklynite had been working as an assistant coach at West Point, and before that had played football as an under-sized offensive lineman at Fordham University. Wellington Mara had been the sports editor of the Fordham yearbook in those years, but the Giants' owner said later that he had never met Lombardi. They became acquainted years later because of Mara's interest in Lombardi's legendary boss at the military academy, Red Blaik, who had once described his assistant admiringly as "a rough soul." It was Blaik who recommended Lombardi to Mara as a coach who could keep pace with the changing pro game. Lombardi carried around a leather satchel that would become known as his "bible." As his biographer David Maraniss would put it, "In Lombardi's bible, the chapters charting the Browns were the book of revelation."

But Lombardi was not as enamored of the passing game as Brown. The core of this rough soul's approach to offense was his experience as a lineman. He became famous for running a relatively small number of plays and not even troubling to disguise them that much. The key was not surprise, not the fancy derring-do of quarterbacks and running backs, but *execution*. Lombardi wanted his entire offense to work together with the precision of a dance company, or an engine (to choose a more appropriately gritty metaphor). The key to his system was not open-field running or a strong, accurate arm, but blocking.

Lombardi looked for linemen who were more in his own mold, not just big and strong, but quick and agile and smart. His most famous play, the sweep, required the guard and tackle on one side of the line to literally pirouette off the line of scrimmage, performing a 180-degree turn at the snap of the ball before leading the running back on a sweep around the end, picking off potential tacklers on the run. The play demanded the precision of a dance number, lest the faster runner get ahead of his wall of protection. Lombardi loved blockers, but he recognized that the flanker position opened up a new range of strategic opportunity.

In the running great Kyle Rote, the Giants had an athlete just like "Crazy Legs" Hirsch, the prototype, so Lombardi moved him out of the backfield and split him wide. The new offensive coach's most significant adjustment, however, was to center his attack around Frank Gifford, the team's first-round pick in 1952, who had not found a consistent role in his first seasons. His coaches shifted him back and forth from offense to defense, and Gifford had yet to really shine in the pros as he had in college. A strikingly handsome, well-spoken man, Gifford engaged the New York press in a Hamlet-like performance every off-season, wondering out loud whether he would return to play again for the Giants or stay out in California to pursue acting, his first love, and a potentially more lucrative career. He had landed small parts in five films. The prospect of success seemed stronger in football, but the potential pay in Hollywood was astronomical by comparison.

Lombardi was determined to keep Gifford on the gridiron. He had coached West Point against USC when Gifford played there, and he remembered the young Californian's talent. When they first met, he told the player, "You are my running back." Under the new offensive coach, Gifford would become the best at that position in the team's history.

As important as Lombardi was to the success of the Giants, Mara's more significant hire may have been Landry, who controlled the other half of the team. Fair-skinned, tall, serious, with thin lips and small eyes, the soft-spoken Texan was in manner and appearance the volatile Italian's opposite. With Landry there were never histrionics. He did not bother to form close relationships with most of his players. He assumed motivation was something private and personal; all that interested him was performance. He would tell his men, "Here is what I want you to do. If you can do it, you will play. If you can't, no hard feelings, I'll find someone who can." A B-17 pilot in the war, Landry had played college ball for the University of Texas, and after a stint with the AAFC, played in the Giants' defensive backfield for four years. He didn't just observe the transformation of the game, he experienced it. He had grown up with Howell's hardscrabble brand of football, and had paid his dues. He liked to tell the story of the time the team's trainer decided that his split lip needed a few stitches, so the old-school trainer pulled out his needle and without a thought of anesthesia started sewing, only to realize that he had forgotten the thread. Landry said he sat on the training table blinking back piercing pain with the needle stuck through his lower lip, while the trainer went off on a casual search for surgical thread. It was just how things were done. Football was always going to demand toughness, and Landry put a premium on it, but the unparalleled success of Brown's Cleveland teams suggested that more than toughness was required.

In the rough meritocracy of the gridiron, football strategy constantly and rapidly evolves. Any new idea that works gets repeated, noticed, and imitated until somebody figures out how to defeat it, often the following week. Survival demands constant adaptation. Losing kills careers. The hard truth of this natural selection breeds desperation. In his first game as a pro with the AAFC New York Yankees in 1949, Landry had been saddled with defending against the dominant Browns star receiver, the aptly named Mac Speedie, who ran past him, under him, and around him all afternoon, catching so many passes from

Otto Graham that he set a league record for receiving yards in a single game, well over two hundred. Landry was humiliated. He realized that the only way to defeat the speed and accuracy of a pro combination like Graham-to-Speedie was to somehow know *in advance* where the receiver and the ball were going.

So, much as Raymond had on the other side of the ball, Landry had turned himself into a student of receivers, scrutinizing them on film until late into the night, memorizing their moves and routes, charting their tendencies. When he made the move to player-coach under Howell, and then gave up playing, shedding his pads for the suit and tie and short-brimmed fedora that would become his trademark on the sidelines, Landry broadened his study to include the entire offense, looking for clues to its intentions in the flickering black-and-white shadows of his sixteen-millimeter film, and devising strategies that didn't just react to plays, but anticipated them. By 1958, he had turned the Giants into the premier defensive team in the league.

As talent scouts, the Maras were alert, and lucky. Emlen Tunnell, the mainstay of their pass defense, had not been drafted, primarily because the league shut out most black players. He walked into the Giants' front office in 1948 not long after Wellington became the team's vice president, and offered his services. Tunnell became the team's first black player and one of the best defensive backs in league history.

The Maras had signed Rote, the triple-threat running back, receiver, quarterback from SMU in 1951, at a time when he was coveted by every other team in the league, winning the chance when the league offered each team a bonus pick. When the own-

ers chose slips of paper from a hat to decide on the order of selection, Wellington had drawn first pick. The next year, with the
third pick in the first round, they drafted Gifford. Players wanted
to come to New York. With the 1956 championship in their
trophy case, the Giants were considered prime contenders. They
paid top dollar for talent, and in the media capital of the world,
achievement was not only noticed, it led to lucrative advertising deals. The Maras tracked down their big halfback, Alex
Webster, in Canada in 1955, playing for the Canadian League
champion Montreal Allouettes. Webster had been a late pick
of the Redskins in 1953, but had been cut before the season
started. Andy Robustelli, the Giants' star defensive end, was
obtained in a trade the Maras engineered with the Los Angeles
Rams in 1956. The Rams threw in another player with that
deal, their third-round pick from Penn State, a massive defensive lineman named Rosey Grier, because the big New Jersey native refused to play away from home. Grier had told every
NFL scout that he would play only for the Giants. He wanted
his family to be able to watch him on Sundays. His stubborn-
ness cost him a hefty signing bonus, and handed New York a
bargain. "That was me," Grier joked many years later, "The great
negotiator."

The Maras traded for the Chicago Cardinals' superb place-
kicker Pat Summerall before the 1958 season, a move which
would pay big dividends, and they gave up a draft pick to acquire
Detroit cornerback Carl Karilivacz. They used their first draft
pick for Phil King, a star fullback from Vanderbilt who stood
six-four and weighed 220 pounds, with a broad face and high

cheek bones. He was part Cherokee, and so was of course immediately christened "Chief." King was a modest fellow with good
work habits and Lombardi liked him immediately. Studying film
of an exhibition game against the Colts one night in the Bear
Martin Inn outside Salem, Oregon, where the team held training camp at Willamette College, the coach barked, "Stop the
picture!"

It froze in the middle of an offensive play. Lombardi
pointed to the screen.

"Who threw that block?" he asked.

Arthur Daley, a *New York Times* reporter, recorded the
moment:

> *There was complete silence.*
>
> *"Speak up," roared Lombardi. "Who threw that block?"*
>
> *There was more silence.*
>
> *"Will someone answer?" said the coach. "Don't be afraid to speak up.
> It was a perfect block. Did you throw it King?"*
>
> *"Well, coach," said the Chief, "It looked like too good a block for me
> to have thrown it."*
>
> *When the guffaws subsided, the modest Alex Webster shamefacedly
> admitted that he was the culprit.*

Deference like that from a rookie earned respect. King became a powerful addition to their running game.

Of all the players Mara had assembled for this team, his biggest coup had come in 1955, with their third draft pick, the
thirtieth player chosen. If there was a player on the New York
squad who stood as a kind of equal and opposite number to the

combination of John and Raymond in Baltimore, it was a broad-shouldered, baby-faced tackler named Robert E. Lee Huff.

The world knew him as Sam.

Sam Huff had been an exceptional 220-pound tackle on offense and defense for the University of West Virginia, helping that team to thirty-one wins and only seven losses in his college career. Son of a coal miner, born in a mining camp, Huff was determined to never go back to the life that defined his father and brothers. There was a deceptive softness to his appearance, a round face and layer of body fat over his big frame, that disguised the powerful athletic build underneath. He was quick and tough and proud to a fault. He had nothing and wanted everything. Huff was an outsized character, with enough ambition on and off the field to frighten the faint of heart. He was outspoken, brash, and unapologetic. Some of the men who played against him swore that he had had the number seventy on the back of his jersey enlarged—"I think he even had seventy painted on the bottom of his cleats, so that on film none of his tackles would be missed," said one. Neither claim was true, but it seemed like something Huff might do. He was not above a little self-promotion and he liked to be noticed. He played football with unmatched ferocity, reveling in the game's violence—"On the field, I try to hurt everybody," he said, cheerfully. He had come to New York City for the first time at the end of his senior season to appear on *The Ed Sullivan Show* with a group of other collegiate football all-Americans.

Huff hit it off there with Paul Hornung, the Notre Dame star, who announced at a rehearsal before the show that he was going to score a date with the movie star Kim Novak, who was also on the show that week.

Penniless, Huff couldn't imagine taking anyone out on a date in Manhattan, much less a movie star.

"How much money do you have?" he asked Hornung.

"Twenty dollars," said Hornung.

Huff was dazzled, both by his new friend's daring and his riches.

It was at the same rehearsal that a dignified man in a business suit approached him.

"Sam," he said, "did you get my letter? I'm Wellington Mara."

Huff shook the Giants' owner's hand and said that he had gotten the letter.

"Well, we drafted you, you know," said Mara.

"Yeah, that's what you said in your letter, number three." Huff sounded slightly displeased.

"I'd like to talk contract with you."

Huff smelled money, maybe even Kim Novak dating money. Mara had brought a contract with him, which the college all-star scanned quickly. It offered $7,000.

"Do you need money right now?" Mara asked.

"Yes, sir," said Huff.

"How much?" asked Mara.

Huff boldly tossed out the first big number that popped in his head.

"Five hundred dollars."

Much to his surprise, Mara didn't even blink. He wrote out a check for the full amount on the spot.

Huff was agog, but wary. Still holding the contract, he said, "I can't sign this." He explained that he had promised his college coach, Art Lewis, that he wouldn't sign anything without first consulting him.

"Well, why don't you give him a call?" Mara suggested.

So Huff called Lewis.

"Coach, I'm here with Mr. Mara of the Giants, and he wants to sign me to a contract for seven thousand dollars."

"Boy," said Lewis, "sign that goddamn thing before he changes his mind."

Huff signed it.

His sudden riches gave him bragging rights that day over Hornung, who still had a few years of college ball to play. Huff didn't score a date with Novak, but it was more money than he had ever had at one time. It lasted him until the season started, when he discovered, to his alarm, that the team had deducted one hundred dollars from his first check. He was told that it would be the same for the next four. He owed Mr. Mara five hundred dollars.

Huff sought out the owner, and complained, "I thought that was a bonus!"

"Son, you may be from West Virginia," said Mara, "but it's time you learned the difference between a bonus and an advance."

Losing his "bonus" was not the only thing discouraging

about that first training camp at St. Michael's College in Winooski, Vermont. Coach Howell tried Huff on both the offensive and defensive lines, and he wasn't impressed. Huff had bulked up to about 235 pounds, but the man he was trying to block, Rosey Grier, weighed 295. Roosevelt Brown, who played offensive tackle, was not much smaller than Grier and Brown was solid muscle, with a narrow waist and broad shoulders, the most athletic big man Huff had ever seen. Huff looked like a high school player alongside him. It was humiliating. Until a rookie settled into a position and was taken under the wing of either Lombardi, Landry, or one of the other position coaches, he belonged primarily to Howell, whose motivational methods burned Huff. The rookie lineman was busting his gut, doing everything the team asked, but it didn't seem to be enough for the old drill instructor.

"You're not running fast enough!" he would shout at Huff. "What the hell is wrong with you?"

Huff hated him. His ebullient, egotistical exterior had a flip side. He chafed at disapproval. He took poorly to the former marine's methods. Shouting at players and insulting them was just Howell's way on the practice field, and it was a time-honored approach in the profession, but it got under Huff's skin. He considered the head coach a dumb son of a bitch from Arkansas, and between absorbing his abuse and his losing battles against bigger, more experienced players, Huff decided he had had enough. He was homesick and felt himself stranded in a hostile place. He had been a standout on the baseball team at West Virginia, too. Now he second-guessed his decision to try football. He told himself, *I think I'm in the wrong game.*

As Huff would remember it years later, he and his room-mate, Don Chandler, a rookie punter from Oklahoma, both felt the same way. They had met at the college all-star game a few weeks earlier.

"I don't like it here," Huff told him one night.

"I don't either," said Chandler.

"And I'm homesick," said Huff.

"I am, too," said the kicker.

And as though listening in on their conversation, the popular country song "Detroit City" came on the radio, with its mournful refrain:

I wanna go home.
Oh, how I wanna go home.

"Let's get outta here," said Huff.

"How?" asked Chandler. They were in rural Vermont.

"Let's just go down and turn our playbooks in and then we'll figure it out," said Huff, determined now.

The two went down two flights and knocked on Lombardi's door, waking him.

Lombardi opened the door and roared, "What the hell are you guys doing?"

"We quit," said Huff.

"What do you mean, you *quit?*" asked Lombardi, angrier now about more than being awakened. Chandler ran back up-stairs leaving Huff to deal with the coach.

"Coach, here's our playbooks," said Huff, handing them over. "We can't take it anymore."

"What the hell do you mean, you can't take it anymore?" roared Lombardi. "Goddamnit, we've had you here for two weeks now. You mean to tell me we wasted two weeks on you two goddamn guys?"

"Coach, I just can't take it anymore," said Huff. "I don't give a goddamn."

Huff went back to his room, leaving Lombardi swearing and sputtering. He and his like-minded roommate were packing when the offensive line coach, Ed Kolman, a former Chicago Bear, knocked on their door. Huff liked him.

"Sam, I talked with Vince, and he said you're leaving," said Kolman.

"Yep," said Huff. "I can't—you've heard Jim Lee Howell yelling at me, screaming at me. Goddamnit, I don't take that from anybody; I never have. Hell, I can go home and teach school and make more money than I'm making here, you know, and be with my family."

This was true. Huff had been a good student and had earned a teaching certificate from West Virginia. Teachers were making more than rookie NFL linemen in 1956. Huff figured he would teach high school and coach, maybe try out for a baseball team.

"Sam, if you leave here, it'll be the biggest mistake you've ever made in your life," said Kolman. "I played this game, and I really believe you can be a star in this league."

"A star?" Huff said, surprised.

"Yeah, I've watched you; I've coached you," he said. "You can play."

"That's not what Jim Lee Howell says, you know," said Huff.

"If you stay—I want you to stay—if you stay, he won't say anything else to you," promised Kolman. "I'll take care of that."

"Okay, I'll stay," said Huff, mollified.

Chandler complained, "Well what the hell am I gonna do?" No coach had come upstairs to tell him he was going to be an NFL star.

So the kicker found another rookie who had a car, and who agreed to drive him to the airport in Burlington. Huff rode along to try to talk Chandler out of it, and ultimately, with Lombardi's intercession—the coach drove out to the airport separately—the kicker stayed. Just to make sure, the rookie with the car got cut the next day.

Just as he had mistaken an advance for a bonus, young Sam Huff had mistaken hazing for disapproval. The Giants saw his talent; they just had not yet figured out what to do with it. He was cocky and proud enough to know he had options in life, and that is an impressive thing in a young man. He continued to play offense during training camp, but unbeknownst to him he had attracted the attention of the team's defensive coach.

Landry had a new idea about playing defense, something to counter the complex Brown-style offenses they were seeing more and more. The standard pro defense for decades had been five down linemen, three linebackers to help plug holes in the line and stop the run, and three safeties who played deeper and guarded against the pass. But as teams began sending tight ends and running backs out for passes along with flankers, there were too many receivers for three defensive backs to cover. Steve Owens, who had been the Giants' head coach when Landry was a player, had converted one of the linebackers into a deep man, creating a formation he called the "umbrella," with five linemen, only two linebackers, and four pass defenders, two "cornerbacks" split wide, and two safeties who covered the middle of the field. Offenses adapted to this shift by throwing more short passes, taking advantage of the opening created by the missing linebacker. So Landry was experimenting with what he called "The Four-Three," a radical departure that simply removed one of the down linemen, restoring the number of linebackers to three. It was radical because it granted offenses a standing mismatch on the line of scrimmage, which invited a running attack. The answer, Landry knew, was the man in the center, the middle linebacker. He would have to be a kind of superathlete, a man as big as a lineman, quick enough and fast enough to play pass defense, and smart enough to recognize which role to play with every snap of the ball. The player he had in that spot was Ray Beck, who was smart and fast, but about twenty pounds shy of the size Landry wanted.

He had been watching Huff in practice. The beleaguered West Virginian with the baby face had improved enough playing against bigger men on the line to make the team as an offensive guard, but in the struggle had lost weight. He seemed doomed, too small for the line, too big for the defensive backfield. When

Beck hurt his ankle in a preseason game and looked like he was going to be laid up for a few weeks, Landry thought about Huff.

Training camp had broken, and Huff was living with a large group of players and coaches in the Excelsior Hotel on the Upper West Side. Landry had an apartment at the hotel with his wife Sheila and their two children. Huff's phone rang one night.

"What are you doing tonight, Sam?" asked the coach.

"I thought I'd just watch a little TV," said Huff.

"Well, good, I'm glad you're not doing anything," Landry said, as he recalled in his autobiography. "Why don't you come down and we can look at some game films?"

With his wife putting the children to bed, projecting film on his living room wall, Landry asked the rookie, "Have you ever thought about playing linebacker? I'd like to try you there and see how you do."

"Tom, I never played linebacker," said Huff.

"Well, why don't you just try it?"

The art of getting a man to excel hinges on understanding his idea of himself, and Landry had read Huff perfectly. The rookie liked to be the center of attention, and liked being entrusted with authority.

"We're going to play this four-three," Landry said, "and I want you to play middle linebacker."

The thing that stuck in the rookie's mind, the thing that clicked, was when Landry said he wanted to build his whole defense around him. Huff stepped into the role in practice, and it was a revelation. He felt like he had found the position he was

born to play. He had spent his entire football career as a lineman, and had begun every play in the three- or four-point
stance, his head craning up no higher than to see the big man
similarly positioned across from him, eyeball to eyeball. That
was what football had meant to him, a man-to-man struggle
on every play. Now he was standing upright at the center of
the line, and he was amazed at how much more he could suddenly see. It was as though he had played the game his whole
life with blinders on, and now they were gone. With his pe-
ripheral vision, he could see the whole field, from sideline to
sideline.

After the first few practices, before he had even played the
position in a scrimmage, Landry told him, "I think you're doing
good."

"What do you mean I'm doing good?" said Huff. "I
haven't even played."

"I really think your catching on as to what, you know, we
need to do," said Landry, "but I want to say something to you.
I don't ever want you to try something in a game that you don't
think you can do."

Huff was startled. No coach had ever talked to him like
this. You never told a coach you couldn't do something. It suggested a lack of heart, a paucity of desire. Here was Landry inviting Huff to declare his own limits. It made him feel less like
a soldier, and more like Landry's partner. They were creating
something new, collaborating. Landry was feeling his way, just
as Huff was. This was exactly the opposite of Howell's heavy-
handed approach.

"If you think you can't do something, you tell me because we're going to develop this defense, and it's going to be developed around you," reiterated the coach.

In his first try against the Giants' offense in scrimmage, Huff was lined up in the middle, just a few steps across the line from the team's great center, Ray Wietecha. On the defensive line, the tradition was to assign each tackle responsibility for a hole, or running lane, either to the inside or the outside of the offensive guard lined up to block them. In Landry's new system, whenever the defensive tackles went to the outside, no one immediately attacked Wietecha. The center had a clean shot and a running start at the new middle linebacker. He knocked Huff on his duff.

"Tom, I can't play that the way you want me to play it," Huff complained to his collaborator. "I can't play off the center like that. He comes right out after me."

Landry made adjustments to ensure that the center always had somebody to contend with, which shifted still more responsibility to Huff. To prevent big holes from opening up in the line, he had to quickly read the play and move toward the ball. And with that, Huff and the four-three defense started to click. Now it was the middle linebacker who had a running start, and he started hitting the runners on his own team so hard they complained.

"What the fuck are you doing?" said Gifford, after Huff flattened him in a scrimmage.

"Come through here again and I'm gonna knock your fucking head off," growled Huff.

Just like Raymond and John, Huff and Landry formed a partnership, spending almost every night studying film on the coach's living room wall. Landry didn't waste a lot of time trying to teach all of his players. He figured there were only four who really understood the lessons he took from his film study: defensive end Andy Robustelli, outside linebacker Harland Svare, safety Jimmy Patton, and Huff. Wellington Mara once sat in on one of Landry's coaching sessions, during which Grier fell asleep. Mara pointed it out to the coach.

"Let him sleep," Landry said. "He wouldn't understand what I'm saying anyway."

Huff understood. He became Landry's prize pupil, and saw very little of New York as a result. He and his coach were perfecting their scheme. Armed with insight into the opposing team's tendencies, Huff felt like he knew on almost every play exactly what the quarterback had planned. What he didn't recognize from his film studies with Landry, he began to pick up on his own. He would notice the way a center distributed his weight before the snap. If he had his weight off the ball, back on his haunches, it meant he was preparing to backpedal and protect the quarterback—a pass. If the guards had their weight off their front hand it usually meant they were preparing to pull—an end sweep. Huff would read and intuit and then shout out rushing assignments to his tackles. Then he would move to the ball and hit somebody. He would later boast that he was "the first designated hitter in football." He wanted his opponents to fear him. If a contending player walked past him on the field after a play, he would sometimes throw an elbow at him, just for the hell of it.

Huff took a job selling cigarettes in West Virginia in the off-season, bought his father a twenty-four-acre farm and set him up as a breeder of Shetland ponies, and for the rest of the year set about making himself the most feared football player of his era. In just a few years, his face would grace the cover of *Time* magazine, a symbol of the hard-hitting game. On their way to the championship that year the New York crowd would chant, "Huff! Huff! Huff!"

Even his name seemed perfect.

Giants quarterback
Charlie Conerly,
Marlboro Man.

Giants running back Frank Gifford. (Courtesy of *NY Times*)

Carroll Rosenbloom, owner of the Baltimore Colts.
(Courtesy of Special Collections, University of Maryland Libraries)

Pat Summerall's game-winning kick against the Cleveland Browns,
Dec. 21, 1958. (Courtesy of AP)

5

Getting There

When the Giants won the championship in 1956, on the heels of another triumphant Yankees season—Don Larsen had hurled the only perfect game in World Series history that October—they became full-fledged celebrities in the city of cities. The New York Giants baseball would soon move to San Francisco and give the football club sole possession of the name. They got the best tables and free drinks and meals at Toots Shor's, the restaurant on Fifty-first Street (Shor insisted it was a "saloon") that was the place to be seen for Manhattan's famous and infamous. The football players shared the spotlight there with politicians, Broadway and movie stars, racketeers, playwrights, and authors—Gifford dined there with Ernest Hemingway. They were introduced courtside at Madison Square Garden, and became hot commodities on Madison Avenue. Gifford, with his matinee idol good looks, was earning $16,000 a year from the team, one of the biggest salaries in the game, and having put his silver-screen ambitions on temporary hold, was starring in TV commercials for shaving cream and hair oil, Jantzen swimwear, and Lucky Strike cigarettes. To his teammates, he was "Hollywood." The veteran quarterback Charlie Conerly, who at age thirty-seven was the most senior player at that position in the NFL, was featured in national advertising as the Marlboro Man, every inch the iconic American cowboy (although he was from Mississippi) with his weathered, chiseled features and dignified graying temples. He and his wife bought a 225-acre cotton farm just outside Alligator, Mississippi. Those few who attracted the attention of advertisers began to make many times more money than their teammates, most of whom were paid less than $10,000 a year.

The extra money was especially welcome because it was nearly impossible to squeeze more out of the Maras. After his freshman season, the twenty-two-year-old Huff had established himself as starting middle linebacker on the best team in the league, and was on his way to defining the position. He asked for a $1,500 raise. In the off-season, Wellington Mara sent him a new contract offering $7,500, a $500 raise. Huff sent it back unsigned. When they met at training camp, the owner upped the offer to $8,000, and Huff tried to stand his ground. Mara threw a tantrum. As Huff would remember it, the pale Irishman's face turned red and the veins in his neck bulged. He stood up, grabbed all the papers on his desk, and flung them in anger around the room. "You will sign this contract or I will trade you so fast you won't even know where you've landed," he said. "Now you *sign this contract!*"

Huff signed. He would get another $1,000 raise after a sterling season in 1957.

Many of the Giants' players and their families lived during the season at the Concourse Plaza Hotel, a large, luxurious complex just a short walk from Yankee Stadium. Its apartments were famous for their sleek modern furnishings and sunken living rooms. The players' children played across the street in Joyce Kilmer Park, often shepherded by the team's biggest star and most famous bachelor, Frank Gifford. Conerly's wife, Perian, occasionally wrote charming columns for newspapers and magazines about the glamour and fun of in-season life, about their outings to Broadway shows, major sporting events, and the city's upscale nightspots. "The managements of our favorite restaurants are extremely sports conscious," she would write in her memoir *Backseat Quarterback,* "and welcome with a broad show of recognition not only the players but also their wives." They rarely paid for a meal or a drink.

The limelight could be fun, but it had a down side. When the Giants were losing a lot in Conerly's early years, and New York's famously outspoken fans were holding up signs in the stands that read, GO BACK TO MISSISSIPPI, YOU CREEP and CONERLY MUST GO, he and Perian stayed home nights because the quarterback did not want his wife to encounter such hostility on the streets. Age took an increasing toll on the quarterback, whose physical stamina seemed to decline as the team's fortunes rose.

In the 1958 season, he would get so beat up during games that on train rides home in sleeping cars, his roommate, Gifford, the running back, would take the top bunk, knowing Conerly would have a hard time climbing up and down. He had stormed the beach at Guam with the marines, and affected an unshakable nonchalance about the pressures of football, which was, after all, just a game, but he relied on sedatives to help him sleep through the night during the season—a problem he didn't have in the off-season when he routinely slept a sound nine hours. Things got better with wins. The bruises and aches went away faster, and Perian wrote chattily again about hobnobbing with movie stars and politicians, shopping at Saks and other fine stores on Fifth Avenue, visiting museums and galleries, and about the exclusive club formed by the players and their wives. Sometimes she would take in a show with her friends and then sit up all night playing cards and talking.

This life was a far cry from the strictly blue-collar existence of pro football families in Baltimore. As Colts, they were working-class members of a decidedly unglamorous city. Encouraged by Rosenbloom to settle there, they bought homes in Baltimore's booming suburbs and sent their children to the local public and Catholic schools. Most of the players held jobs in the city, many of them working right through the season. Tight end Jim Mutscheller sold insurance at a firm downtown, where people would stop him on the street to congratulate or commiserate with him about the latest game. He would report to work early, work all morning in the office, and then take off in the afternoon for practice. He would then return to the office most evenings to work into the night. Art Donovan was a liquor salesman, and would take off after practice to visit stores through Maryland, Delaware, and even Virginia, wining and dining store owners who were always delighted to see the hilarious "Fatso" walk through their door. John Unitas, Gino Marchetti, and other players worked shifts at Bethlehem Steel, the mammoth industrial facility in Dundalk, along the city's waterfront. Raymond Berry tried a job at the steel plant for a few weeks, and while he found that his repetitious chore, drilling holes in steel beams, helped strengthen his lower back, it bored him so that he quit and went back to his film studies.

The Colts' players enjoyed celebrity status, but it was a strictly local variety, akin to playing for the high school team in a very big small town. But the team was a phenomenal success. Season ticket sales had nearly doubled. Memorial Stadium was packed for home games, and the town had formed booster clubs and a marching band that traveled to every away game. Local sportswriters coined the term "Coltsaphrenia" to describe the local excitement generated by the "Steeds." The city was hooked on football, from the steel mills in Dundalk to the surgical theaters of the city's world-renowned medical school at the Johns Hopkins University—as noted by the team's most famous literary enthusiast, Ogden Nash:

> The lucky city of Baltimore
> Is famed for medicos galore.
> It's simply teeming with fine physicians,

With surgeons, occultists, obstetricians,
All dedicated men in white,
All at your service days and night
Except—and here's the fly in the ointment—
When with the Colts they have an appointment.
And the vast Memorial Stadium rocks
With the cheers of fifty-thousand docs.

In a way that would be impossible in years to come, as athletes began to earn millions, the team was part of the community. They would be stopped on the sidewalk, or in restaurants, or out grocery shopping by those fans who recognized them without their pads and helmets, and would receive congratulations or commiserations or long-winded theories for how to approach their next opponents. But they were not besieged. The local embrace was enthusiastic but polite. It was part of what made playing in the city a pleasure.

That pleasure was shared by the team's black players, but mostly in segregated terms. The Colts' blacks—the terminology then was "negro"—were celebrated by all of Baltimore, but they often found they were only welcome off the field in the city's black neighborhoods. Their superiority on the gridiron made all the more galling their inequality off of it. On road trips to southern states, they were often forced to stay in "negro" accommodations, which, because it got them out from under their coaches' watchful eyes, was sometimes more fun. It was also humiliating, but as such was just part of the general experience of African Americans in an overtly racist country.

It was widely believed, and the pro rosters provided ample evidence, that NFL owners had an unspoken agreement to employ no more than seven black athletes per team. The Washington Redskins, owned by the outspokenly racist George Preston Marshall, had none. Marshall did not integrate his team until 1962, when the federal government effectively forced him to—and he died the following year. The Giants in 1958 had just four black players: Rosey Grier, Roosevelt Brown, Emlen Tunnell, and Mel Triplett. There were six on the Baltimore roster: Lenny Moore, Lenny Lyles, Milt Davis, Jim Parker, Johnny Sample, and Eugene "Big Daddy" Lipscomb.

Lipscomb, a giant at six-foot-six and 288 pounds, towered over most of his opponents but, surprisingly, he was not that strong. He rarely managed to throw off a blocker and sack the quarterback, as his linemate Marchetti did several times in almost every game. What made Lipscomb effective was his speed: he had terrific lateral moves. His specialty was gliding sideways to plug holes in the line, stopping runners cold. He was so big that halfbacks would seem to disappear in his grasp.

Big Daddy had been signed right out of high school. On a form he filled out for the team, where it asked for his alma mater, he had forthrightly written, "No College." Someone inserted a period after the "No." For years afterward he was introduced on radio and television as a graduate of "North

College." He was a pro wrestler in the off-season, and was known for his ferocity on the field, even in practice; he often got in fights with his own teammates. He had been let go by the Rams because his behavior was considered ungovernable—he kept getting thrown out of games for fighting or for threatening referees. Yet when the mood lifted he was genial and quick-witted—the Colts considered him, next to Donovan, the funniest man in the locker room. He was haunted by childhood fears—as a boy he had seen his mother stabbed to death in Detroit—and when he was forced to room by himself on the road would slide a dresser in front of the door to secure it before climbing into bed. Black men as a rule were considered menacing and dangerous, and Big Daddy was not above using the stereotype to his advantage. The mustache that wrapped around the corners of his mouth seemed to fix his face in a dangerous scowl.

At one training camp, after the annual physicals, the team doctor announced that one of the players was infected with crabs. This was a potential catastrophe in a setting where players shared a locker room, towels, toilets, and shower stalls. Something of a prude anyway, Weeb was beside himself.

"I don't know how a pro football player could do something like this," he complained to his son-in-law, assistant coach Charley Winner.

At a team meeting, the head coach announced that the team doctor would be driving back to Westminster to treat everyone, but in the meantime asked, "Does anybody have any home remedies?"

Big Daddy put up his hand. He had the fixed attention of the eighty-or-so players and hopefuls in the room.

"Coach, whenever I get them, I take them to the movies," he said. " I feed them popcorn. Whenever they go out to get a drink of water, I change seats."

On the practice field during one particularly hot summer workout session, Big Daddy called across the field to Jim Parker, who sold cemetery plots as one of his off-field jobs. Parker was called "Boulevard" because he was so wide.

"Hey, Boulevard, I'll take two of them plots, but I want 'em both in the shade!"

Blacks were considered suitable only for positions that were presumed to call for primarily physical, as opposed to mental, acuity. They were running backs, wide receivers, defensive backs, and linemen. Like so much of racist logic, the presumption that such positions didn't require intelligence was clearly false and widely accepted. Raymond, the most cerebral of receivers, was not the most intellectual player on the Colts' roster. That would have been Milt Davis, the team's right cornerback, whom his teammates called "Pops" even though he was only twenty-eight years old. The scholarly Davis was a polymath who would eventually earn a doctorate in education from UCLA and become an avid ornithologist and teacher of natural history. In 1958 he was not considered civilized enough to drink, dine, or sleep in the same establishments as his white teammates.

Lenny Moore, who was a jazz lover, had a part-time job as a disc jockey on a "negro" radio station in Baltimore. He played his way into the Hall of Fame catching passes and taking handoffs from Unitas, whom he looked up to as an inspirational leader, but in later life he would say, "I wish I could tell you I knew Johnny better. As with the other white players on the team, we never mingled."

White teammates were friendly and even supportive, but it depended on the circumstances. On the field, they were brothers. If a black player was taunted or hit with a cheap shot by an opposing player, the team's white players would exact revenge, just as they did for each other—"Daddy, who we gotta kill?" asked defensive end Don Joyce in one game where Lipscomb got poked in the eye. That comaraderie sometimes was extended off the field. When Davis was refused admittance to a movie theater in Westminster in company with Alan Ameche during his first year with the team, the star white fullback complained to the theater manager, "Is this the land of the free and the home of the brave or are you some asshole?" He refused to enter the theater without Davis, who would never forget the gesture, and instead took the black player with him to his dorm room and introduced him to his collection of opera records. But there were limits to even Ameche's colorblindness. The same Ameche, a few years later, would approach Parker, who had opened many holes for him on the offensive line, and apologetically ask him to leave his new restaurant in Reisterstown, where the offensive tackle had driven out to eat in a show of solidarity for his teammate. Ameche, ashamed and embarrassed, explained to his teammate that if a black man were seen eating in his establishment in that part of Baltimore it would kill his business.

There was a kinship born of solidarity among the Colts' black players. They kidded each other and played practical jokes. Lipscomb developed a cunning imitation of Parker, who was a ponderously thickset fellow with a massive brow. Big Daddy delighted in goading Parker to do silly things, and the offensive tackle had enough of a sense of humor about himself to oblige. He loved soda pop, and was challenged one day by Lipscomb to drink three at a time. He stuffed the tops of three open bottles in his mouth and drained them all at once, pouring soda down his throat and out the sides of his mouth. Lipscomb would collapse with gleeful giggles.

The African American players gave each other nicknames. Parker was "Boulevard," Moore's "Spats" morphed into "Sput" in honor of the Russian satellite, which was too high and fast to be caught; Lyles was known as "LP Piles," because of an unfortunate recurring gastrointestinal problem; Lipscomb was always just "Big Daddy."

Rosenbloom may have adhered to the policy limiting the number of black players on his team, but he was sympathetic and supportive of those he did sign. He obtained first-run movies and set up a private movie theater for his players so they wouldn't have to deal with the racist cinema in Westminster. He personally lured Parker back to the team after the number-one pick quit training camp on his first day. When the enormous tackle showed up in Westminster, he found practice helmets, pads, socks, and sweats in a heap on the gymnasium floor. At Ohio State, the team had hired a tailor to custom make shoulder pads and a helmet for him because

119

nothing in the normal size ranges fit. He had brought along the shoulder pads, but he couldn't wear his Ohio State helmet for Colts practice. When he told Freddie Schubach, the equipment manager, he needed a special helmet, he was given a patronizing chuckle and a reminder that he may have been drafted, but he had not yet made the team.

"You make the team and we'll buy you one," Schubach said. Meanwhile, Parker was invited to fish a helmet off the pile at the center of the gym like everyone else.

He walked out to his car and drove back to Ohio.

Three days later Rosenbloom called to ask what had happened. When Parker explained, the owner hired the same man who had made his college helmet to outfit him with several Colts ones.

Weeb wanted to convert Parker into a pass blocker to guard John's blind side, but pass blocking was something new to the offensive tackle. Ohio State was famous then for running the ball on almost every down. In his first scrimmage, Parker was matched against Marchetti, who was considered the best pass rusher in football. It was the kind of matchup—the top pick versus the star veteran—that drew a small crowd of players onto the practice field. On his first try, Parker stood too upright and Marchetti cut right underneath him, knocking him down for a clear path to the quarterback. Parker dusted himself off and endured the hoots of his new teammates. Advised now to stay lower, on the next play Parker crouched. The agile Marchetti simply hurdled him. Now Parker was embarrassed, and the crowd was taunting him. On the third try, he tried to strike a balance between being too high or too low, but was clearly thinking about it too much, because Marchetti just threw him aside. Parker got up stuttering, "Wwwwhat do I do now?"

Donovan said, "If I was you, Jim, I'd just applaud."

Parker learned the ins and outs, and would become one of the best to ever play his position. But in the larger world he was still just a black man, albeit a big one. He and his black teammates endured such blatant racism in Westminster that Rosenbloom offered to move the camp to someplace more enlightened —further north, maybe even Canada. The African Americans opted to stick it out where they were because it was close enough to Baltimore for them to go home several times a week.

The owner didn't just encourage his players to settle in Baltimore, in some cases he helped them with loans or even down payments on their homes. Most needed it. The highest-paid player was Ameche, whose $20,000 reflected his status as the first pick in the draft. Marchetti, a six-year veteran, was making $11,250. Buzz Nutter, the center, was making the least, just $6,500. Davis made $7,000, despite being named all-pro in the previous season. Moore was earning about $12,000. Raymond was particularly careful about his contracts, as he was about everything. He had contacted other pro receivers before signing his first one, and had asked for $10,000. Kellett agreed to pay him $8,500 and offered a bonus of $1,500, which Berry accepted. But when it came time to renew the contract, after the receiver had begun posting big numbers, he was startled to find Kellett ready to start negotiating from a base salary of $8,500, not $10,000. Raymond was one of the team's stars at that point. John Unitas had started with a $7,000 salary and by the time he was the league's MVP in 1957, he was making $12,500. His salary was up to $17,550 by 1958. Even the lowest of these paychecks was reasonably good pay, considering the American family's average annual income that year was $5,087. The cost of a car was between $2,000 and $3,000, and a nice home in the suburbs could be had for $20,000.

Despite their contract battles with the team's tight-fisted management, the players adored the Colts' fun-loving, free-spending owner. The Giants may have had more celebrity and glamour in their lives, and more chances to earn advertising and promotional dollars off the field, but the Colts had Rosenbloom. They called him "Rosey." He looked after them like a rich uncle, and adored flamboyant gestures.

At the beginning of every season he promised that he and his friends would start a special victory fund for the players, depositing $10,000 after every winning game. At the end of the season, the money was paid out evenly to the entire roster. Several days before Thanksgiving each year, he had gift baskets with turkeys, hams, fixings, and bottles of booze delivered to the locker room—there was always a rush on Raymond's locker on those days, because he didn't drink and would give away the bottles to whoever asked first. When L.G. Dupre complimented Rosenbloom on his suit one day, the owner, who was about the same size as the running back, had several delivered to the running back's house. In addition to helping them buy houses, he cosigned loans for those trying to start businesses, and offered players chances to invest in real estate deals in Florida that he personally guaranteed—and that for many would prove quite lucrative.

Just weeks before the championship game, when the Colts were in a San Francisco hotel readying for a game against the 49ers, Marchetti was cornered by Schubach, who told him, "Mr. Rosenbloom wants to see you."

Marchetti's heart sank. *What had he done? Were they trading him? Releasing him?*

He went up to the team owner's suite, where Rosenbloom challenged him.

"You dumb Okie, what are you gonna do with your life?"

"What do you mean?" asked the defensive end.

"I want to know what you're gonna do with your life."

Marchetti was a happy man at thirty-one years old. He had survived two years as a grunt in Europe during the war, including the Battle of the Bulge. He felt lucky just to be alive. The Colts not only paid him to do what he enjoyed most, which was playing football, but more than he could make doing anything else. He lived in nearby Antioch, California, with his wife and three children in the off-season. He told Rosenbloom that he hadn't given the future that much thought.

"Listen," said the team owner. "I want you to move to Baltimore. I want you to go into business and I'll help you."

Rosenbloom talked to Mrs. Marchetti, who had driven from Antioch with the kids to watch Gino play that day. It wasn't all altruism; the owner saw promising opportunities in the rising popularity of his players in Baltimore. His original idea was to help Marchetti invest in a bowling alley. Eventually, backed by the owner and some of his friends, Marchetti and Ameche would open a chain of fast-food restaurants in the Baltimore area modeled after the then-growing phenomenon of McDonald's. The defensive end visited some of that booming chain's outlets in the middle of the night, shining a flashlight through the windows to scrutinize the layout and the design. He and Ameche would make millions with a regional knockoff hamburger chain called Gino's.

There were chances like this for the industrious and lucky, but Baltimore's players, on average, earned less than their New York counterparts. The prize money from the big game would more than equalize things. Each member of the winning team would receive $4,718.77, which Rosenbloom promised to match; altogether, this meant some of them could more than double their salary.

"Coltsaphrenia" grew throughout the '58 season as the team rolled over one opponent after the other. Baltimore lost two meaningless games on the West Coast at the end of the schedule, finishing with a record of nine and three, and arrived at the championship game healthy, rested, and ready. The Giants had an identical record, but their season had been a struggle from the first game to the last.

Frank Gifford had opened the season with his usual public expressions of reluctance. He gave several interviews early in the year to local sportswriters suggesting that he might not be returning to play another year. He had taken some acting classes, had secured bit parts in two James Garner vehicles, *Darby's Rangers* and *Up Periscope*, and had signed a long-term contract with Warner Bros.

"I loved my pro football career, but the movies have a lot more longevity with any sort of luck and breaks," Gifford told a UPI reporter in February. The best Jack Mara could come up with in response was to warn Gifford that he was contractually forbidden to take a role in a "football picture." In a June profile of the "blithely audacious" halfback by Gay Talese, then a features writer at the *New York Times*, Gifford announced that he had decided on acting full-time. He was now twenty-seven years old, and had just returned to New York looking tan from a swimwear photo shoot in the Bahamas. In an interview at Toots Shor's, Gifford said he was "through with football." He had been engaged, he said, to play a recurring role in an upcoming TV series to be called *Public Enemy*.

"I'm the hero," he told Talese. "I catch 'em."

This came as news to Jack Mara, whom Talese reached on a golf course that day.

"I saw Gifford this morning and at no time did he say that he was going to quit this year," the team owner said. "The decision is still up in the air."

Gifford was backtracking before the day was out. He told Talese in a telephone interview from his hotel, "There is a remote chance I will play . . . but I don't know whether Jim Howell (the Giants' coach) will allow me to go to camp late. He's running a ball club, not a TV station. He might frown on it, and I wouldn't blame him."

Gifford may just have been playing the time-honored game of a veteran scheming to avoid some of training camp. He reported for work at the club's distant training grounds in Salem one week late. *Public Enemy* never got beyond the pilot episode.

The team dropped all five of its exhibition games that summer before opening against the Chicago Cardinals. They lost two of their starting offensive linemen to injuries in those games, but Mara alertly picked up Al Barry from Green Bay and Bob Mischak from Cleveland. Both lineman were just coming out of the service and had landed with teams that had a surplus of talent at their position. Mischak was from New Jersey and his wife had just given birth to twins, so he was delighted with the move. Barry had played with Gifford at USC, and was thrilled to be coming to a potential championship team. The Packers had lost nine of their twelve games in 1957, and would lose ten in 1958. Gifford picked up the new offensive guard and his wife, Phyllis, at the airport when they arrived in late September. Both Barry and Mischak were thrown right onto the field for the opener, which caused some predictable confusion.

Lombardi used a system to number players and holes that was, in some respects, the opposite of what Barry had learned in Green Bay. Famous for pulling his guards, the coach sent in such a play early in the Cardinals game. It called for Barry, who weighed about 250 and was quick enough to play linebacker, to lead the running back. At the snap of the ball, Barry turned, pivoted, ran to his left, and was startled to find the field ahead completely open. For a fleeting moment he thought they had a touchdown for sure, until he heard a disheartened crack at the other side of the field. Gifford had run headlong into the Cardinals' defense without a blocker. On the sidelines, Lombardi huddled with his players. "Let's run this play over again," he said, "but this time keep an eye on Barry." They got something right, because Gifford went on to score three touchdowns on the way to a victory. The team's bruising halfback, Alex Webster, bulled in from short yardage to score two more.

They lost the following week, then won again, then lost again. Then they won three in a row, including victories over the eastern division–leading Browns and the victory over the Unitasless Colts. In that victory over the Colts, receiver Kyle Rote spent some time setting up Baltimore's fleet cornerback Milt Davis, running a zigzag pass pattern where he cut toward the sidelines and then reversed direction, coming back across the middle of the field. After running it several times, the veteran receiver noticed that Davis was accustomed to it, following the outside zig halfheartedly, waiting for Rote to cut back inside. So as the Giants threatened in the third quarter, trailing 14-7, a quarter of the field away from the goal line, Rote saw his chance.

"Okay, Charlie," Rote told Conerly in the huddle. "I've got this guy all set up. Throw the ball in the corner of the end zone."

Rote's catch over the off-balance Davis's outstretched hands was cited by New York sportswriters as the game's turning point. The Giants scored another touchdown in that quarter —a thirteen-yard end run by Gifford—but Baltimore tied the game in the fourth quarter. Summerall kicked a field goal with just under three minutes to play, giving New York the 24-21 lead that they held for the rest of the game, the one that had Donovan pelting them with stones.

It was during halftime of that game, going over the problems the offense had faced in the first half, that Weeb asked, "Well, what do we do about Sam Huff?" The middle linebacker had been wreaking havoc along the Colts' blocking front.

There was a silence, and then the center, Buzz Nutter, suggested, "I think we should trade for him."

The win tied the Giants with the Browns for first place in their division. They lost the following week to Pittsburgh, but then went on a three-game winning streak that set up a final do-or-die game against the Browns on December fourteenth. A win would force a play-off game for the eastern division championship, a loss meant the Giants would go home. The Colts by now had wrapped up their division and were playing out meaningless games on the West Coast, resting their starting players for the championship game. New York played a thrilling game to save their season, before 63,192 fans in a snowstorm so heavy that Summerall never saw his amazing, forty-nine-yard winning field goal fall through the uprights. The kicker had hurt his leg the week before, and in warm-ups before the game was worried enough about it to tell his backup, Don Chandler, to be ready to take his place.

"I don't think I'm going to be able to kick," he said.

Beating Cleveland was about one thing: stopping its agile fullback Jim Brown. With Huff assigned to dog Brown one on one, Cleveland had been held to just one touchdown and field goal, but with less than three minutes remaining, the Giants had managed only to hold their own. Summerall's leg felt stronger as the game wore on, but he had missed twice already, including a thirty-one-yard field goal try just minutes before. Howell debated with himself before sending the kicker in to try from midfield. The coach would have liked to move his team in closer, but Conerly had just missed three passes in a row, including a long one that had slipped through Webster's fingers at the goal line. It was fourth down. They might not get another chance.

When Summerall showed up in the huddle, Conerly asked, "What the fuck are you doing here?"

It wasn't encouraging. The snow was coming down so thick that the yard lines were all buried. Conerly took a knee and brushed the snow away from the spot on the field where he would hold the ball. Summerall reminded himself to keep his ankle locked. He felt like he had let it flop a little on the earlier misses. From that distance he was going to have to hit it hard.

This time he remembered. The Giants won 13-10.

The victory set up a one-game play-off for the following week. Holding the Browns to only ten points in that game had been quite an accomplishment, but Huff knew he could build on it. Jim Brown had been a nemesis for the linebacker ever since their college days, when West Virginia played Syracuse. The running back got under Huff's skin, not just because he ran so hard it hurt when you hit him, but because he played nice. Huff worked himself into a fury to play football. He tried hard to hate his opponents for those rough sixty minutes. Brown would pop up after Huff knocked him down, pat him on the shoulder and tell him, "Nice tackle, Sam."

"Leave me alone, goddamnit!" Huff would growl.

He had gone into the game knowing that Brown would carry the ball on probably half of Cleveland's offensive plays. The middle linebacker had to watch the Browns' center, Art Hunter, and the guards to either side of him, Jim Ray Smith and Chuck Noll. Behind the center was quarterback Milt Plum, and behind him, Brown. In one of the game's first plays, Huff could tell a run was coming by the way Hunter positioned himself over the ball. He had his weight forward. Huff knew that the offensive line would take on each of the Giants' four linemen—Robustelli, Dick Modzelewski, Grier, and Jim Katcavage—which would leave him free to hit the runner head-on. Except on this play Cleveland pulled a stunt. The linemen all blocked down to their right, ignoring Katcavage, the man at the end of the line, who was busy rushing into the backfield and too far from the hole to stop the play. This left Noll free to hit Huff. Brown had breezed through the opening and sprinted sixty-five yards for a touchdown.

But Huff saw what they had done. Cleveland coach Paul Brown had clearly designed the play to thwart Landry's new four-three system. What he hadn't counted on was that a player might recognize the stunt and design a countermove on the spot. On the sideline Huff told Katcavage, "If you see the tackle blocking down, don't charge in [as he had done on the touchdown play]." Instead, he told Katcavage to just drift down the line laterally, plugging the hole. The strategy effectively bottled up Jim Brown for the rest of the game.

When they met again the next Sunday, a frozen afternoon, Huff played the game of his life. He would later explain that he and Landry and his teammates, playing the Browns for the third time that season, had simply figured them out. They knew exactly what Cleveland was going to do on every play. They shut out Paul Brown, and held his superstar to just eight yards on thirteen carries. They won 10-0.

It was time to play the Colts.

Alan Ameche tackled by Sam Huff (70) and Jim Patton (20).
(Courtesy of Hy Peskin/*Sports Illustrated*)

Gino Marchetti (89, white) bats down the first attempted pass by Giants quarterback
Don Heinrich (11). (Courtesy of Hy Peskin/*Sports Illustrated*)

Frank Gifford (16, blue) catches a lateral as Colts Gene 'Big Daddy' Lipscomb
(76, white) makes chase. (Courtesy of Hy Peskin/*Sports Illustrated*)

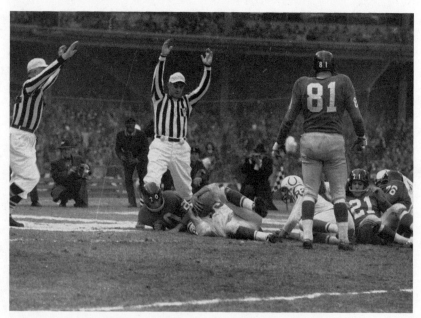

Ameche crosses the line for a second-quarter touchdown.
(Courtesy of Hy Peskin/*Sports Illustrated*)

6

Fumble-itis

The Colts flew to New York on Saturday morning, December 27, landed at LaGuardia Airport and boarded a bus that took them across the Triborough Bridge into the Bronx, and then uptown to 161st Street and the Concourse Plaza Hotel. Much to the amusement of his teammates, Raymond wore a blackout mask on the plane and bus to shut out the card games and foolery that always accompanied team travel. He carried an overnight bag and his personal scale, which he used to take daily measure of his weight. He had determined that 186 pounds was his ideal playing weight, and he monitored it scrupulously. Over the season he had dropped down to almost 175, so he was concerned, and had been trying to bulk up through relatively light practices in the previous two weeks. Weeb had put them through their usual steps the week before, easy workouts, some film study, walk-throughs at Memorial Stadium, but nothing strenuous.

After six months of practice and twelve games there wasn't must left to teach.

The Concourse Plaza was a towering maroon-brick structure with a popular bar and restaurant on the ground floor. It sat at the southern end of a four-and-a-half-mile stretch of towering apartments, retail shops, groceries, and Art Deco office buildings on both sides of the Grand Concourse, which was marketed locally as "the Champs-Elysées of the Bronx." Harry Truman campaigned there. It was a magnet for autograph-seekers, because not only did many of the city's home-town heroes live there in season, the hotel also hosted visiting baseball and football teams. It was just a short walk from the hotel to Yankee Stadium, and as the Colts' players strolled down for their afternoon workout that day, locals welcomed them in time-honored Gotham style.

"You guys are gonna get killed!"

"Yer gonna get the ball shoved up yer ass!"

The Colts' garrulous defensive tackle Artie Donovan had grown up in the Bronx and he enjoyed mixing it up with his old neighbors. He had a storied connection with New York sports. His grandfather, "Professor" Mike Donovan, had been the world middleweight boxing champion, and his father, Arthur Sr., was a famous boxing instructor at the New York Athletic Club and had officiated many fights in Madison Square Garden, including heavyweight champion Joe Louis's bouts. The football-playing Donovan had attended Boston College after four years in the marines, and was now a beloved journeyman, a mainstay of the powerful Colts defense, and a big, lovable clown. His neighborhood was just a few blocks away, in Bedford Park, or as Catholics of that era would have said, in St. Angela's parish. For him it was a holiday homecoming.

A fireman shouted, "Hey, Donovan, I hope this team is better than the one you played for at St. Angela's!"

The lineman's schoolboy team had lost most of its games. When he and his teammates walked back to the hotel later that afternoon, the same people who had heckled them invited them in for free sandwiches and beer.

The team offered a big dinner spread of hamburgers and beer that night, but Donovan skipped it. He was used to his late-night binge before falling asleep, so instead of chowing down with his teammates he went over to his parents' house. He came back in time to make the ten o'clock team curfew, carrying two pizzas, and sat up late with his roommate, Art Spinney, polishing them off and washing them down with beer before the television. They went to bed at eleven.

Just before curfew, Gino Marchetti and Bill Pellington took a walk along the Concourse. As they stopped at a corner, a bus filled with raucous Baltimore fans pulled up to the stoplight.

"Yeah, go Colts!" Marchetti shouted at them.

Assuming two big men standing on a Bronx street corner were making fun of them, some of the fans on the bus hurled beer cans at them.

"Yeah, you bums, we'll get you tomorrow!" one shouted.

Weeb liked to keep the team together on the road, so the night before a game it was his tradition to take breakfast orders from everyone. He wrote down the orders himself.

"Anything you want," he said. Many of the men wanted steak and eggs. Donovan, who was so nervous on the morning of games that he couldn't eat anything heavy, ordered two bowls of consommé soup. Big Daddy Lipscomb ordered a root beer float. Breakfast wasn't served until ten o'clock, because on Sunday morning the team's Catholics, and there were many, including Unitas, Donovan, Sandusky, Mutscheller, and Marchetti, attended Mass at nearby St. Angela's. Weeb wasn't Catholic, but he went along. He had done so in a gesture of solidarity some years earlier, and the team had won, so he kept it as part of his game day routine, like wearing the same lucky brown suit. You looked for any edge you could find.

Any edge. In the week before, the Colts had spied on the Giants' practices from the roof of an apartment building outside the Yankee Stadium right centerfield wall. Bob Shaw, a former player who worked as an advance scout, attending the game of the team's next opponent, had worried about getting caught and incurring the wrath of the NFL. Rosenbloom had promised him a job for life in one of his other companies if that happened. So Shaw just strolled into the chosen building's lobby, took the elevator to the top, and then found a flight of stairs to the roof. He sat up there with binoculars, watching the Giants run through the assortment of plays they would employ against the Colts. He hadn't seen anything new or radically different, which was welcome news to Weeb. Coaches lived in fear of teams inventing a new trick play, or suddenly unveiling a completely new approach. He couldn't prove it, but Weeb was certain that the Giants had spied on his team, too.

Mornings in the hotel on a game day were tedious. Nervous players watched the clock and wandered the halls and lobby. Walter Taylor, the *Baltimore Evening Sun* reporter, happened to be seated at a table in the coffee shop next to Huff, who lived in the hotel. Taylor tried a small joke, suggesting that there was still time for the linebacker to catch the morning train back to Morgantown.

Huff was not amused.

"I can always take the train for West Virginia," he said, "I can't always go out and win a world championship."

The Colts were showing their nerves, too, only a little more boisterously. John Steadman, a reporter for the *Baltimore News-Post*, observed the players reporting to a room on the sixth floor in groups of four to have their ankles and wrists taped. Donovan had showed up in his underwear and announced, "I'm going to get so rich today, here's what I'm gonna do!" He put his thumb in a hole in his boxers and tore them off. Fatso twirled before them, naked from the waist down, and the room erupted in laughter.

Lipscomb spent much of the morning singing loudly to himself. Lenny Moore and Jim Parker, the jazz enthusiasts, had chatted away about Moore's new stereo player until it came time for Parker to be taped. He crossed the room and set his 272-pound bulk on the chair, only to have it give way. This prompted more gales of laughter. Buzz Nutter, the center, came in asking, jokingly, "Who won that play-off game last week, the Browns or the Giants?" He complained that in all Weeb's efforts to prepare them, he had forgotten to tell them who they were playing.

They took a bus for the short drive to the stadium at 12:30, just an hour and a half before game time. In the small visiting team

locker room, seated on stools, Unitas, Spinney, and halfback
Art DeCarlo gently tossed a football around. Off in his own
world as usual, Ameche practiced some lines he had memorized
from the Gettysburg Address. Rosenbloom walked around the
room, stopping to chat with players one by one, wishing them
well. His two sons, Danny and Steve, were at one end of the
locker room helping the trainer chop ice. Steadman approached
Don Shinnick, one of Baltimore's linebackers, and asked him if
he was ready.

"Yes, I think we are," he said. "You can feel it. This place
is ready to explode."

Ever the showman, Donovan honored his own game-day
ritual by vomiting loudly and theatrically in one of the bathroom stalls. His teammates were used to it. The sound echoed
horribly through the locker room.

To Raymond it sounded like a hippopotamus heaving a goat.
He understood that the big lineman's rowdy displays just
masked his anxiety, but it annoyed him anyway. Different players had different ways of coping with tension. The receiver's was
to absorb himself in preparation.

He was mightily prepared. He pored over and over the
twenty-five pages of notes in his microscopic handwriting that
he carried in a binder: insights he had gleaned from hours of
solitary film study, plays that he wanted to try, reminders to
himself about everything he needed to remember, from head
fakes he had designed for specific routes to basics like remem-

bering to watch the ball all the way into his hands. "WATCH YOUR FOOTING ON STARTS," he had written in large block letters in the middle of one page. He had the careful planner's habit of dividing each page into segments with perfectly straight lines. Under the heading "DURING RUNS," he had written, "BASIC THREE," which were:

CK [check] *FEET*
GET DOWNFIELD FAST
BE BULLDOG ON YOUR BLOCK

Below that, with stars penciled in alongside, referring to safety Jim Patton, who wore number twenty, and Karilivacz, who wore twenty-one, was written:

* BE BEST COMPETITOR ON FIELD
* KNOCK #20 & #21 ASS OFF
* *GO ST* [straight] *AT 21 TO SET UP 136* [a play]

Under the heading "DURING SHORT YDG & GOAL LINE" he had written:

* KNOW SNAP COUNT
* *DO YOUR JOB*

There were meticulously drawn plays on pages and pages divided into twelve neat squares, with arrows indicating every pattern he had ever run against the Giants and cornerback Carl Karilivacz, with tiny notes about outcomes. He knew at least some of this would remain in Karilivacz's head, and he wanted his own thinking to be one level deeper—he wanted to anticipate the cornerback's thought process. He had almost an entire page devoted to #84, Giants outside right linebacker, Harland Svare, one of Landry's star pupils. Some of the notes were cryptic, others straightforward:

> When you squat to block 71 [tackle M.L. Brackett] he
>   will grab you
> Will hold you on GL-6-1, short yardage, too, possibly
> He might play outside on OH from FR
> When standing up on special, get under him, step with out
>   foot first, possible body block
> Will stay on your nose, then jump back when count starts
> Gets to outside fast!
> KNOCK HIS BUTT OFF EVERY CHANCE YOU
>   GET

Raymond often wondered whether such obsessive preparation really paid off in any concrete way. There were few games where he could point to a specific insight or trick that had made a big difference. It was just his way, part of an overall approach that worked for him. Long before the fans began to file in, Raymond was out on the field carefully inspecting the turf. He did it primarily to decide what kind of cleats to wear, but also to look for wet, loose, or frozen patches he might be able to exploit during the game. He had his regular cleats and his "mud" cleats, which had two extra-long spikes under the ball of each foot, on which he would pivot. If the turf was wet and soft, the mud cleats gave him advantage, but on a hard field the longer cleats hurt the soles of his feet and slowed him down. It was a tough call for this game because most of the field was dry, but there were a few wet spots. Raymond knew where to find them. There was a pattern to the way the grounds crew removed the tarp after a snowfall or rain. If they weren't careful, the water tended to pool toward the center and then drain out the edges of the covering as they removed it, leaving wet spots on both sides of the field near the fifty-yard line. Sure enough, he found a big wet patch at midfield right in front of the Giants' bench. He found another in the far southern corner of the field, which during the winter was almost always in shade. Raymond didn't want to get caught at a critical moment in the game on one of these slippery spots, so he decided to wear his mud cleats. They would prove useful.

Raymond's parents were going to be at the game. It was rare for them to see him play any more, but Ray Berry's high school season in Paris, Texas, was over so they had come east. Raymond had an aunt who lived in Philadelphia with her husband. The whole family was coming up on the train to see the big game.

With them were thousands of Baltimore fans, so many that New York transit workers stood on the platforms at Penn Station shouting directions for how to get to the subway line that ran up to the Bronx.

✻ ✻ ✻

Both teams took the field an hour and a half before the game wearing their uniform pants but with no shoulder pads under their wool warm-up jackets, jogging back and forth and doing calisthenics as the first fans began to fill the seats. Teenage photographer Neil Leifer was at work wheeling in the disabled vets, setting them up behind the eastern end zone against what in baseball season was the left field wall.

In the radio broadcast booth overhead, NBC announcer Joe Boland began introducing the game to millions of listeners all over the city and nation:

—*The weather conditions are almost ideal, surprisingly enough. We have sunny skies with a bit of a haze. The temperature is a pleasant forty-seven degrees. The wind very slight. The field surface is good, but in spots may be a bit loose because of the surprisingly mild weather, comparatively speaking, we've had in the last few days after the recent frigid spell. The frost is coming out of the ground in a few spots, and there are a few spots that are a bit moist. On the whole, I would say that the playing surface is as fine as you can possibly get in northern climes for a game this late in the year.*

As befits the title game in the fastest-growing league in the nation, two great teams will collide on this Yankee Stadium turf today. The New York Giants have had to fight two furious battles with the Cleveland Browns the last two Sundays to gain credentials to play today. . . . To give you an idea of the size of the mountain the Giants had to climb, they defeated the Browns three times this season, a performance that had never been accomplished over that tal-

ented group of Clevelanders. Baltimore, right on schedule on the other hand, for the five-year plan Coach Ewbank announced in 1954 when he took over, arrived at title status by winning the western conference race with a record of nine and three. The Colts got off to a fast start, winning six games before losing to these New York Giants, and then won three more to lock up the title with two weeks to go in the regular season. . . . So the heat was off them, while the Giants had to go into a pressure cooker for the last several weeks of the campaign to win. New York today shows the wear and tear of the eastern race, with a well-bruised team that has had to produce a pair of monumentally emotional efforts these last two Sundays. Baltimore is well-rested with everyone healthy and ready to go this afternoon.

Boland introduced John Unitas as "The Cinderella Kid," noting that he had now thrown a touchdown pass in twenty-five consecutive games, and pointed out that the Colts were a new team in their first-ever championship game. The Giants, he reminded, had been in the title game nine times, and had won it just two years ago. So while Baltimore fans were greatly outnumbered in the stands, they had arrived with a disproportionate share of enthusiasm.

In the press box, the *New York Herald Tribune*'s Red Smith, was leveling his wry wit on the pregame festivities. He was one of the few New York sportswriters whose account, because of the strike, would be published around the country the next day.

"From the start of the sunny afternoon," Smith wrote, "the play ground had presented a spectacle rarely seen in this blasé town.

Fog horns and sirens hooted and shrieked. Bands tootled and postured. Antlered ballet dancers in bright red union suits impersonated cottontail reindeer, a rare breed. Fillies of provocative design paraded wearing the letters COLTS across bosoms that pointedly contradicted the label."

Down on the field, Weeb was wearing his lucky suit under a long wool overcoat buttoned to the top with the collar turned up to his ears. His dark fedora was pressed down low on his forehead. He watched his team loosen up and paced the sideline waiting for the game to start. When he noticed two old men sitting on the Colts' bench who didn't belong there, he waved for a cop. He didn't know it, but one of the two men was his rowdy defensive lineman's father, the locally famous Arthur Donovan, and the other was a plainclothes New York City police captain, John Brady, an old friend of Fatso's, who was responsible for security at the stadium that day. Donovan had invited his father to watch the game from the sidelines. His father had run into Brady, and the two were relaxing on the empty bench, passing a bottle of whiskey back and forth, waiting for the pregame festivities to end.

Weeb demanded that they be removed. The cop saw that one of them was his commander.

"Coach," he said, "You go before they do."

Back in the locker room, Weeb got the team together. He always scripted the first three plays of the game, and after that he left the game to God and John Unitas. He was convinced that the Giants had the locker room bugged. He looked under the benches and then pointed at the ceiling to let the players know that he knew that they were being overheard. Then he mouthed the first three plays.

That business concluded, the head coach loosened his vocal cords and gave the motivational speech of his life. Pro football players have heard just about every possible variation on the locker room pep talk, so there is little a coach can say that will surprise or effect them, but on this day Weeb truly rose to the occasion. He praised his players for their achievement, one by one, and cataloged the disrespect other teams and coaches had shown for their talent.

"Nobody knows you guys, and we're in a good place to get known, New York City, so we're going to have to win this game," he told them. He pulled out some handwritten notes from his pocket. "Nobody wanted you guys," he said. Then he went around the locker room, singling out most of the starting players. To John: "Pittsburgh didn't want you but we picked you off the sandlots." To Milt Davis: "Detroit didn't want you, but I'm glad we got you." Most of his players had been cut or rejected somewhere along the line, and Weeb cited every slight. Cornerback and kick-returner Carl Taseff had been cut by Cleveland. To Big Dadddy Lipscomb: "The Rams didn't want you. We picked you up for the one-hundred-dollar waiver price. You've come a long way. When you start rushing the passer more you will become one of the greatest tackles the game has ever seen." To Bill Pellington, the linebacker: "The Browns cut you after one scrimmage; you had to hitchhike to your first practice with us!" To Raymond: "Nobody wanted you in the draft. You are a self-made end." Even for his first-round draft picks and stars, those who had gotten an easier ride, he found soft spots. To Ameche: "I caught hell for taking you first in the draft. There was a guy at Maryland they wanted me to take. I didn't take him and that made a lot of people mad. Then on your first play you went seventy-nine yards for a touchdown against the Bears and they got off my back quick!" To Lenny Moore: "You can be as good as you want to be. That's what they said when we drafted you, but the idea was presented that we might have a hard time getting you to practice." To Jim Parker: "They didn't know where you could be used as a pro. They said you couldn't play offense and were so-so on defense. But we sure used you." To Marchetti: "In ten years of pro coaching, you are the finest end I have ever seen. They said you are the greatest end in the league and that you just couldn't get any better, but you continue to get better every week and you will today."

The coach also talked about himself. He noted that he had not been the Colts' first choice for the head coaching job when they had gone looking in 1954, and they all knew how close he and his staff had come to being fired after the 1956 season. The message was, they were a team of self-made men, playing against the glamour boys of the NFL, the only team that had beaten them in a game that mattered that season. In a ghostwritten column the Giants' Conerly produced for a wire service, he had said after that game that the Giants had "out-gutted" them. The article had been posted in the Baltimore locker room all week.

Linebacker Don Shinnick led the team in the Lord's Prayer, and then they set off for the field like men with a score to settle, not just with the Giants, but with the world.

* * *

In 1958, the NFL was not full partners with television the way it is today. Today's gridiron is miked and wired for dozens of cameras that record the action from every conceivable angle. The pace of the game has been altered to allow for television commercials and commentary. For this championship game, television was strictly an observer, its cameras, microphones, and commentators consigned to the press box on the periphery. NBC had just five stationary cameras, one of which was trained on an easel that held flash cards to display down and distance. The others viewed the action from afar. There were no slow-motion replays, overhead cameras, or close-ups. There were no microphones to capture the sounds on the field. The action did not stop for TV commercials and the referees did not wait for broadcasters to return from commercial breaks to whistle the ball back in play. As a result, the game moved faster. On the radio broadcast, Boland and his partner McColgan just stayed silent as the distant sound of the national anthem filtered up from the combined Baltimore Colts and Wayne (New Jersey) High School marching bands down on the field. The effect for a viewer or listener was much like sitting in the grandstand.

New York won the coin toss, and Bert Rechichar, the Colts' kickoff man, thumped the ball with the hard toe of his cleats, high and deep into the Giants' end zone, where rookie Don Maynard caught it—*A tremendous boot!* said McColgan—and the championship was underway. Maynard opted not to run it out, so New York's offense started on its own twenty.

Early in the season, Lombardi had begun using both of

his veteran quarterbacks, Conerly and backup Don Heinrich, in every game. It was, and remains, unorthodox. Heinrich started the game, and would stay in until the coach decided it was time to insert Conerly. Usually this was after two or three offensive series, but once he kept Heinrich behind center until the third quarter. The "starting" quarterback would bide his time, watching the game with Lombardi, noting wrinkles in the opposing team's defense. Conerly never liked doing it this way. He felt he learned more, and more quickly, about his opponent when he was in the game. He didn't understand why Lombardi did it, and the coach never bothered to explain. Heinrich disliked the practice, too, and would sometimes complain bitterly and profanely when Lombardi yanked him. But for the opening drive, it was once again Heinrich who trotted out to run the offense. His first attempted pass was batted down by the leaping Marchetti, who, at six-five and with very long arms, was a formidable obstacle.

Both offenses sputtered. When Baltimore took over for its first drive, it pulled one of the surprises that Weeb had mouthed to them in the locker room. It was a trick play. The offense lined up with only one blocker on the right side of the line; the rest of the team's linemen, four of them, were all stacked to the left. It was a bizarre, lopsided arrangement, and it had the desired effect. Giants defenders scrambled to figure out where to play. John capitalized on their confusion by starting the play on a quick count. Out-of-position New York defenders responded with a chaotic rush, but an effective one. Ameche missed the quick count and got a late start leading

Lenny Moore on a sweep around the left end, and a number of Colts missed their blocks entirely. Tacklers swarmed all over Moore for a three-yard loss. The Colts returned to a more conventional formation after that, and on their third play from scrimmage, a quarterback keeper, Huff tackled John and forced a fumble.

Heinrich trotted out and returned the favor, bobbling the snap and losing the ball. Marchetti pounced on it. Then John attempted a little swing pass to tight end Jim Mutscheller that Karilivacz read all the way.

—Intercepted by Karilivacz at the Giants' forty! He's across the forty-five to the forty-seven, where it will be Giants ball, first and ten. L.G. Dupre made the tackle. The forward pass thrown by Unitas intercepted by the former Syracuse University star . . . so it's New York's ball.

It looked more like amateur hour than the NFL championship. Three of the first four drives had ended with turnovers. Twice, Baltimore handed New York the ball with less than half a field to score, but Lombardi's offense could not move it. Al Barry, the left guard New York had picked up from Green Bay at the beginning of the season, was struggling. He always had a hard time blocking Lipscomb, who was about six inches taller and fifty pounds heavier. Over the years Barry had tried every trick he knew, legal and illegal—holding, tripping, cut-blocking —to knock him out of the way, and had only mixed success, but enough to make Big Daddy angrier and angrier. Once, the furious Colts lineman had sought him out after a game to vent his disgust. Barry had begged forgiveness. "Big Daddy, you are such an amazing athlete, how do you expect somebody like me to block you? I have to do those things." At the beginning of this game, Lipscomb had hailed Barry as they untangled themselves after an early play. The Giants' blocker had spent a week in the hospital with an injured foot, and news of it had made the papers.

"How's your foot?" asked Lipscomb.

"Pretty good, thanks," said Barry.

"Which one is it?" asked Lipscomb, with an evil grin.

Lombardi's offense had yet to move the ball ten yards to sustain a drive. After Karilivacz's interception they ran three plays and gained only five yards. Don Chandler punted for the second time, and the Colts tried again from the fifteen, deep in their own half of the field.

On the first play, John heaved a bomb down the right sideline to Moore, who was shadowed step for step by right cornerback Lindon Crow. Crow was from a big California family, and had grown up playing football with his four brothers. He had been a pro for eight years, and in three of them had made the Pro Bowl, the league's all-star game. The Giants had obtained him from the Chicago Cards in 1958 to help shore up their secondary. Coach Landry had worked with him in the Pro Bowl at the end of 1957, and had made acquiring him a priority. It had been one of the team's major upgrades going into this season. But Crow, like every other cornerback in the league, was no match for the lanky speedster from Penn State. On most plays, Landry had two defensive backs keying in on the Colts' right flanker. But whenever safety Jim Patton had to watch for the run, it left

Crow lined up one-on-one with Moore, as on this play. Because most of Moore's patterns—Landry had, of course, counted them—were to the inside, he instructed Crow to anticipate that by lining up two or three steps inside him, toward the center of the field. It was a gamble based on the odds, which favored Crow, but it left him flat-footed when Moore instead broke to the outside and sprinted downfield. Crow recovered well, and when the pass hung up a little too long, he actually overtook the receiver. Moore had his eye on the ball over his left shoulder all the way. He slowed and jumped slightly behind Crow to catch it, then turned inside and opened up his long stride. The cornerback tried to pivot and grab him, but his feet slipped out from under him and he went down. When safety Jim Patton caught up, running from the center of the field, Moore put a move on him and broke for the goal line, but Patton pulled him down.

—Lindon Crow was defending on the play but Moore made a great catch. A fifty-five-yard pass play from quarterback John Unitas to the speedy halfback, Lenny Moore, and the Colts come up with the first big play of the afternoon. They now have the ball on the Giants' twenty-five yard line, first and ten.

The Colts couldn't make much headway from there, however, and after failing to get a first down, the team's big erratic kicker, Steve Myhra, trotted out to try a thirty-one-yard field goal. It was on the outer edge of his range.

Myhra was a Midwesterner whose family owned a tractor franchise. He had grown up with money, so the pro paycheck didn't mean as much to him as it did for most players.

As a result, he played with a cheerful, devil-may-care attitude that endeared him to his teammates but that rubbed Weeb the wrong way. He kicked in the way most football place kickers did at that time, by lining up directly behind the ball and booting it with his toe. It was good enough for extra points, which were close in, but he lost accuracy rapidly the farther away from the goal line the ball was placed. Weeb had coached Lou Groza, the Cleveland kicker considered the NFL's best. He once observed that when Groza kicked the ball ten times in practice from the same spot in the dirt, his footprints for each kick traced the same precise pattern. Myhra's footsteps after ten kicks, Weebs complained, looked like "chicken scratchings." To Weeb, Myhra was just a bad place kicker, a position he had not yet been able to upgrade—few teams then had place kicking specialists like the Giants' Pat Summerall. Most booters were on the roster because they were versatile; Myhra usually doubled as linebacker, where he was playing in this game, filling in for the injured Dick Szymanski. His uniform was already covered with Yankee Stadium dust and muck. His kick was well short of the goalposts, but the Giants had jumped offside, so he got another chance from five yards closer. Baltimore seemed poised to score the first points of the game.

—The signal is being called. It's spotted. It's blocked! It's blocked by Sam Huff and Carl Karilivacz, and the Giants take over. Sam Huff, number seventy, came driving through to block it.

Huff had an easy time of it. He was standing full upright before the kicker as the ball left his toe. Donovan, the Colts defensive star, who was a blocker on kicking downs, had turned the wrong way and been knocked, as he would later put it, "on my fat ass." Huff came breezing through so unblocked that he would have had time to shake Myhra's hand before batting away the kick.

It was beginning to seem like neither team could score.

Lombardi chose this moment to pull Heinrich and send Conerly into the game. The old pro got a roaring ovation from the crowd as he trotted out—*The old master,* said McColgan— and promptly steered the Giants to their first points. The big play came on a sweep by Gifford around the left side. New York stacked its strength on the right side, and then Conerly made a quick pitch to his halfback, who had lined up on the weak side. The lateral got the fleet Gifford around the end very quickly. Rote came across to trip up the Colts' right-outside linebacker, Myhra, and a lunging block by the big New York right guard, Jack Stroud, sent two more pursuing Colts sprawling. Gifford cut back, dodging through tumbling white uniforms and almost losing his balance before sprinting down the left sidelines.

> —*He gets yardage! He's at the thirty-five, the forty, the fifty, the Baltimore forty, the thirty-five, and he's down at about the thirty-one-yard line! Bill Pellington makes the tackle. Gifford doing some fancy running, circled his own left end, cut back, and goes all the way down to the Colts' thirty-one-yard line. A good block thrown by number sixty-six, Jack Stroud, who is back in there this afternoon after being out with rib injuries.*

The Giants failed to move the ball much further in three plays, so Summerall came out to kick a thirty-six-yard field goal, and New York took an early, slender lead.

That's how the first quarter ended. In its four offensive possessions so far, the Colts' vaunted offense had turned the ball over three times, and had managed only one first down. The Giants' offense had done little better, managing only one first down. Neither team looked much like a champion. The difference in the game so far had been blocking on the two field goal attempts.

—*It has been a defensive battle so far, which is what most experts figured it would be.*

The Giants opened the second quarter with another blunder. From deep in their own side of the field, Conerly tossed a flare pass to Gifford on his left, and the star running back started around the end with Lipscomb in pursuit. Still in his own backfield, Gifford spun away from the tackle, but the move gave the Colts' other tackle, Ray Krouse, a chance to catch him. Krouse hit him hard and knocked the ball loose. Lipscomb fell on it, and the big game had produced its fifth turnover.

The stadium was quiet now. The gleeful sound of scattered Colts fans sounded small as John trotted out. Baltimore was just twenty yards from the Giants' goal line. From here they just ran the ball, which they were doing with increasing success, alternating handoffs to Moore and Ameche, who pounded forward steadily until they were on New York's one-yard line, from where Ameche plunged over the goal line. It took them just five plays.

When Myhra's extra point went through the uprights, the Colts were up 7-3. Two things of note had happened in that short drive. On the Colts' first play from scrimmage, Lenny

Moore had taken off with the ball around the left side. He dodged inside, avoiding one tackler, and was then snared by Huff, who caught him at an angle, wrapped both long arms around his midsection, and stood him up. Moore kept his balance but stopped running. The powerful middle linebacker pushed him a few yards backward, and then lifted him completely off the ground, inverted him, and slammed him down hard on his back. The running back got up with a sharp pain between his shoulder blades. He finished the drive, but on the sidelines told Weeb that he was hurt.

"Man, when I lift up my arms it feels like somebody is sticking a knife in the middle of my back," he said.

"Can you run?" the coach asked.

Moore said he could still run, but he wasn't going to be able to catch the ball very well.

"I want you to stay in the game," the coach told him. New York was double-teaming Moore on the right side, which potentially opened up more chances for Raymond on the left. So far, Baltimore had not taken advantage. Raymond had yet to be thrown a pass. John had been biding his time, letting the plays he had worked out with his alter ego ripen like fruit on a low branch, which was one of his specialties. He had been setting up the Giants with all these running plays and deep passes to Moore. If the flashy receiver came out of the game, the Giants would surely double-team Raymond.

"We can use you as a decoy," Weeb told Moore.

The touchdown had come on a play that in the Colts' book was called "17": Ameche over the left tackle. Raymond's job on the play was to line up just to the left of Jim Parker, the Colts' left tackle, and then plunge right, into Rosey Grier, New York's gargantuan right defensive tackle. Ameche would come banging in right behind him. Raymond was a great believer in *The Power of Positive Thinking*, Norman Vincent Peale's huge best seller, and he resolved to overcome the mismatch with Grier by girding himself with confidence. He also had the advantage of knowing the snap count. He figured that a much smaller man, coming off the line quickly, could knock over a much bigger man if he caught him off-balance. Remembering his personal admonition to "be a bulldog," the tight end closed his eyes and on the snap launched himself furiously at Grier, who outweighed him by more than a hundred pounds. When Raymond opened his eyes, he was on the ground in the end zone. Colts fans in the lower seats were cheering wildly. He heard the big drum of the team's official marching band banging in celebration. Ameche was on top of him, and he was on top of Grier. Touchdown! He got up and brushed off his uniform, mightily impressed with himself. It wasn't until a few days later, watching film of the play, that he realized what had happened. Parker had gotten off the snap even faster than he did, so when Raymond launched himself, he had smashed full bore into his own left tackle's rump. Parker was the one who had flattened Grier, but somehow in the jumble of big bodies had ended up rolling to one side. Raymond had wound up on top of the felled Giant. Still, for the rest of the game, Raymond was puffed up with a sense of accomplishment.

In fact, Grier was hurting. He had injured his knee the week before in the play-off game against the Browns, and had warned his coaches that he wasn't his usual self. He couldn't push off with much strength, or make the quick side moves he needed for a pass rush. Landry had wanted him to try anyway. Grier was such a presence on the Giants' defensive line that teams usually worked around him. Maybe Baltimore wouldn't notice, and sometimes in the game, when the adrenaline flowed and a player loosened up, he discovered that he had more to give than he thought. But two things were made clear by this play, and neither of them had anything to do with Raymond: one, Grier was not able to match up against Parker; and two, the Colts had noticed. They had aimed Ameche at what was normally the strongest point on the New York front, and it had folded like cardboard. Grier came out, replaced by Frank Youso, a rookie from the University of Minnesota who weighed about thirty pounds less. It was a big advantage for Parker, who would have little trouble for the rest of the game protecting John's blind side. Grier spent the remainder of the game watching sadly from the sidelines, draped in his long blue team cape.

Sloppy play continued. A Gifford fumble had set up this Colts first touchdown, and another would set up the second. Unable to move the ball on the drive after the Colts' score, the Giants were forced to punt it away, but the kick was dropped by Jackie Simpson, a fast rookie halfback who Weeb sometimes used for kick returns. His timing was disastrous.

—There's a fumble! Let's see who comes up with it; I believe Taseff [Colts safety Carl Taseff] recovered it. It is ruled that Carl Taseff recovered. Don Chandler punted and in the face of—Now it's ruled that the Giants recovered! It's the Giants' ball, Roosevelt Brown. On the eleven-yard line!

The New York crowd roared happily. The Giants' fumble had set up the Colts, and now Baltimore had returned the favor. But the cheers didn't last long. On the first play from scrimmage, Conerly pitched the ball to Gifford again for a sweep around the left side, but Kyle Rote failed to block cornerback Milt Davis, who with a running start hit Gifford immediately and knocked the ball loose. It was recovered by Baltimore's right end, Don Joyce.

So after two fumbles on consecutive plays, the sixth and seventh turnovers of the game, the Colts started the first truly sustained drive of the afternoon. Their offense was finally hitting its stride. They marched steadily upfield, mostly with modest gains of between five and ten yards. The Stadium crowd grew quieter and quieter. Raymond caught his first pass of the game for a five-yard gain. Ameche picked up a key first down with a ten-yard broken-field run. Then Moore, bad back and all, picked up another ten yards on a shifty run up the middle. The two backs took turns picking up yards for another first down. When the drive stalled on a third down play at midfield, John tucked the ball under his arm and with his peculiar shuffling gait took off, traveling sixteen yards before the surprised Giants defenders brought him down. Raymond made a diving sidelines catch and Ameche picked up another first down, so as the clock ticked off the final minutes of the first half, Baltimore was just fifteen yards away from the goal line.

When the Colts broke their huddle, they lined up in a formation that the Giants recognized as a running play, not unlike the "17" with which they had scored the touchdown. Raymond again took a three-point stance just to the left of Parker, and as the ball was snapped, ducked his head and threw himself into the line. Only instead of following through with the block, he lifted his head and slipped stealthily through the scrum and raced straight downfield. John faked the pitch to Ameche, which had the desired effect of fooling safety Patton, who took a long step forward as Raymond ran past him, and never recovered. The receiver was alone in the end zone when he caught John's softly thrown pass.

—*The Baltimore Colts drove eighty-six yards in thirteen plays. . . . Steve Myhra on the field to attempt the extra point. The snap, the spot, the boot. It's good, and it's now a fourteen-to-three football game. Joe?*

—*Well, the league's best offense against the league's best defense, and they really ground it out. The Colts this year gained over four thousand yards, forty-six hundred and fourteen to be exact, . . . so you can see this march of theirs was not a strange thing at all. They seemed to be inspired when they recovered the Giants' fumble on their own fourteen and proceeded to go to work with tremendous dispatch. Unitas guided them skillfully. . . . The Colts are supported today by some twenty-thousand of their fans who have made the trip, by bus, rail, car, and by plane. . . . It has been a first half full of surprises, full of the pressures of a championship game, because fumbles and pass interceptions have played major roles in the action here to date. The second quarter belonged entirely to Baltimore.*

The Giants ran three futile plays before the clock ran out. Backpedaling to pass, Conerly slipped and fell. On the last play of the half, fittingly, Alex Webster fumbled.

Giants Sam Huff threatening Colts head coach, Weeb Ewbank,
as trainer Dimitri Spassoff looks on.

Raymond Berry (left) and Johnny Unitas (right) led the Colts during a thrilling
fourth-quarter comeback. (Courtesy of Hy Peskin/*Sports Illustrated*)

Steve Myhra's game-tying field goal. (Courtesy of *Sports Illustrated*)

Overtime. (Courtesy of *Sports Illustrated*)

7

Three Plays

In their locker room at halftime, the Giants' players felt they were lucky not to be further behind. Gifford's fumbles had cost them dearly, and their offense had failed to move the ball. Landry, who never had much to say, told his defense to have faith in his game plan.

"If you keep doing what I've told you to do," he said, "We'll win."

As the game moved into the third quarter, cold and darkness settled down on Yankee Stadium. In the stands, fans burrowed deeper into scarves and blankets. Pocket flasks came out as men fought the chill with hard liquor. The lights overhead began to throw the game into eerie contrast, the field brightly illuminated against the darkening stands, just in time for more and more TV sets around the country to tune in. Families were settling in for the evening, and many, finding this gritty drama unfolding on NBC, one of only two or three channels available in most places, were twisting their aerials to sharpen the image. And at just the right moment, the Giants made the game more interesting, first with a dramatic goal-line stand, and then with that grand and goofy play—Conerly to Rote to Webster—to set up the first New York touchdown.

Suddenly the score was New York, 10, Baltimore, 14. Up in the NBC radio booth Joe Boland took over the play-by-play from Bill McColgan, and noted the shifting tide.

> —*New York has definitely come up with a more inspirational brand of play since that goal-line defense fired this crowd as I am sure it fired you listening across the nation. . . . Now let's see whether that high emotional supercharge of the New York Giants team, which seemed to be lifted by that goal-line defense that stymied the Baltimore Colts, will enable them to stay alive.*

At one end of the field with the wheelchair-bound vets, sixteen-year-old Neil Leifer had been snapping pictures with his camera, but he envied the more sophisticated equipment carried by the pro photographers, and the sideline passes that allowed them to move up and down the field with the action. He was trapped behind the end zone with a simple Yashica Mat camera and the lens that came with it. There was no chance of the close-ups sought by the newspapers, magazines, and wire services. Once or twice during the game he took a cup of hot coffee to the cop at his end of the field on the sidelines, and the cop winked at him and let him creep up the field a little. He took a few pictures before one of the pro photographers made a beef and the cop waved him back.

Emotions on both sides of the field were high. When Raymond was tackled before the Colts' bench after snaring a fourteen-yard pass, a furious Huff, arriving moments late, threw himself on the downed receiver's back. The next sensation he felt was a blow. Weeb had come flying out to defend his star receiver, and had punched Huff in the face.

—— *There is a disturbance directly in front of the Baltimore bench.*

It startled Huff more than it jarred him. A sidelines photographer caught the moment, the angry coach, his gray overcoat flapping, being separated by a referee from the linebacker, who is standing with his back to the camera, towering over both men, his wide back with the big number "70" filling one-third of the shot. Huff looked like he was capable of devouring Weeb— years later, without a hint of sarcasm, he would say, "I was about to kill him." Donovan and Marchetti and the other Colts defenders thought it was hilarious. For years Donovan would tell the story of how the diminutive coach—"that weasel bastard"— charged after Huff, "until he turned around and noticed none of us were following him."

Watching from his own sidelines after the touchdown, Giants halfback Alex Webster could feel the shift in momentum, like a sudden strong wind. His teammates had stopped the Colts on the one-yard line, and seconds later, the Colts had been unable to stop the Giants from banging in from the same distance. The Giants' stellar defense was like a force of nature. All season long the team had been coming back from behind to win big games because its defense allowed opponents so little. When the Huff-led defense caught fire, as they had since that goal-line stand, it could take control of a game. Here was the league's best, on both sides of the ball, in full collision, the unstoppable force meeting the immovable object. The general wisdom about football was that great defense beat great offense. Stopping the Colts four times on the one-yard line seemed to underline the truism. Just minutes later, put in the exact position, the Colts' defense had buckled. If you were looking for a small sample of plays to divine an outcome for the whole contest, these back-to-back goal-line stands, one successful, the other not, seemed made to order. It was as though New York, while still trailing, had gained a purchase on victory. The whole team now began playing with authority.

When the Colts took over again after the Giants' kickoff, the third quarter was drawing to a close and Baltimore seemed suddenly overmatched. John was sacked on the first play from scrimmage after the Giants' touchdown, and wound up scrambling away from the rush on third down and being tackled after just a short gain. They punted the ball away.

Still, as dominant as the New York defense was, the team still had to score, which had been their problem all season. The disparity between the two halves of the team was felt most oppressively by Landry's defense. Huff would goad the offensive players as they passed each other coming off and on the field. "Try and hold 'em," he would sneer. "Try not to give up too many yards." The defensive players all knew that their counterparts on offense tended to make more money and get their pictures in the papers with movie stars, and it was hard for them to contain their scorn in games where the hotshots failed to do their part. They were acutely aware of "Hollywood" Gifford's two fumbles—Huff always felt that the running back was a show-off who tended to carry the ball away from his body in one hand, a maneuver that looked good in the stop-action photos but that made him vulnerable to being stripped. So as he and the rest of the defense blew hard on the sidelines after another successful effort, they watched skeptically as the offense tried once more. Conerly and company had managed only two first downs in the first half.

But the magic of that goal-line effort was still in the chilly Bronx air. The offense suddenly sprang to life. On the last play of the third quarter, Conerly faked a handoff to Gifford, then wheeled and threw a seventeen-yard pass to tight end Bob Schnelker, a canny veteran from Bowling Green who had played as a marine for the Corps' team at Parris Island before joining the pros. He had been traded to the Giants two years earlier by the Eagles, and while never considered a star, he was a steady performer who rarely made mistakes. A future coach, he was having his finest moment as a player. The seventeen-yarder, his first catch of the game, gave the Giants a first down on their own thirty-nine-yard line. Then, on the next play, the first of the fourth quarter, with the offense aligned in the T-formation, Schnelker bolted straight downfield from his tight-end position. It was a classic "post pattern," down the right center hash marks angling toward the goalpost. Ignored by the Colts' right linebacker, Bill Pellington, he sprinted toward the center of the field between Baltimore's right and left safeties, Andy Nelson on the outside, and Raymond Brown on the inside. Neither safety seemed too concerned about him, a fact Lombardi had anticipated.

The tight end was used as a blocker on most plays, and although he had caught more passes and scored more touchdowns that season than the team's star receiver Kyle Rote, the Colts did not apparently regard him as a deep threat. They were aligned in a "cover three," with the two safeties and the right cornerback each covering a third of the field, deep. Brown, in the center, let Schnelker run right past him, leaving Nelson to pick him up one-on-one. Only, as the tight end raced toward the open center of the field away from Nelson, the cornerback continued to play him loose, as if protecting the sideline. He let Schnelker get behind him. Conerly faked a handoff to Gifford, then set, and heaved the ball high and far. Brown threw his hands up in despair when he turned and realized that the tight end had gotten too far upfield for him to overtake. Once the ball was in the air, Nelson closed in fast, but not fast enough. Schnelker gathered in the ball in full stride, deep in Colts territory. The safety caught him on the fifteen-yard line, dove for his legs, and spun him down. Apart from the fluke play that had set up their first touchdown, this would be the longest Giants gain of the day.

—*Joe, I don't know who was supposed to cover Schnelker on that play but he certainly outmaneuvered him. He was out there all alone!*

With a first and ten on the Colts' fifteen, the Giants again assumed the conventional T-formation, with Gifford, Mel Triplett, and Phil King lined up directly behind Conerly. All three backs sprinted out of the backfield at the snap. The quarterback backpedaled, looking to his right, and slipped on loose turf before regaining his balance. He turned to his left and threw to Gifford, who caught the ball along the left sidelines just a few yards from the goal line. Before him was Colts cornerback Davis. Gifford ducked his head and plowed straight into the defender, who pounced on his back but failed to stop him. Gifford stumbled forward and fell into the end zone with Davis draped all over him for the Giants' second touchdown.

The crowd erupted with joy as Summerall kicked the extra point to give the Giants a slim fourth-quarter lead, 17-14. They had come all the way back. Strips of paper flickered in the lights as they floated down from the darkened stands to the field; Giants fans were tearing up their programs and the tissue paper that vendors wrapped around their hot dogs and using it as confetti. New York could smell another championship.

Up in the press box, N.P. "Swami" Clark, the Colts' beat writer for the *Baltimore News-Post*, vented his disgust, loudly throwing in the towel.

"They're going to get routed!" he announced, referring to his hometown team. "Have you ever seen such a bunch of fucking clowns?"

Word filtered down to the New York sidelines that sportswriters upstairs had voted Conerly as *SPORT* magazine's Most Valuable Player of the game, an award that came with a new Corvette.

Baltimore was not about to give up, but even on their own sidelines they felt the game slipping away. Draped in their long blue capes, Donovan stood next to his linemate Marchetti.

"Gee, this is the first championship game we've ever been in," Donovan said wistfully. "We've took a shellacking in all these years of pro football. We're so better than these guys, and here we are fighting for our lives. If we lose this game, what a mistravesty of justice."

"Yeah, you're right, Fatso," said Marchetti.

Time was running out, and for the next two possessions, the game seemed to be headed for the expected finish. The Colts' offense sputtered. John passed them into the Giants' half of the field, and Rechichar tried and missed from forty-six yards out. The crowd gave Huff and the Giants' defense a standing ovation as they left the field.

Then Conerly began to maneuver his team smoothly upfield again, four yards, then three, then four more, completing one first down, then another. The Giants were grinding it out on the ground. The Baltimore defense looked tired and beaten.

—They are chewing up that clock with seven minutes, fifty seconds to go.

The Colts got another chance, gift-wrapped, when this workmanlike march ended with still another Giants fumble. Conerly handed the ball to King, who was hit by Lipscomb before he had a firm grasp of the ball. As he fell, it skittered on the turf behind him.

—A scramble for the ball, and . . . ah, a Baltimore recovery, I believe! Looks like Lipscomb came in and hit them and forced the fumble, with Myhra making the recovery of the ball for Baltimore on New York's forty-one-yard line. So Baltimore takes advantage of a hard-hitting defense, a resultant fumble, and a break with this fumble in New York territory, with

New York leading seventeen to fourteen . . . it's Baltimore's ball on the, looks like the forty-two-yard line!

A huge break for the Colts, the play set up their potent offense on the Giants' half of the field. They needed only to get in field-goal range to tie it up. But again the New York defense rose up. Two big defensive plays pushed Baltimore backward and well out of field-goal range. First, Andy Robustelli, exploiting a mistake on the Colts' line, sprinted into the backfield, unblocked, and dropped John for an eleven-yard loss. Then left tackle Dick Modzelewski came straight up the middle to tackle the quarterback nine yards further back. The threat of a field goal was erased. It had the feel of a decisive stand, an exclamation point on what was beginning to look like a certain New York victory.

Joe Boland smelled it up in the radio booth:

—This New York team is aflame defensively. They fired through on Unitas and dropped him for another loss. . . . Five minutes and forty-nine seconds still to go in the ball game. Bill, can New York run out most of that clock?

—Well, I know they hope they can. This is a mighty big drive.

Taking their time between plays, letting it tick off in great chunks, the Giants' offense began moving methodically upfield again, grinding out a critical first down, and then another. Baltimore had to stop them now or its offense would not get the ball back. Two more plays brought the Giants to another third down, this one on their own forty-yard line with four yards to go. There were under three minutes left in the game. It was dark now, and every minute that passed added hundreds of thousands of TV viewers. At this point, up in the mezzanine, league commissioner Bert Bell could hardly have asked for more. The game was close, and every play was charged with excitement.

— Joe, the thought just occurred to me that this is the closest-matched championship game in the last five years.

—There's no question about it. It is. And an amazing comeback by these high-flying New York Giants. That clock keeps running and New York is taking all the time in the world, waiting until the last second to get up and out of their huddle and over the ball. It's third down and, make it about four yards, just a shade under four yards to go for the first down on the New York forty-yard line. Two-fifty left to go in the ball game. New York leading seventeen to fourteen in the final period here in Yankee Stadium for the biggest of all prizes, the world championship of professional football.

If the Giants could make one more first down, they could probably run out the clock. Baltimore fans watching on TV saw their hopes fading.

New York coach Jim Lee Howell sent in a play—"Shoot-25 Trap"—which called for the left halfback to follow the other two backs into the right side of the line, off tackle, between Donovan and Marchetti. It was a gamble. The more likely move would have been to run at the other side of the Colts' line, away from Baltimore's strongest tacklers. Howell was betting that the Colts would overshift the wrong way, and he guessed right. They had a balanced front line, three down linemen to the left and the right, but Don Shinnick, the middle linebacker, positioned himself forward and to the right, and the rest of the defensive backfield shifted with him. The alignment left only cornerback Carl Taseff in the defensive secondary on the weak side. If the ball carrier could make it past Donovan and Marchetti, he would only have to dodge the smaller defender to pick up the first down or more.

As Marchetti got into his three-point stance, he was so sure the play was going away from him that he reminded himself to get off the ball quickly in order to evade the block and pursue the play to the other side.

New York again assumed a T-formation, with Webster, Triplett, and Gifford in a row three yards deep. Ordinarily, Webster would have carried the ball on a Shoot-25 Trap, but Lombardi wanted to give the ball to Gifford. At the snap, Schnelker and guard Jack Stroud hit Marchetti and tried to drive him out. Behind them, Webster and Triplett ran interference for Gifford, who saw an opening and cut inside them. Marchetti had come off the ball so fast that he had surprised the two Giants blockers, who were wrestling with him when Gifford shot past. The defensive end fought away from the two, twisted his body awkwardly and lunged at the running back, catching Gifford's legs from behind and hauling him down. The end, the running back, Stroud, and Schnelker tumbled forward in a flailing heap. Marchetti had just made the biggest tackle of his career. Up in the radio booth, McColgan thought Gifford was shy of the first-down marker on the forty-four-yard line, but in the tangle of bodies he could not be sure. He estimated that Gifford had been stopped on the forty-three.

—It's going to be close!

Trailing the play, Donovan, Shinnick, and Lipscomb had all thrown themselves on the pile, hoping to prevent Gifford from squirming forward the extra inches needed for the first down. Together it was three-quarters of a ton landing hard. Absorbing this blow, stretched out beneath the running back, was Marchetti. When Lipscomb came down on him he heard his ankle snap and felt a blinding pain.

He howled, and struggled to pull his wounded limb clear of the pile. The men slowly untangled, grunting and swearing at each other, "Motherfucker!" and "Get yer ass off me!" But as they peeled away, Marchetti stayed on the turf, holding his leg, rocking back and forth, bellowing. His parents in San Francisco, who were watching the first pro football game they had ever seen on television, looked on with alarm as their son writhed. In the midst of this commotion, Charley Berry, the line judge, a former pro baseball player, tried to stay focused on the football. He retrieved it and set it down close to the forty-four-yard marker.

Gifford was certain he had made it. He hadn't even glanced back as he got up. He eyed Marchetti's performance cynically. They knew each other. They had played each other often over the years. The running back thought his canny old friend was pulling a typical ploy, angling for a delay to stop the clock without wasting a team time-out.

"Get your damn butt off the ground, Gino," he said. "The play's over."

"Frank, I can't get up," said Marchetti.

—*Marchetti is down on the field for Baltimore as time-out is taken for him and a measurement. Time-out taken for Gino Marchetti, and time in for Bill McColgan.*

—*Well, Joe, Marchetti has been chasing Charlie Conerly throughout much of the afternoon, and he now goes over to see what's wrong with Gino as the Baltimore trainer comes out on the field. Two minutes and thirty-two seconds. That's unofficial time, of course, the official time is kept right on the playing field by the back judge. . . . This is a mighty important measurement coming up right now. The trainers are still working on Gino Marchetti. It was Marchetti who was on the bottom of the pile in stopping Frank Gifford on that play. The Giants have the ball on about their own forty-two-and-a-half, forty-three-yard line, and most important to them right now is to pick up this first down and run the clock out. Gino Marchetti is going to be taken from the playing field. Regarded by most football observers as the most outstanding defensive end in pro football, he is being helped off the field. . . . The Giants did not make the first down!*

When the chain was run out to the spot and stretched, it confirmed that the ball was inches short. Jack Stroud, the offensive guard who had been battling Marchetti with only marginal success all afternoon, was delighted to see him being carried off the field on a stretcher—he would later complain to him, "Gino, if you were gonna get hurt, why couldn't you have done it in the first quarter?"—but he was furious with the spot of the ball. He was hopping mad. Stroud told the line judge that he had made a mistake; coming in from the sideline he had set his right foot down to mark Gifford's forward progress, but after he found the ball, distracted by Marchetti, he had inadvertently set it down in front of his left foot, which was about a yard short. Berry serenely ignored the protest.

Gifford also complained loudly, insisting, "I made it! I made it!"

"Why don't you shut up?" said Donovan.

Gifford would be voicing the same lament a half century later.

But the ruling had been made, which meant that it was now fourth down and inches. The Giants' argument shifted from the field to their own sidelines, where coaches and players crowded around Howell. With the injury time-out and the measurement, there was time to debate. Jack Kemp, the rookie backup quarterback, was in the middle of it. He would remember Gifford and Lombardi begging Howell to let them try.

"We gotta go for it," said Gifford. "We can do it."

The Yankee Stadium crowd and all of New York wanted Howell to go for it, including his wife in the stands (who would tell him in no uncertain terms later), but it was the head coach's call. In Don Chandler he had one of the best punters in the pros, and his defense had been playing inspired ball. With the game on the line, Howell was being asked to lay down his chips on one half of his schizophrenic team, and without much hesitation he chose the defense. As Red Smith noted with characteristic understatement, "Later, the wisdom of this decision would be debated, but it seemed wise then." Giants fans would be debating it a half century on, but such is loneliness at the top.

—And we see that Don Chandler, the punter, has come into the football game. So the Colts will get the ball once more . . . and, Joe, it looks like this one is going right down to the wire.

—It's not only going down to the wire. . . . There is a possibility that Baltimore might tie this up at seventeen-seventeen and we might see a sudden death, but that's only a "might."

That possibility receded with Chandler's punt, which went high and far. Taseff signaled for a fair catch on the Colts' fourteen-yard line. With two minutes and twenty seconds left in the game, the Colts had a long way to go. The game had come down to the perfect matchup again, the league's best offense against its best defense. Howell had gone with the established wisdom.

As Huff took the field with the rest of Landry's squad, he was pleased. He would have been angry if the coach had decided the other way.

Exuding the calm surety that always inspired his teammates, John leaned into the huddle and said, "We've got eighty-six yards and two minutes. We're going to go straight down the field and score. Let's get to work."

He led off with a bomb, launching the ball fifty yards upfield for his tight end Mutscheller, who had caught a thirty-two-yard pass early in the third quarter with the same route, straight up the middle. This time he was bracketed with New York defenders, who were watching for anything deep. John had seen it and threw the ball well over all three men's heads.

Marchetti was watching from the sidelines, sitting up on the stretcher. His litter-bearers had been ordered to take him off the field, but the big defensive end demanded that they set him down. The Colts' fans in the stands behind him began chanting, "Gino! Gino! Gino!" All he could do now was watch. After every play the bearers would move him further down the field, prodded by the police, but as the Colts broke their huddle he would insist that they put him back down so he could watch the next play. A sideline photographer caught him, soiled and battered, a towel draped over his broken right ankle and foot, sitting up on the stretcher, craning his thick neck to see downfield, a study in intensity.

John's deliberate overthrow brought the game to the two-minute warning, which gave Landry and his defensive captains a chance to plan their strategy for the final stand. Everything was in the balance. It had been a very physical game, but at this critical moment, a delicate war of tactics would play out. Landry was a diligent student of the game, and of the Colts. He had spent many hours charting tendencies and trying to climb into the head of John Unitas, and he knew exactly what to expect.

All game long they had been double-teaming Lenny Moore when he lined up as a flanker to the right, and the Colts had countered by throwing often and successfully to Raymond Berry on the other side. He had caught seven passes, including a touchdown. He was clearly the quarterback's favorite target in second-and-long and third-and-long situations, and it was equally clear that the Giants' right cornerback, Karilivacz, was struggling to stay with the canny Colts receiver one-on-one. So

Landry decided to do something drastic. On certain throwing downs, he would take away Raymond Berry. If Unitas wanted to move the ball upfield in this final drive, he said, he was going to have to do it without his favorite target. Landry instructed his right-side linebacker, Harland Svare, to abandon his usual position and split way out, lining up directly in front of Berry, head-to-head. His assignment was to stay with him, get in his way, prevent him from running his route.

The move was radical. It was designed to rattle Unitas, who would be in his hurry-up offense, calling two or three plays at a time in the huddle. From all of his film study and charting of tendencies, further confirmed by what had happened in this game, Landry *knew* that in this critical moment of the game, the Colts' quarterback would go to Berry, and that the route would almost certainly be a sideline pattern, which would stop the clock whether the pass was caught or not. It was basic clock-management strategy, and nobody was better at the sideline pattern than Berry. If the Giants could take it away, it would throw the Colts off-stride. Once derailed, in the hurry-up offense there wouldn't be time to regroup.

And Landry was right. John completed a key eleven-yard pass to Moore for a first down, and then missed on a short pass to running back L.G. Dupre, which stopped the clock and allowed the Colts to huddle. There was only one minute and fifteen seconds left to play. This was the Colts' last chance. Failure to make a first down or score here would give the Giants victory. What followed were not just the most important three plays of the game, but the most important three plays of Raymond's and John's careers.

At second and ten, it was a clear passing situation, and John called two consecutive passing plays, both sideline patterns to Raymond. On the first, the receiver was to run an "L-cut," just a simple down-and-out toward the Giants' sideline, exactly what Landry had guessed they would do. Karilivacz had been playing well-off, guarding against a deep route, more or less conceding a short sideline pattern, and now the Colts would take advantage of it. But when Raymond trotted out to his spot along the left sideline, much to his surprise, Svare came with him. The linebacker set himself directly across from the receiver, just three yards deep.

—*Here's Berry, flanked wide to the left now.*

In all of his meticulous pages of notes for this game, in all of his film study of the Giants, Raymond had never seen one of their linebackers do this. It was the perfect counter to the play John had called, because even if he could shake Svare on the route, he would be slowed enough for Karilivacz to jump him from above—just as he had done in the first quarter to intercept. It appeared as though Landry had outsmarted them.

But the one thing the Giants' coach could not have known was that he was facing two players who were as obsessive about film study as he was. Years earlier, in one of their private film sessions, Raymond and John had seen this play. It wasn't Svare. It wasn't even the Giants. Raymond could no longer recall which team it was. But he and John had seen on the flickering image on his white apartment wall a linebacker drift out and line up nose-to-nose on a wide receiver. It had surprised them, and they had come up with a countermove. This exact situation. They had decided that Raymond should make a quick outside release to fake the linebacker, and then just slant pell-mell toward the center of the field. When you split a linebacker wide like that it leaves a gaping hole in the secondary. John told Raymond he would hit him in stride.

In the seconds before the ball was snapped, Raymond looked over at John and their eyes briefly met. *Does he remember?* He guessed that the quarterback did. Raymond assumed his three-point stance, and at the snap of the ball took two steps wide, pulling Svare outside, and then broke toward the middle at such an angle that Svare couldn't touch him. John's quick pass reached him six yards downfield, in full stride. He had remembered.

—Berry in the middle of the Giants' secondary, shakes one man off, shakes another as he's finally caught up with at about the fifty-yard line where he is brought down by Sam Huff, the middle linebacker in that Giants defensive platoon. A twenty-five-yard gain.

Huff was so surprised that he had run right past Raymond as he angled across the field. He had turned upfield and caught up to the slow-footed receiver from behind. Baltimore called time-out. There was one minute and five seconds remaining, and the Colts had just leaped to the middle of the field. A game-tying field goal suddenly seemed very much in reach, and with it the first ever overtime period. The successful second-down play had stunned the Giants. It was spooky. Landry and Huff felt like this Unitas was inside their heads.

Upstairs in the radio booth, for the first time the game announcers began to seriously contemplate a tie score.

—Joe, you are quite familiar with what a minute and five seconds means in the National Football League, and right now I know what Johnny Unitas and Weeb Ewbank would like to do, not go all the way but pick up another ten to twenty yards and get in position for a field goal. For the first time in the history of the National Football League we would witness a sudden-death play-off. And in case you are not familiar with the ruling on such a thing, if the game came to regulation time and was tied, then there would be a three-minute delay. There would be a toss of a coin, a new kickoff, and the first team to score would be declared the winner. If they went through a period without a score, then there would be a brief intermission and they would go right back out to play again.

The Colts could not afford to waste a play now. John called two in the huddle, the first to Raymond. The Giants gave up on moving Svare out wide directly in front of the receiver. He lined up this time split about halfway out. Huff was no longer positioning himself at the center of the line. He was cheating a little backward and to the right, something John, like a boxer noticing a weakness in his opponent's technique, noted and filed away. The most likely move was to the sideline, to stop the clock, but what John had called for was a square-in pattern. It was a gamble, John was opting here for surprise over caution. If it was successful, it would not stop the clock, and every second now was precious. Raymond broke straight downfield, and then cut across the middle behind Svare and in front of Karilivacz. Again, Raymond caught it in stride and turned up the center of the field. This time he was hauled down on the Giants' thirty-five-yard line, another gain of fifteen.

With less than a minute to play, the Colts lined up again without huddling. In the pro game, the clock did not stop while the team moved downfield to set up after a first down. The second of the two plays John had called was known as the "come open late." He would drop back and check off three receivers, Moore on the far right, Dupre in the middle of the field, and if both were covered, he would look last to Raymond on the left. The pass routes were staggered so that each of the three receivers would make the final cut on their routes a few seconds behind the other. In all the years they had run it, Raymond had never known John to decline throwing to one of the first two targets.

Before the game started, when Raymond had scouted the field looking for wet spots, one of the ones he had found was right in front of him, right where Karilivacz was standing. It was the place where water tended to drain off the tarp as it was removed from the field. Raymond had gone back to the locker room and changed into his mud cleats, and now it was going to pay off. When the ball was snapped, Raymond ran about ten yards upfield, and then curled back two steps to the wet spot, which had begun to ice. John rapidly looked to his two primary receivers, and drilled the pass to Raymond. As Raymond caught the ball he pivoted sharply to his right on his long cleats, and when Karilivacz tried to make the same cut his feet slipped out from under him. Raymond had nothing but open field ahead, up the sidelines. He made it all the way to the thirteen-yard line before the Giants' pursuit caught him from behind.

Three plays, three passes to Raymond Berry, sixty-two yards. "Unitas to Berry," said the Yankee Stadium public address announcer for the third consecutive time. Huff was sick of hearing it. The Giants' defense was reeling. There were fifteen seconds left. The referees called a brief time-out to move the first-down sticks upfield again. The Colts' offense raced off the field, and the field-goal kicking team sprinted on.

Back in Baltimore, Toni J. Carter and her brother had been watching the game together on TV, finishing off their Christmas turkey, and when Myhra trotted out for the kick, they both got up off their chairs and knelt before the TV set, holding hands and their breath. At the home of William S. Emrich in Arnold, Maryland, poor Barbara Emrich, William's wife, was banished to the second floor. Her husband was convinced that every time she came downstairs, something bad happened to the Colts. Barbara humored him. She took a seat on the top step.

George Shaw was the holder for Myhra, who was thinking what a long cold winter it was going to be for him back in the wheat fields of North Dakota if he missed. He also thought about the attempt that the Giants had blocked in the first quarter, and resolved to get this one off more quickly. Shaw took a knee and scratched an X in the turf where he planned to set the ball. Myhra stood behind it, took one long deliberate step back, and readied himself. It would be a nineteen-yard try. There wasn't much time to think about it, or to fret over the kicker's poor percentages. The ball was snapped, Shaw placed it, Myhra took one step and swung the wide toe of his cleats into the ball. He glanced up in time to see it sail cleanly over the crossbar.

In Baltimore, a driver listening on the radio ran his car into a telephone pole. Toni Carter's brother picked her up and threw her so high that she cut her shoulder on a ceiling fixture.

The score was 17-17. Myhra and Shaw were leaping for joy as they came back to the Colts' sideline.

Most of the players on both sides of the field thought the game was over. In the entire previous history of the NFL, when a game ended in a tie it had gone in the record books as a tie. Many of the players bolted for the locker room, eager to escape the mob that generally raced across the field at the end of a big game. But this game wasn't over yet. The NFL was about to play its first ever sudden-death overtime.

The largest audience to ever witness a pro football game was watching and listening. Bert Bell was in heaven.

Injured Marchetti watches
from the sideline.

Neil Leifer's famous photograph of Alan Ameche's game-winning touchdown.
(Courtesy of Neil Leifer)

Game over. (Courtesy of Hy Peskin/*Sports Illustrated*)

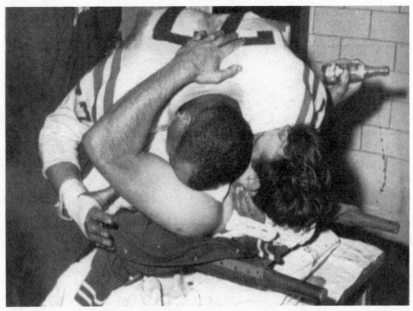

Gino Marchetti and Jim Parker in a post-game celebration.

8

Living to See
Sudden Death

Sam Huff thought the game was over. It was disappointing to tie, but as he trotted in off the field from the failed attempt to block Myhra's field goal (he played on special teams), he was already calculating his share of the take. He figured both teams would share the winnings equally, which he added up to something like $3,700. It was a thousand less than for winning, but almost a thousand more than he would have received for losing. Not too bad. He was bone-tired and even a little happy.

With seven seconds left on the clock, the Colts kicked off to Don Maynard, who caught the ball in the end zone and ran it back to the eighteen-yard line. Conerly just fell on the ball at the snap, and the regulation game was over.

Then the referee came over to the Giants' sideline.

"All right, we got sudden death coming up in three minutes," he announced. "We're gonna kick it off again. The first
team that scores wins."

The revelation that they would get another chance to win,
or lose, was not universally welcome news on the Giants' bench.
Huff turned to one of his teammates.

"Sudden death? What the hell's he talking about?"

Few of his teammates knew. It was news to lineman Al
Barry. Somebody told him that it had apparently been spelled
out in the program for that day's game.

"Who reads the program?" asked Barry.

"What happens now?" Pat Summerall asked Kyle Rote.

"I think we play some more," said the receiver.

"Shit, man, I'm tired," said Huff.

Gifford was sitting next to Conerly on the bench, and the
veteran quarterback looked beat.

"Wow, I can't go any more," said Conerly, surprised at
how exhausted he felt.

"Boy, you're gonna have to go some more," said Gifford.

"I can't," said Conerly. "I just can't."

Colts safety Andy Nelson didn't know about sudden death
either. After Myhra's kick, he had run off the field and was half-
way to the locker room when he heard a voice behind him.

"Andy, come on back! We're going to play it out."

He was delighted. Unlike Huff and most of the Giants'
team, he had never played in a championship game before. He
wanted to win.

Raymond had also bolted for the locker room. Several weeks earlier, when the Colts had come from behind dramatically to defeat the 49ers at home, the Memorial Stadium fans mobbed the field so quickly that he feared for his life. He saw people getting knocked down and trampled, and was amazed when there was no report in the *Sun* the next morning about people being killed or injured. He didn't want to be in the middle of a mob like that again. But when his teammates started calling out, he came back and saw the referees assembling in the middle of the field.

Bert Bell had fought the owners for this years ago. The commissioner had argued to the traditionalists that you could not end a championship game and a season on a tie. The only purpose was to crown a champ. This was the first time a sudden-death opportunity had presented itself, and it could not have come at a better time. He knew that millions of fans were watching all over the country. They were caught up in the most dramatic showdown in the league's history, two heroically talented teams playing their hearts out. Now they would fight to the finish. It was doubly pleasing that one of the teams was the Colts, the new franchise that he had midwifed five years earlier with his old friend and former player Carroll Rosenbloom. A healthy league had to be structured in a way that would let new teams from small markets, like Baltimore, compete with the established clubs in big cities. Bell had appeared before Congress just months earlier to successfully defend the staggered system he had invented for drafting college players, arguing that it was not a monopolist conspiracy but a vital tool for ensuring equity in his league. On both counts, this suspenseful season-ender proved his point.

At midfield, referee Ron Gibbs stood between the Giants' cocaptains, Rote and linebacker Bill Svoboda, in their blue capes, and John Unitas, who was filling in for the Colts' fallen team captain, Marchetti. Gibbs explained that Baltimore, the visiting team, would get to call the flip. John shouted "tails," but the coin dropped—all four men stooped to see—heads.

—And the Giants won the toss, and they are going to receive!

A roar arose from the dark wall of people around them. The crowd was on its feet. This may have been the first sudden-death overtime ever, but this primarily New York audience knew that in sudden death, winning the toss was a huge advantage. John looked disgusted, his hands on his hips.

At Henny Mack's pub on Ritchie Highway in Glen Burnie, Maryland, Ed Chaney Jr., one of about three dozen Colts fans watching on TV, called his boss at a nearby service station to say he was going to be late for work. The boss fired him. Chaney hung up happily and ordered another beer.

—A most historic moment in football history . . . A sudden-death play-off with all the marbles on the line. Members of the winning team will receive about five thousand dollars. The members of the losing team will receive slightly less. Seventeen-to-seventeen thanks to some brilliant passing by Johnny Unitas to get the ball into field-goal-kicking position. Joe?

—Bill, I was just hoping to call attention to the fact that the first team that scores, field goal, safety, touchdown, will win the game now, and the game will be over with the first score. That's what the sudden-death rule means, and the Giants, as you pointed out, are in a favorable position because . . . they will get the first opportunity with the ball. Here we go. We're almost set for the kickoff.

It was now fully a night game. The stands were completely dark and the field shone like it was spot lit from heaven. There was a sense throughout Yankee Stadium and in homes all over America that something truly memorable was unfolding. It was television prime time. The nation was experiencing what was still a new kind of human experience, a truly communal live national event, something made possible by the new medium. In future years the phenomenon would become familiar, but no less powerful, as the nation gathered to watch rocket launches, the aftermath of assassinations, a magnificent civil rights speech, an astronaut stepping on the moon, a presidential resignation, and someday even the slow-speed highway chase in Los Angeles of a former NFL football star charged with a double-murder—O.J. Simpson was still in grade school in 1958. In this moment, football itself was about to step fully into the age of television, of multimillion-dollar player contracts, slow-motion replay, cable sports networks, Super Bowls, and franchises with market values exceeding the gross national product of many small countries. Not even Bert Bell could imagine where his sport was heading.

At ground zero it was now freezing. The wet spots Raymond had noted before the game had turned to ice. Players were chilled to the bone and exhausted. On the Baltimore sideline, Weeb stood at the center of a circle of worn out, muddy players, and reminded them to block and tackle the way they knew how. He added, pointing down to the end zone where Marchetti was still sitting up on his stretcher, refusing to leave the field, "Win it for Gino."

Colts kickoff man, Bert Rechichar, booted the ball into the end zone, so the Giants started on their own twenty-yard line. Conerly rallied and dragged himself back out on the field, but his prediction to Gifford was true. He couldn't go any more. They could not make a first down. Gifford picked up four yards on the ground, then Conerly gambled, throwing another deep pass to Schnelker, running the same route that had produced the big play earlier. The pass was incomplete. He couldn't find a receiver on third down and had to try and run for it himself—Conerly hated to run with the ball—and he almost made the first down. Bill Pellington tackled him one yard short. New York had lost its last chance. Pellington would later say that as he trotted off the field after that tackle, "I knew right then that they had to turn the ball over to us and that Raymond and John were going to lead us to a score."

Indeed, Howell once again gave little thought to going for it on fourth down. A failure that deep in their own side of the field would almost certainly hand Baltimore victory. Don Chandler trotted back out.

—*Again, a tremendous vote of confidence in the New York defensive team.*
New York is going to punt.

The kick flew high and deep into Baltimore territory, and Huff and the rest of the tired Giants defense came back on the field to resume battle. John was about to top his just-completed, game-tying drive with a masterpiece, a thirteen-play performance that would secure his reputation as football's premier play-caller. These back-to-back, critical scoring drives would enter the NFL history books as the most dramatic performance ever.

The first play was a handoff to L.G. Dupre, who ran through the right side of the Giants' line, broke into the secondary, and scooted eleven yards before Frank Youso, playing for the injured Rosey Grier, leapt on his back and dragged him down. On the second first down, John went back to the play they had tried twice earlier, the bomb to Moore down the right sideline. The first time it had worked. The second time Moore had caught the ball but stepped out of bounds. This time he had a step on cornerback Lindon Crow. John flung the ball sixty yards, a high, arcing pass that seemed to hang forever in the stadium lights against the black backdrop of the stands, where the New York crowd was holding its collective breath, and fell right into the racing Moore's hands. But this time Crow's hand was there, too, and he knocked the football away.

Sensing triumph, hundreds and then thousands of Baltimore fans had begun to leave the stands and crowd behind the goalposts at both ends of the field. It was the tradition, borrowed from the college game and soon to be banned by the NFL, to storm the field after a victory and tear down the goalposts. After this game, everybody wanted a souvenir. As

Moore trotted back to the huddle, a police captain walked over to Marchetti's stretcher bearers, who were now surrounded by spectators. If the mob moved, the injured Colts captain might be trampled.

"Get him out of here," the captain said. So they carried the protesting lineman down the dark tunnel and into the visitors locker room, under the stands. The men set him down, draped a blanket over him, and then ran back out to the field to see the game. There was no TV or radio in the locker room. The big defensive end lay there alone, in suspense, trying to divine what was happening by the rumble of thousands sitting overhead.

On second and ten, Unitas handed off to Dupre again, for only a two-yard gain. A time-out was called by the officials to push back the crowds in the end zones.

When play resumed, it was another critical third and long from the Giants' thirty-three-yard line, a Raymond Berry situation. Landry again moved his right linebacker, Svare, all the way out to line up nose to nose with the receiver. This time Raymond ran a deep route, pulling both Svare and Karilivacz downfield with him, while John threw a swing pass to Ameche, who raced along behind Raymond up the left sideline. By the time Svare recovered and came back to tackle the running back, Ameche had gained eight yards and another first down. A big cheer went up from Colts fans.

The Colts' patient progress continued. Unlike the drive minutes earlier at the end of the fourth quarter, John now had plenty of time. He could chip away, mixing the run and pass, taking short bites like quick jabs, keeping the Giants' defenders off-balance. On first down, Dupre again plunged into the right side of the line and gained three yards. On second down, John dropped back to pass and was sacked for an eight-yard loss by left tackle Dick Modzelewski. Once again the Colts had a critical third-down play. They needed fifteen yards to sustain this all-important drive.

Raymond lined up on the left side, out just a few yards from the line. Having been twice burned lining up Svare on Berry's nose, this time Landry positioned the linebacker half-way between the receiver and the line, and at the snap of the ball, Raymond took off upfield, heading for the left sideline, again to the icy spot in front of the Giants' bench. Karilivacz played him loose, backpedaling, determined to keep Raymond in front of him. John looked for Moore on the right side, but he was covered, so he began drifting to his left out of the pocket, searching for Raymond. His favorite target had stopped suddenly about twenty-five yards upfield, reversed direction about five yards, and stopped again. He was standing all alone, twenty yards downfield. Karilivacz, working on that slippery patch, could not reverse direction as quickly. John's rifled pass reached Raymond before the cornerback did. The receiver tried the same move he had made earlier in that spot, spinning to his right, but this time Karilivacz got hold of one foot and would not let go. Raymond pulled and pulled, and finally ducked to the turf as a wall of angry Giants flung themselves at him. He was down on the Giants' forty-four-yard line with another first down.

—Carl Karilivacz, the defending back, lost his footing when the end, Ray Berry, made his cut there on the forty-five-yard line. Karilivacz fell down and Berry hauled in the pass.

"Unitas to Berry," came the public address announcement. "First down."

Huff was tired, frustrated, and confused. He didn't know what to expect. He felt like Unitas knew what he was thinking. The whole Landry defense was premised on anticipating what the other team was going to do, being one step ahead mentally, but time and again this Unitas seemed to be not one but *two* steps ahead—as though he knew what Huff thought he was going to do, and so did something else. Every play was a surprise. The New York defense was like a fighter who had been hit once too often by the same left jab. When an offense was clicking the way the Colts were, even the most disciplined defense begins to crumble. Mounting failure has a cumulative effect, taking defenders out of their carefully wrought schemes. Players begin to improvise adjustments, just as a fighter will start raising his right glove to ward off the annoying jab, only to leave open his midsection. This is what was happening to Huff.

The left jab was that damned Raymond Berry. It was obvious to the middle linebacker that Karilivacz, the right cornerback, was overmatched, and moving Svare out to help him hadn't worked. John and Raymond had a countermove for everything they did. The loudspeaker kept echoing, "Unitas to Berry." "Unitas to Berry." It hit Huff's ears now like a taunt.

So on this first down, the middle linebacker lifted his right glove. He cheated a little bit, stepping back away from his usual spot in the middle, between his tackles, and drifting a yard or two to his right, daring Unitas to throw that way again.

Crouched behind his center, waiting for the snap, John saw it and immediately changed the play. He had the perfect play to exploit the situation, in fact, he had been waiting for this opportunity. It was based on everything he had observed in the game so far, but particularly on what had happened on the two previous plays. Two plays earlier, Modzelewski had come crashing into the backfield for a sack. The Colts' right guard, Alex Sandusky, was having a hard time stopping him. So John called a trap play that would bring his left guard, Art Spinney, up behind the center and across the backfield to deliver a surprise blow to the charging Giants tackle from the right side. It would knock him to the ground. The center, Buzz Nutter, would snap the ball and then charge hard to his left to hit Spinney's man, right tackle Frank Youso, and drive him out. The key to these maneuvers, however, was Huff. Normally, if the middle linebacker was lined up in the middle, the stunt by Nutter and Spinney would leave him un-blocked at the center of the line, ready to eat whatever came through. But Huff wouldn't be there this time. The completion to Raymond on the previous play, along with the eleven catches that had preceded it (eleven receptions was a remarkable achieve-ment), had drawn Huff out and off to his right despite his better judgment. John *was* inside Huff's head. He knew the linebacker would be leaning backward and to his right, and would never re-cover in time to plug the hole in the middle. The capstone on this play's design was Colts right tackle George Preas, who would forego blocking defensive end Jim Katcavage, who would be too far from the direction of the play to matter, and instead charge across the backfield to deliver a running hit on Huff at precisely the moment he realized he'd been had.

And the trap sprung exactly as Weeb had drawn it on the blackboard. Modzelewski crashed to the ground. Nutter stood Youso up and knocked him backward. John faked a handoff to Dupre, and gave the ball to Ameche. Huff realized too late, tried to reverse direction, and then Preas flattened him. Ameche raced straight up the middle of the field, right past the falling Huff, and into the Giants' secondary. He sprinted between safeties Emlen Tunnell and Jimmy Patton.

—Ameche's at the thirty, the twenty-five, down to the twenty-yard line! So the Baltimore Colts have first down and ten yards to go on the Giants' twenty. . . . The handoff to Alan Ameche and up the middle he went, going twenty-four yards from the forty-four yard line.

It was the knockout punch. Forty-nine years later, a still vital and formidable Huff would throw his long arms wide and complain, "John had me psyched, you know? I thought he could read my mind after a while because it seemed like the son of a bitch knew every defense I was in. You know, it was frustrating to play against him, he was just a mastermind at it." Ameche's run up the Giants' guts was virtually a game-winner. The crowd groaned and then grew silent. The Colts were now in easy range of a winning field goal, just one yard further out from where Myhra had kicked the game-tying one minute earlier.

But Weeb was not about to wager victory for a second time on the unreliable leg of Steve Myhra. Later, sportswriters would speculate that the Colts' owner, Rosenbloom, whose fondness for gambling was known, had ordered his coach not to kick a field goal in order to preserve a more favorable point spread, but the owner was upstairs and Weeb was on the sidelines. Myhra was notoriously erratic, time wasn't a factor, it was first down, and John was like a heavyweight champion finishing off a challenger with wobbly legs. Weeb wasn't going to send out his kicker unless he had to.

It wouldn't come to that. The Colts tried a running play around the right side that went nowhere. On second down, John took one step back from center and rifled a pass to Raymond, who slanted across the field and caught the ball behind Svare and in front of Karilivacz. He fell down immediately, and realizing that he had not been touched, got up and lunged for the goal line. He was downed eight yards short. It was his twelfth catch, for 178 yards, the most ever by a receiver in a championship game. In this one game he had nearly matched his performance during his entire rookie season. Huff had to hear the loudspeaker once more announce, "Unitas to Berry."

The play earned another first down. Now the Colts were looking right up at the goalposts, and the Giants had their backs to it. New York called time-out.

And then, as the climactic moment approached, TV sets in millions of homes went gray. NBC had lost its connection.

Nowhere was this taken harder than in Maryland. The well-watered Colts fans at Henry Mack's pub in Glen Burnie groaned and started throwing things at the set. Henry put himself between the mob and the screen. As William Gildea wrote in his book *When the Colts Belonged to Baltimore*, Joey Radomski, a dockworker in Locust Point, who was watching the game with his eighteen-year-old daughter, Mary Margaret, who was praying the rosary throughout, got up and smacked the top of his set hard with a calloused hand. When nothing happened, he swore like . . . well, like a dockworker. In the novitiate, the nuns-in-training around the blanket-draped set worried that their dodge of the ecclesiastical ruling against watching the game had angered a higher power. In the relatively posh Baltimore suburb of Riderwood, the poet Ogden Nash and his wife, Frances, who were watching the game with four generations of Nashes, went temporarily mad with frustration. Shouting and oaths echoed from the normally dignified poet's residence, as a rapid search was undertaken for that recently antiquated device, a radio. When one was located, an urgent dispute erupted over where to find the game on the dial. Nash's daughter would say later, "Our behavior was something absolutely appalling."

Someone in the crowd milling behind the end zone had kicked the network's cable and unplugged America. The Colts broke huddle and approached the line of scrimmage. The NBC TV sports directors upstairs were frantic but, remarkably, prepared. In years to come, the marriage between television and football would be so complete that games would routinely stop to allow time for commercials and broadcast emergencies, but in

1958 television was still just a spectator. The game would proceed with or without television coverage. But the TV men were clever. Two months earlier, in an article about TV coverage of football games in the *New York Times*, a CBS producer had speculated about ways his network might stop action on the field in a pinch.

"Maybe we could cue a drunk to go out and interrupt things," he told *Times* reporter John P. Shanley.

—Play will be held up now. A fan running out on the field with three of New York's finest trying to corner him.

The runner, a giddy-looking young man in a flapping winter coat, gave the cops a good run. He moved well, covering most of the length of the field before police reinforcements from the other end zone intercepted him.

—and they get him [chuckling here] *down at about the twenty-two-yard line. Now there are four or five policemen escorting him off the playing field.*

"God-dang, shouldn't be getting me" said the man. "You should be getting that number nineteen [Unitas]. He's the guy that's killin' us!"

Newspaper reports would later refer contemptuously to the "drunk" who held up action at the penultimate moment of the game, but the man who ran out on the field was not drunk. He hadn't been drinking, he had been working. His name was Stan Rotkiewicz, and he was business manager of NBC news, who on game days doubled as a sports statistician. He had played some college football, and in the service of his network dusted off his broken-field running just long enough for television engineers to find the plug and reconnect their cameras. Television sets blinked back to life in time to see the Colts line up, first and goal on the eight-yard line.

On a play called "16 Power," Ameche bulled his way forward two yards on first down, and was tackled by Huff. Then John once again did something unexpected. He made up a play. The Giants were digging in to stop the run. With the championship just six yards away and with the chance of an almost certain field goal if they reached fourth down, the last thing New York figured he would do is risk an interception by putting the ball in the air, but as the quarterback would later calmly instruct sportswriters, "If you know what you're doing, you don't get intercepted." John had been watching Emlen Tunnell, the Giants' strong safety, cover his tight end all day. But in this goal-line position, he knew Mutscheller would be covered by linebacker Cliff Livingston, who would be trying to take away an inside pattern. If the tight end broke wide, it left only Lindon Crow to pick him up, and Crow had been preoccupied all afternoon with Lenny Moore. He told tight end Jim Mutscheller to run a diagonal route to his right, angling for the goal line. "Get out there real quick," he said.

Once again, John's play calling took the Giants completely by surprise. Nobody followed Mutscheller as he ran toward the sideline. The pass was lofted gently. The tight end turned and caught it with both hands on the two-yard line, right on another of the wet patches Raymond had noticed before the game, in the corner where the sun never shone. It was now ice. There was no one to keep Mutscheller from the end zone, but his feet wouldn't take him there. He slid helplessly out of bounds at the two-yard line.

So it was third down, two yards to go. If they blew this, Weeb would have to chose between trying a fourth time for the touchdown, or betting once more on Myhra. John leaned into the huddle and looked at Ameche. "This is the 16 Power," he said. "This is the game right here. We can win the ball game with this play." Two downs ago, on the same play, Ameche had altered course. He was supposed to plunge off the right end, but he had seen an opening and tried to cut up the middle, where Huff was waiting. This time it worked exactly as drawn. Mutscheller blocked left linebacker Cliff Livingston toward the middle of the field, and Lenny Moore stopped safety Emlen Tunnell with the best block he had ever made. The hole they opened up was so wide that nobody laid a finger on Ameche as he lunged into the end zone. He lowered his head and shoulders expecting to get hit, and when he met no resistance his momentum threw him face first into the cold turf, the end zone turf.

—And the ball game is over! Alan Ameche has scored the touchdown, and the Baltimore Colts are the professional football champions of the world! Baltimore twenty-three, the New York Giants seventeen.

Neil Leifer got the picture. He stood surrounded by drunken Colts fans and wheelchair vets, and by the accredited photographers who had crowded behind the end zone for the winning points. At the climactic moment of the game, the remote space in which he had been confined was suddenly the right place to be. The birthday-boy's shot would be one of many trained at

Ameche's winning plunge. In film of the game there would be an explosion of light behind the end zone as the flash bulbs on all the cameras popped. Leifer envied the pros and their more sophisticated cameras with adjustable lenses. With those, they could focus in tightly on the fullback as he crossed the line, get the close-up. His Yashica Mat had only a normal lens, which meant that his picture would be not just of Ameche hurtling toward him, but of a broad panorama, John watching from behind the line, the hand that had given Ameche the football still outstretched, the long empty, illuminated field behind him, the encircling stands, the dark sky. Leifer didn't consider it in that moment, but his picture told the bigger story, of a team that had just driven the length of the field, of a game that had stretched from early afternoon into night. It would be the first picture he ever sold, and would become the most famous photo of the game.

Up in the owner's box, Bert Bell was beside himself. He bellowed, "This is the greatest day in the history of professional football!" He told *New York Times* reporter Louis Effrat that it was, simply, "The greatest game I have ever seen."

Ameche was immediately mobbed by fans, one of whom stripped the ball from his hands. Buzz Nutter, the center, knocked the fan down, recovered the souvenir, and raced with Ameche for the locker room.

Their quarterback wasn't watching. By the time the running back hit the ground, John Unitas, now the most famous quarterback in football history, had turned his back and was coming off the field the same way he did in victory or defeat, shoulders stooped, head down, a man walking home from work.

Ameche, a hero. (Courtesy of Hy Peskin/*Sports Illustrated*)

Johnny Unitas driving the Corvette awarded to him by *Sport* magazine.
(Courtesy of *Sport* magazine)

Colts return home. (Courtesy of Special Collections, University of Maryland Libraries)

9

Epilogue

Alone in the locker room, Gino Marchetti got the news when his teammates burst in shouting it, "We're world champions!" Years later he couldn't remember whether it was Bill Pellington or Ray Brown. There is a picture of him on the stretcher, being embraced by Jim Parker, the great offensive tackle he had humiliated on that day long ago in training camp. Parker is stooping, still in his full uniform and pads, the tape on his hands and wrists unraveling, his head resting on his injured teammate's shoulder. Marchetti is clutching a bottle of soda pop.

They celebrated with Coke and Nehi Orange, these new champions, many of them veterans of hard combat, because the NFL was squeamish about alcohol. The beer would come later, in cases, loaded into the charter plane for the quick flight home.

Once Raymond saw Ameche cross the goal line, he ran for the locker room as fast as he could. In the earlier crush weeks before at Memorial Stadium, the noise level had been so great that if he had yelled at the top of his lungs he could not have heard himself. Strangers had scooped him up on their shoulders and swept him along. He hadn't liked the feeling of being so out of control, so much at the mercy of a mob. In his rush at the end of this game, he was out of the arena before the sense of accomplishment fully hit him.

Raymond had not had the religious experience that would shape the rest of his life, so he had no words yet for the feeling that overcame him in that moment, but later he would arrive at the understanding that would frame it properly. At the time he just felt overwhelmed with the perception that he had been touched by something powerful and other. Maybe destiny, although the term was hackneyed. Whatever it was, it shook him.

"WHO OUTGUTTED WHO!" screamed offensive guard Art Spinney, referring to the Conerly newspaper column that had hung on their locker-room wall in Baltimore as a motivator all week. As more and more of the players made it off the field, the laughter and hooting and shouting created a happy din.

Raymond retreated from it. He found an empty toilet stall and closed himself in for more than five minutes, a tall, lean man in a dirty white-and-blue uniform, his shoulder pads filling the small space. He thought about the high school team he had fought to make, the college scholarship he didn't get, the provisional scholarship that allowed him to stay with the team at SMU, and the fluke of being drafted as a "futures" pick by the Colts. He thought about the desperation he had felt two summers ago, and about meeting John and their fortuitous partnership. And now they had done it. They were the best team in all of football, at the pinnacle of their sport, and he was not just a member of the team, but a key player. His catches today had set an NFL record, but, more importantly, along with key plays by a lot of his teammates, they had enabled victory.

He thought about the three pass plays in the critical fourth-quarter drive, and about the pass he and John had improvised when Svare drifted out wide to take him out of the play. For the first time, he knew there was a moment in a game where they had triumphed for no other reason than preparation. He often had reason to believe his obsessive habits proved only that he was the nut his teammates said he was. There were times when even John treated him that way, like the time when he had suggested that they get together and go over some things, and the quarterback had protested, "Oh, Raymond, here you come again." That had stung. But he could see why John might have felt that way from time to time. In all the years of his obsessive work habits, the pages and pages of handwritten notes he kept in worn three-ring binders, he had never been certain himself that it was worth it. He believed that it made a general contribution, but day in and day out he did it mostly on faith; it was something he *had* to do. Now there had come a moment that rewarded everything. Fate had delivered a moment that proved its worth, and not just in any game at some random point. It had come in the pivotal moment of the ultimate game of their careers. It had come on what was the most important play of his professional life. It was hard not to feel how spooky that was, and how wonderful. The timing . . . well, it went beyond just being good, or being lucky. He would come to see it eventually as the hand of God.

When he emerged from the stall he ran into Tex Maule, a writer from *Sports Illustrated,* and told him, simply, "It's the greatest thing that ever happened." That's how he felt.

Out on the field, the visiting Baltimore fans were in a frenzy. *News-Post* writer John Steadman would describe the scene in his 1988 book about the game, *The Greatest Football Game Ever Played*:

> *The noise factor from the applause may have broken the sound barrier. . . . The din . . . was charged with electricity and almost pleading personal involvement. The instant the overtime period ended, we climbed from the press box, game notes in hand, to make our way to the second deck of the stadium. . . . The field was being picked clean of grass. . . . They were tearing up the sod to take home as souvenirs. The goalposts had been dismantled and were being fought over . . . Don Bruchley, a radio/TV broadcaster from Baltimore . . . one not normally given to being caught up in the frenzy of the moment, was down there among the fans ripping apart the grass. . . . The Colts' band, making jubilant music . . . went up and down the field, goal-line to goal-line.*

Steadman ran into Commissioner Bell, who was with his son and daughter and Art Rooney, the Steelers' owner whose team had let Unitas get away. Bell pronounced it, "The greatest game I have ever seen! John, old boy, I never thought I would live to see sudden death." Baltimore Mayor Tommy D'Alesandro, Jr., who had maneuvered to bring the Colts to his city and was pink-faced from the cold and the liquid cheer, was also making his way to the victorious locker room, as happy, Steadman wrote, "as a schoolboy."

In the New York locker room, the defeated Giants peeled off their gear in silence. Sweat-soaked player after sweat-soaked player saluted the performance of the Colts. "They deserve it," said Dick Modzelewski. "They're great and we have nothing to be ashamed of. That Unitas was just terrific with his passes. . . . We out-fought Baltimore, but they out-played us." Howell politely defended his decision to punt in the fourth quarter over and over again. He would be defending it for the rest of his life. "I didn't think it was a good gamble," he explained. "Remember, we stopped them on the one-yard line in the third quarter by loading up the defense." Then the next group of reporters would wander over, and ask the same question.

Gifford wept. He told every reporter who asked that he thought he had made the first down in the fourth quarter. "The officials ruled otherwise, so what can you do?" Later, he claimed that the referee, Ron Gibbs, had come up to him after the game and admitted that they had blown the call.

The gloom in their locker room stood in sharp contrast to the gleeful noise down the hall. Chuck Thompson, the slender, balding man who had become the voice of the Colts on

WBAL-TV, Baltimore's NBC outlet, cornered Rosenbloom, who had an enormous grin.

"I just can't say enough about these kids," he said. "They are the greatest."

"We are the best in the world!" shouted rookie cornerback Johnny Sample, to no one in particular. "We are the best in the whole universe!"

It went on like this for as long as it took the reporters to gather the quotes they needed to file their stories, and for the players to shower and dress. Donovan stayed in New York as the team boarded a bus for the airport. He would spend the night with his family just a few blocks away, the toast of a family dinner populated mainly by disappointed Giants fans. Raymond also stayed behind, stopping on his way out to introduce himself and shake the hand of Commissioner Bell, who had tears in his eyes. The receiver rode back to his aunt's house in Philadelphia on the train with his parents, just another slender young man in glasses. He was back in Baltimore on Monday morning, knocking on Weeb's door, as usual to borrow game film.

Ameche stayed in New York. There was no more- fitting symbol of the NFL's arrival in prime time television than the appearance he made that night—for $750—on *The Ed Sullivan Show*. Dressed in a smart suit, Ameche did little more than awkwardly smile, wave, and shake Sullivan's hand. America's favorite impresario showed a film clip of Ameche crossing the goal line with the winning touchdown. The Colts had made the big time.

John had turned down the show. He said he wanted to "go home with the guys." He would come back to Manhattan a few days later to accept the Corvette offered by *SPORT* magazine to the MVP of the game, the one prematurely awarded to Conerly. John posed seated behind the wheel, leaning out the window, grinning and waving. Perian Conerly later complained, jokingly, "Mrs. Unitas is driving *my car!*" Not likely. Married with three children, John traded it promptly for a family-sized vehicle.

He went right back to his suburban life in Baltimore, not fully realizing how much his life was going to change. Overnight "Johnny" Unitas was a household word, not just the most famous football player in America, but a cultural phenomenon. As one of his biographers, Lou Sahadi would write,

Every high school and college quarterback wanted to be like Johnny Unitas. The barbershops put down their combs and scissors and began using electric haircutters to sculpt crew cuts. High-top shoes were a must for every kid who dreamed about being like him. If there was a cult hero in professional football, it was Unitas.

The team rode the bus to LaGuardia Airport and flew home immediately. They landed just after seven o'clock that evening, where an estimated thirty-thousand ecstatic Baltimoreans were waiting at Friendship Airport. The players' bus was mobbed on the way out. Firecrackers exploded. Fans climbed on the roof of the bus and struggled to keep their balance as the crowd rocked it back and forth. Children had to be lifted to safety. Women screamed. The roof of the bus buckled and players started looking for a way out. Police reinforcements arrived and tried with little effect to suppress the havoc as the crowd clambered up on the roofs of patrol cars. Beer bottles flew. The celebration finally broke up on its own after the bus driver took on the crowd, rolling forward defiantly into the crush and defying the people to get out of his way. Survival instinct prevailed, the masses parted, and the busload of frightened world champions escaped.

Carroll Rosenbloom saw to it that his team got the biggest payday of their lives for the championship. Each man got a check from the league for $4,718, which, good to his preseason promise, was matched by the owner. The victory fund was $90,000 and it was split down the roster evenly. The National Brewing Company, which sponsored the Colts' game broadcasts, kicked in another $25,000, and a check for the same amount came from an anonymous benefactor, thought to be Rosenbloom's Florida real estate friend Lou Chesler. Steadman wrote, "Winning was a bonanza for the Colts, unlike anything that had ever happened to a professional football team."

The Giants each got a check for $3,111.

The day after the game, Jim Lee Howell invited the local press, whose strike had just ended, to review the game film with the team's coaches. In the *Daily News*, Joe Trimble wrote, "It was almost as exciting as the game itself. Couldn't change the 23-17 ending, though."

The film showed, according to Trimble, that Gifford had not made a first down on the critical fourth-quarter play.

The third-down play shows Gifford reaching the forty-three-yard line, plus maybe a few inches. He didn't reach the forty-four, which was necessary for the first down. Howell stopped the action and reran it a couple of times, almost in the hope that Giff might get that needed distance. But each time the play ended, Frank was in the same place.

In the *New York Times*, columnist Arthur Daley wrote:

If this . . . wasn't the most exciting football game ever played, it will do until an even more implausible cliff-hanger is performed. This was one for the book, an unforgettable episode crammed to the gunwales with dramatics and heroics.

Daley defended both of Howell's decisions to punt in the fourth quarter and again in overtime: "It would have been sheer idiocy for him to have done other than what he did."

Daley saved his highest tribute for Raymond:

The astonishing thing about Berry is that his eyesight is so poor he wears thick glasses offstage. He can't even read the letter 'E,' the biggest letter on the chart. Hence he wears contact lenses on the gridiron. They have made him the best pass catcher in the league. 'Berry is so blind,' remarked the whimsical Jack Mara . . . , 'that the only thing he can see is a football.'

"The Best Football Game Ever Played," as it was soon dubbed by Tex Maule of *Sports Illustrated*, vastly increased the profile of pro football and fattened the league's paycheck. The game's attraction helped spur the creation of the rival American Football League in 1960, and by mid-decade the three networks, ABC, CBS, and NBC were competing to broadcast games. By the midsixties, they were paying a combined total of almost

$50 million to the two leagues for the rights, an amount which kept escalating. Today it is well into the billions. Franchises grew unimaginably rich. When Norman Braman bought the Philadelphia Eagles in 1982 for $65 million, he was thought by many to have overpaid. He sold the franchise twelve years later for $185 million. In 2006, *Forbes* magazine estimated the same team's worth at more than a billion. Bidding for players went sky-high. The AFL gave quarterback Joe Namath a $200,000 bonus to sign with the New York Jets, and paid him $427,000—just five years after John Unitas was paid $17,500 to lead the Colts to the championship.

The Colts and Giants met again for the championship the following year, and the results didn't change. Baltimore won convincingly, 31-16. Howell retired after that season, but stayed on as director of player personnel for the Giants until he retired in 1981. At home in Arkansas he was elected to the state legislature. He died in 1995. Bert Bell collapsed and died of a heart attack in 1959, watching an Eagles game at Franklin Field in Philadelphia, where he had played in college and fallen so in love with the game.

Vince Lombardi left New York after the 1958 season to take over the Green Bay Packers, and made such a mark in that place that soon few people other than old Giants fans even remembered he had once coached in his hometown. His Packers would crush the Giants in the 1961 championship, 37-0, the first of five he would win in Green Bay, along with the first two Super Bowls. Tom Landry left New York after the 1959 loss to take over an expansion franchise, the Dallas Cowboys. It took him a few years to build a talented roster from scratch, but he had the Cowboys in the championship game in 1966, and then kept them in firm contention for the next twenty years, taking them to five Super Bowls, and winning two. The great Giants team assembled by Wellington Mara collapsed in 1964, after Huff was traded to Washington.

Frank Gifford remained a star with the Giants until he retired that year, after being elected to seven Pro Bowls. He never made it as a Hollywood star, but he did become very famous as an ABC television sportscaster, working for twenty-seven years in the booth for that network's *Monday Night Football* broadcast. His teammate, kicker Pat Summerall, left the field for the booth in 1962, and became the most famous of American football voices. He is still working as a broadcaster, and few people who hear him remember that he was once the best field-goal kicker in football.

The great Baltimore Colts team stayed great for most of the sixties, and then unraveled, as they all must. The memory of Coltsaphrenia is still cherished by older Baltimoreans, but the city's love affair with its team came to a cruel end. Rosenbloom swapped franchises in 1972 with the owner of the Los Angeles Rams, the infamous Robert Irsay, who packed up the Colts' uniforms and gear in moving vans on a snowy night in 1984 and shipped it all to Indianapolis. He stole more than a football franchise from the city. He took a piece of its soul. Rosenbloom had drowned swimming in the ocean near his home in Florida five years earlier.

The Cleveland Browns moved to Baltimore in 1996 and became the Ravens, but nobody who grew up in the city during the golden era of Johnny Unitas and Raymond Berry, of Gino Marchetti and Artie Donovan, roots for it without mixed feelings.

Of the great New York players, Charley Conerly, Jim Patton, Phil King, Kyle Rote, Emlen Tunnell, and Rosey Brown are all deceased, as are Howell, Lombardi, and Landry. Rosey Grier was traded to Los Angeles, having grown out of his desire to play only close to home. He became part of the "Fearsome Foursome," along with Deacon Jones, Merlin Olsen, and Lamar Lundy, one of the most famous defensive fronts in the history of the game. He retired in 1967 to his Christian ministry, and was working as a bodyguard for Sen. Robert F. Kennedy when the senator was assassinated in Los Angeles a year later. Grier helped pry the gun out of the hand of Kennedy's murderer. I met him in the offices of the Milken Foundation in Santa Monica in the summer of 2007. Grier is the foundation's community director. He says that when Landry began experimenting with the four-three defense, he didn't trust it:

> *We ran a play and I went away from the system. I made a sensational play, I really did. So Tom Landry said to me, he said, "You made a great play, but if you didn't make that play, Harland Svare would have made the very same play," because it was coming right to him. So next time, we ran that same play, and I could have got the guy. I let him go, and Harland Svare tore him up, and I knew then that I could trust the defense.*

He says he still remembers the shock of being shipped out of New York.

To be traded is a heartbreaker. Particularly when you feel that you devoted your time and your energy to the team. I mean, you put your own interests aside for the good of the team. If there was grumbling on the team, I went to the grumblers and said, "Don't mess the team up." I was always speaking out for the team. It's a concept that I carry into my life, in my real life, that we're all part of a team and we all have contributions to make, and so I have great love for these guys. In fact, I used to say we love one another . . . they say it all the time now. I mean, guys were funny back then about what they said concerning their relationship with men; and to me, it was just words of unity, words of saying we're together, you know, like family.

Sam Huff still feels the pain of his trade. It was one of the most bitter disappointments of his life, and even though he went on to a stellar career with the Washington Redskins, for whom he still does radio commentary, Huff gets hot describing what he sees as a betrayal.

My last game with the New York Giants was in Chicago in the World Championship Game, which is now the Super Bowl, and we lost 14-10. And our offense turned the ball over to the Chicago Bears seven times, and they only scored fourteen points on two quarterback sneaks. And who gets traded? Me, Dick Modzelewski, Erich Barnes, and five guys off the defensive unit. . . . The old saying is you gotta trade a guy when he has a year or two left, to get a younger ballplayer. Oh, it was a great run, great players, and guys that are still friends today, great ownership. I mean, Wellington Mara and the Mara family were just great. When they started trading people away,

223

dismantling the team, I go talk to Wellington Mara. I said, "What are you doing?" Because I work in New York, JP Stevens. So I go talk to him. I said, "I don't understand, you know, what's going on with this club? You're getting rid of everybody, and you traded Rosey Grier last year . . . and now you got rid of Modzelewski." He said, "Yeah, we did do that." I was real happy playing with the Giants. That's the only team I ever played for, only team I ever wanted to play for. I told Wellington, "I don't want to be traded." He said, "You don't ever have to worry. You're part of the family." Good enough for me. I go back to work.

A few days later I'm out in Cleveland, Ohio, making calls for JP Stevens. I'm at Modzelewski's restaurant. He had a restaurant. And I get a call from my wife, "Sam, bad news for you." I said, "What's the bad news?" "Allie Sherman [the Giants' head coach] just called me. You've been traded to the Washington Redskins." I said, "He can't trade me. Wellington Mara told me I'd never be traded. I was part of the family." She said, "Allie said you ought to be happy because he got two ballplayers for you, Dick James and Andy Stynchula." I said, "I ain't happy; I ain't happy." I came home the next day, the next night. I lived in Flushing, New York. There was cars all around the neighborhood. Media parked everywhere. When they traded me, it went over the Wall Street ticker tape. I was traded; it stopped Wall Street. It was unbelievable what took place. I mean, I was really shook up about it.

So the next day I go to work, Forty-first and Broadway at JP Stevens. I get a call from Wellington. He said, "I think we need to talk." Wellington Mara, probably the most honest man I've ever known. I said, "Well, yeah, I think you have some explaining to do." He said, "I'll meet you at the New York Athletic Club. We'll have lunch."

I meet him there. He wouldn't look me in the eye. He looked out over Central Park. He said, "What can I say?" I said, "What can you say? You

goddamn lied to me. That's what you can say. You told me I'd never be traded;
I was part of the family." He said, "I know, but you know that's just part
of the game." I said, "Part of the game? Wellington, you're a goddamn liar."

Huff has partly forgiven Wellington Mara, who died in
2005, but will never forgive Sherman.

"He destroyed the whole team, and Wellington let him
do it."

I visited Gino Marchetti in 2007 at his home in a gated development outside Philadelphia, where we sat in a small den filled
with memorabilia from his playing days. He is still big, tall,
strong, and active, although he moves a little slowly and gin-
gerly. The shock of black hair that used to fall across his forehead is thin and gray now. He has raised his children and become
a grandfather, helped steer a hugely successful hamburger franchise that was sold for millions, and has enjoyed years of active
retirement. As he eases into his big chair he seems immediately
overcome with mirth and pleasure summoning those old football characters and those times. I had not yet asked a question
when the first cheerful anecdote spilled out.

Have you met Donovan? That guy. Here's what you need to know about
Donovan. He tells the story all the time about the chicken contest between
Joyce and I. So, he tells it, like, one Sunday me and Joyce got in a chicken-
eating contest because that was our best meal in training camp, on Sunday.
And the way he tells it, he says that Champ—we called Joyce "The Champ"—
beat me and that then he ate mashed potatoes. He ate all that. And then he got

us coffee and he put saccharin in it. "Why you put saccharin in?" we ask. "I gotta watch my weight," says Champ. That's how Donovan tells it. But the real story is, I was living with Shula, Art DeCarlo, and myself. We were baching it. And I sent home, I asked my mother to send me some spaghetti sauce. She made homemade spaghetti sauce and spaghetti. Donovan was there and Joyce had just joined us. He had gotten cut by the Cardinals. So he just joined us. . . . So we sat there and we drank wine and ate the spaghetti. Joyce musta ate three pounds. Three pounds, *I kid you not. And then he reaches in, pulls out this little pill and puts it in his coffee. I said, "Champ, what the hell's that?" He said, "That's saccharin." I said, "What's that for?" He said, "I gotta watch my weight." See how the gentleman Donovan turns it around? It's a chicken-eating contest. It wasn't. There's more to that story. Donovan ate so much he threw up. He's in the bathroom hollering, "I need some help!" "What's wrong?" I ask. "I'm heaving blood," he says. "That's not blood, that's all the wine you drank." You know, so—well, anyway I didn't mean to disrupt you.*

I tried to interrupt his flow as little as possible. People often ask me, as a reporter, how to get people talking. The answer is usually, "Show up." Of no story was that more true than this one.

Visiting retired football players almost a half century after their glory days is, in one sense, a bracing lesson in the ravages of time, because I saw many legendary athletes who have undergone knee and hip replacements and whose once large and mighty frames have shrunken and grown frail, but in another sense it is a testament to the undying joy of fellowship and accomplishment. And of personality. Donovan's once enormous body now shuffles behind a walker, unsteady but still formidable, and he motors around his small country club estate north of Baltimore on a four-wheeled cart, but when he starts reeling off the stories about Marchetti and Unitas and Weeb—"That weasel bastard"—he is a man of limitless appetite at an endless feast. And "Fatso" never tires of the fare.

My older sister held her wedding reception at Donovan's beautiful old clubhouse twenty-five years ago, and I remember him sitting on the sofa with my sister's new father-in-law, a huge Colts fan who was very ill and would die not too long afterward. Fatso had never met him, but he entertained him for hours, the two of them rocking with laughter and slapping their thighs. My brother-in-law Milt was so touched that he told me once that I ought to consider naming a child "Fatso."

"But I don't think people would understand," he said, sadly.

I had a long and hilarious lunch in Annapolis with Fatso and his old teammate, Alex Sandusky, along with Al Brennan, Raymond Berry's old neighbor from Lutherville, who is now a retired Baltimore County judge. Wherever they go in the Baltimore area, these old football heroes are still treated like royalty. Donovan's head still sports the same buzz cut he wore fifty years ago, and his dome rises slightly to a rounded narrow peak. He affects a look of absolute amazement when he tells his stories, wide-eyed astonishment, as though each one is coming out for the very first time. He and Sandusky were remembering cornerback Carl Taseff, whom they called "Gaucho" because he was so bowlegged he looked like he had grown up on a horse. They told their stories . . . well, like teammates.

"How about when he hit Weeb with the water?" asked Donovan.

Said Sandusky, "That's a funny story. That's a true——"

"We were throwing buckets of water in the locker room during the season, and we had a guy, from Louisville, Lenny Lyles."

"And Ameche."

"But Lenny Lyles was in the whirlpool and they hit him with a bucket of water and he jumped out and hit his ankle on the heater."

"The radiator."

"The radiator, and he fractures his ankle," said Donovan.

So Weeb sends John Sandusky——he was our defensive line coach, we called him Spanky because he looked like Spanky McFarland in the Our Gang comedies. So Spanky comes out and says, "Weeb says if he catches anybody throwing another bucket of water, he's gonna fine him five hundred dollars." So everybody stops. But Gaucho was a little bit of a jerk. So Marchetti says, "Gaucho, one more bucket of water and then we'll stop." He says, "We're gonna get the Horse [Ameche] when he comes around the corner. Gaucho, that dumb asshole, goes, he says, "Okay, Gino."

And here comes Weeb out of his office all dressed up to tape his weekly show, and Marchetti says, "No go." But Gaucho doesn't hear him and he unloads the bucket. Gaucho is going, "Jesus Christ!!" He's brushing Weeb off, "I'm sorry. I'll never do it again." Guys are rolling on the floor of the locker room. Guys were crying they were laughing so hard.

One story led to another.

"Lenny Moore was the best offensive football player I've ever seen," said Donovan. "He could just play."

"Put him anywhere," said Sandusky. "Put him in the backfield, it's six points. Put him on a flank, it's six points."

"How about the catch he made against the Lions?" asked Donovan.

"Most fantastic catch I've ever seen."

"He was out like this, parallel to the ground—"

"—catches the back end of the ball like this," Sandusky gestured with both hands outstretched. "We ended up losing that game."

"I got kicked out of the game."

"Yeah, you're the reason we lost."

"I know. They had to call a time-out."

"Detroit gets the ball back and Donny [Donovan] gets us a fifteen-yard penalty for some kind of reason, kicking somebody."

"I kicked the guy in the face," said Donovan, shrugging.

"Why did you do that?" I asked.

"Because he hit Alex Hawkins, who wasn't one of my favorite football players, but he was my teammate, and it was a late hit. I'll tell you who it was, it was the tackle, what the hell was his name? Anyhow, he had been known for being really dirty and I was just running out on the field, and I see him hit Hawkins. I went by, he was laying on the ground. I kicked him in the face. Out and fifteen yards. We lost the game."

"Tell him about the time Big Daddy lost his money," said Donovan.

"We're playing in Griffith Stadium. I'll tell you, the locker room was about as big as a girl's locker room. Christ, Big Daddy was right beside me, we were all squeezed in. We beat the Redskins."

"But you got to tell him what he did with his money, he gave it to Eddie Stearns."

"Eddie Stearns was one of the trainer's helpers."

"So everybody used to put their wallets and their money in the valuables box before we left Baltimore. So Big Daddy, he's got a wad, he was gonna buy shirts or something in Washington, he gives his money to Eddie to hold it. So anyhow, right at halftime, Eddie has to go to the john, he pulls his pants down and the money fell out of his pants. So during the third quarter, Big Daddy asks Eddie, 'You got my money?' Eddie says, 'I lost it. I lost your money.' Big Daddy says, 'It's my alimony money!' "

"We beat the Redskins," said Sandusky.

"Big Daddy didn't go in the game after that. He sits on the bench crying."

"Now we're in the locker room, and Big Daddy is still sitting down crying, and Rosenbloom comes over and asks, 'Big Daddy, what's the matter?' 'Eddie Stearns lost my money.' Rosenbloom peels off four hundred-dollar bills."

"He only lost about eighty," said Donovan. "He told Rosey it was four hundred!"

"Let me tell you something," said Sandusky. "Everything you ever read about Raymond Berry is true."

"Yeah, but Raymond took a long time to get open," said Donovan. "John could eat a sandwich before he threw the ball. I mean, our offensive line could pass block usually for about three seconds."

"And Raymond had all these zigs and zags and zooms and booms and what have you, you know, and him and John would practice during the week, you know, it would be a tough game and Raymond would come back and say that this certain play would work. Preas and I would bump each other in the huddle and look at one another because our bung holes would start quivering because we knew it was a five-second play.

"Many times, John would say, 'Raymond, I don't have time.' But Raymond was just super."

"He could catch the ball."

"Raymond could catch the ball. Raymond was great."

"How about the time you two assholes shot the groundhog?" asked Donovan. "I was gonna say that, too. Two goddamn hillbillies, you and Nutter, huh? Was it you and Nutter?"

"It was me."

"It was you? You lying son of a bitch. It was you!"

"At training camp, you know," explained Sandusky, "I used to go after practice—a lot of times I didn't go down and drink beer till six—so I'd get in my car and ride the country roads. And I'm a big hunter, and I had this deer gun that I used to shoot groundhogs. One day I shot one right through the eye. I come and put him in Donny's bed."

"I come back from the movies and Spinney says, 'There's some beer for you underneath the blanket.' I said, 'Oh, boy.' I pull the blanket and there's this one-eyed son of a bitch looking at me. Spinney says, 'What is it?' I said, 'How the fuck do I know what it is? It could be a lion. I'm from the city, I don't know these things.' There was blood all over my bed; I had to go upstairs to sleep. The next day I go over, it's the last day of practice, I open my locker, and there's this thing, hanging from the—"

"I short strung it and put it in the locker on the shelf. Then he goes to open the door, and here comes the fucking groundhog! Hit him again."

"I made out I was really pissed off but I got behind the door, laughed my ass off," said Donovan.

He's still laughing.

When the '58 game was played my family lived in Chicago. I may have seen some of it on television. My father would certainly have tuned in. But I have seen so many film clips of it over the years I don't know if my memory of that brightly lit field against the dark backdrop of Yankee Stadium is the real thing or an implant. I do know that my interest in pro football began along with millions of others around that time. I was seven and would soon be playing the game myself on sandlots and in community leagues. My uncle bought me a full football uniform complete with everything except the cleats, and I remember desperately wanting a pair of high-top black ones like Johnny U.

When we moved to Baltimore a few years later, the Colts were in the middle of a resurgence. Weeb was gone. He was coaching the New York Jets in the upstart American Football League. In 1968, he would lead that team into the third Super Bowl and defeat the Colts, led by Don Shula, in the game made famous by Joe Namath's bold guarantee of victory—this was at a time when the AFL was considered subpar and the Colts were being touted as the best team in the history of the game. The win made Weeb the only coach to lead teams from both leagues to championships, and established the AFL as its rival league's equal. They would merge two years later. It was the first of the absurdly named uberchampionships to live up its "Super" billing, and launched pro football even further into the stratosphere of money and global media attention. John Unitas played in that game, too. He was an aging superstar by then, and had watched from the bench with a sore arm for most of it, but when Shula put him in, in desperation, in the fourth quarter, John briefly lit up the field. He threw for one touchdown, and ended up with more passing yards that Earl Morrall, the Colts' starter, but the Colts had fallen too far behind for it to matter. John played for a few more years, including a brief sad stint with the San Diego Chargers, but I will always remember his stooped, bow-legged appearance in that Super Bowl as the final chapter in a great, great career.

Even in the late sixties, the old Colts remained members of the community in Baltimore. Growing up there I saw many of them, like Donovan at my sister's wedding. John had his restaurant in Towson, The Golden Arm, and if you went in he was often there to loan his star status to the place, his hair stylishly longer and his torso a bit thicker. The restaurant eventually went out of business, and John, the quarterback who worked on saying boring things to sportswriters, put himself back on his feet financially as a banquet speaker, traveling the country giving talks for various corporate sponsors. He died of a heart attack, working out on a treadmill, in 2002.

Ordell Braase and Bill Pellington had more successful restaurants in the Baltimore suburbs. Shula's house was just up the street from mine, and my younger brothers used to play with his boys, who would go on to become NFL assistant coaches themselves. I ran into Dave Shula on the turf at Veterans Stadium once in the early 1990s when I was the Eagles' beat reporter for the *Philadelphia Inquirer*, and we chatted about the old neighborhood. He was born too late to remember the '58 and '59 team, and I had come to Baltimore too late. But we both knew all the players as local celebrities, as neighbors.

That is how most of the old players remembered it, a team in a great big neighborhood, and as such it belongs to a now-distant era in the pro game, like an old black-and-white photo on a postcard. Roughly half of the players in the great game of 1958 have died. Big Daddy Lipscomb went, in an overdose of heroin, in 1963, which was puzzling to many of his old teammates who remembered his outsized fear of needles whenever the team doctor scheduled inoculations. Alan Ameche is gone, as are Steve Myhra, Bill Pellington, Don Joyce, Jim Parker, George Preas, L.G. Dupre, and Don Joyce.

Jim Mutscheller became a successful insurance man, his years as a Colts tight end no doubt opening many doors and wallets in Baltimore. I met him in his office at an industrial complex north of the city, and as we talked his secretary interrupted, despite his request that we be left alone.

"I'm sorry," she said, "but I have someone on the line who insists on talking to you right now. He said to tell you that it's the 'Pope.'"

Mutscheller grinned and looked up at me. "Donovan," he said.

He took the call and then we talked about some of his other teammates.

"Alan Ameche was such a good guy, funny, fun to be around," said Mutscheller.

He was quick, clever. A big joker. Weeb didn't like him because he arrived as a bonus baby. Alan didn't care, which bothered Weeb all the more. He was a bright guy. After he made all that money with Gino, I called him once for a fundraiser.

It's the kind of call anybody hates to make, leaning on a friend for money. "I've got to hit you up for some money," I told him. "How much do you want?" He asked. "Hell," I said. "I don't know." He gave me fifty thousand dollars, which was about a hundred times more than the largest figure I had in mind.

He remembered Weeb fondly:

He had all these little sayings, clichés mostly. Lenny Moore called him 'The Little Mentor,' or the 'The Little Quaker.' He says, 'That little man, he knew more than we did!' He never made any money at football, and he was tight. A frugal little Quaker. He had to look up at us. He'd say, 'I never cut anybody, I help steer them into their life's work.'

I don't think winning that game changed me or the rest of us at all. We all still had the same attitude. I might have made a little more money. I do think it changed pro football, though. Prior to that game we always had decent crowds, but afterward we always had <u>huge</u> crowds wherever we went. The game just turned popular.

Charley Winner picked me up in Ft. Myers, Florida, in his tennis whites, wearing his '58 championship ring, a handsome nugget of gold with a big horseshoe carved into the side. Winner has other championship rings from his long coaching career, "but I like this one the best. It was my first, and the rings today are big and gaudy, and I'm not a very big guy and they just dwarf me." He coached with Shula after his father-in-law was fired, and then became head coach of the St. Louis Cardinals for five years. He worked again with Shula in Miami, and for a few years in Cleveland, and has been living with his wife, Nancy, Weeb's daughter, in Florida since his retirement in 1992.

"Big Daddy used to crack me up," Winner said.

He was really clever. Part of the annual physical was a rectal examination, where the doctor puts a little glove on, sticks his finger up your rear to check your glands. Our doctor, Dr. McDonald, was known to be a pious Catholic, so Big Daddy bends over, he says, "Hey, Doc, what are you going to do?" He said, "I'm going to give you a rectal examination. We do this every year." Big Daddy says, "Well, get that thing off your finger. I'm Catholic."

He remembers how hard it was for some of the players from that team to call it quits—Donovan, in particular. Fatso was forced to hang up his pads three years after the '58 game.

Artie did not want to retire. He still holds it against Weeb for letting him go, you know, because he said he could still do it. He couldn't. He stayed longer than he should have. And Marchetti made the statement one time that I'm going to quit while I still have some left because I don't want people to see me like they see Donovan. We brought Donovan in one time to go over the films with us because he was bitching that we weren't grading him right. And he says, "Look, I'm getting by the guy." And he was, but it was too late. He wouldn't admit it to himself at the end.

Winner pulled a photo album down from his shelf and turned the pages slowly.

"Those were the days," he said.

They were the best days of professional football. I don't care what anybody says now. They're making all kinds of money. We had fun. We knew the players, and our families on Sunday during the preseason, our families would come to training camp, and we would all have dinner together. The kids would play together, the black kids, the white kids. One big family, one big family. We had so much fun. I went to work for the Cardinals and our first preseason game was against the Colts in St. Louis, and they beat us. So I'm putting my oldest daughter to bed and she was about maybe eight or nine at the time, and she's crying. I think she's crying because we lost the ball game. So I say, "Cindy, don't worry about it. It's just a preseason game. It doesn't mean anything." She says, "I don't care about the game." She had stood out by the bus, kissing the players good-bye, Jim Parker, Lenny Moore, Johnny Unitas, and all that. She said, "This will be the last time I'll get to see my Colts friends."

He wiped a tear from his eye.

"I get emotional about it," he said.

Raymond Berry came out to meet me at the airport in Nashville. He stood at the bottom of the escalator by baggage claim, jotting notes to himself on a small slip of paper, which he slipped into his shirt pocket when I introduced myself. Back at his home, in a spacious office, he showed me the faded, worn loose-leaf binders that filled an entire upper shelf, one for each of his thirteen years as a player, containing the detailed preparatory notes and play diagrams he made before every game.

His career was just getting started when he helped the Colts win their first championship. He told me that he didn't really start to work on serious head and body fakes until after that season. He kept on getting better. His catch total went from fifty-six in 1958, to sixty-six the following year, and then to seventy-four, and stayed in that vicinity for most of his thirteen years as a player. When he retired in 1967, he owned the record for the most receptions in a career. When Weeb introduced Raymond at his induction into the Hall of Fame five years later, he noted how unlikely it was, given his physical limitations, that Raymond had ever even played pro football, much less become the most successful player at his position in NFL history.

"Raymond and Raymond alone turned himself into the receiver he became," the coach said. "If I had a son, I would want him to be like Raymond."

This is his legacy. Today many of the techniques Raymond employed are standard at all levels of football.

After the first four years of being in the league, you know, I asked myself, 'Were does this drive come from?' I began to realize that I was doing this so differently than everybody else that was playing in the league. I began to get very curious about the source of this <u>drive</u> that was—it was a powerful thing. I began to realize it was a tremendous gift. It had everything to do with how I was playing and it just did not get deterred by obstacles, it just drove me to beat all these people and keep on going. I got very curious about the source, and I finally realized God gave me that drive. It was just as much a part of what you bring to the table as speed, jumping ability, strength, the weight, you know? The desire and the drive was more important than all of them. It totally made me.

No one was surprised when he became a coach after his playing days. Raymond became head coach of the New England Patriots in 1984, and took them to the Super Bowl the following year. He was a head coach for six seasons in Boston before the team let him go and he retired from the game.

*   *   *

Gino Marchetti wasn't on the bus that night they got mobbed by Baltimore fans, returning home as the conquering heroes. He had been placed in an ambulance right off the plane, and was driven directly to Union Memorial Hospital. He had downed a few beers by then, and was feeling no pain.

As the ambulance left the airport, pulling away from the swarms of people who had come out to cheer the team, Marchetti saw a man and a boy standing alone by the side of the road. This was miles from the airport. The man had pulled his car off onto the shoulder, figuring the team bus would eventually pass that way, and was holding a flashlight to illuminate his sign, which read, WELCOME HOME CHAMPS.

Marchetti shouted for the driver to stop. The gesture moved him. He wanted to stop and thank the man personally, reward him and the boy for the effort. How good would that be? They would have a story to tell everybody. But the driver couldn't hear him. Gino hollered and the ambulance kept on going. A half century later, sitting in an easy chair in his living room outside Philadelphia, his once powerful shoulders stooped, Marchetti shook his head sadly.

"I always regret that I couldn't make that guy stop," he said. "I didn't think fast enough. I was gonna make him stop and say hello to them, you know, 'cause I thought that was probably the greatest thing I seen, you know? Anybody can be a part of a crowd but . . . you know?"

Author's Note

Any attempt to tell a true story is to discover how much more your readers know about the matter than you do. Of no subject is this truer than sports. Passionate fans and professional sportswriters are zealous guardians of the historical record. They cherish details, and, I am happy to say, tend to be generous and forgiving of amateurs who stray into their turf.

I am grateful to the dozens of correspondents who pointed out errors in the original text of this book, and to none more than *Sports Illustrated*'s "Dr. Z," Paul Zimmerman, who waded through the manuscript correcting everything from my inept characterization of the gambling rumors that followed Carroll Rosenbloom (he was suspected of "meddling to cover" the point spread, not "tampering to meet"), to player history (Jimmie Lee Howell, who in his younger days had played on both offense and defense, had been primarily a "pass-catching tight end," not a "defensive lineman"), to how long before kick-off the teams took the field for warm-ups (an hour-and-a-half instead of a half hour), to the correct vital statistics of certain players (Big Daddy Lipscomb was only six-six, 288 lbs; he only *looked* six-eight, 300 lbs.). This edition has been much improved by Zimmerman's patience, generosity, and encyclopedic recall.

Betty Anne Diefenbacher wrote to me about how she and her friends, all students at Goucher College in Towson, Maryland, in December, 1958, enjoyed a kind of rolling party on the afternoon of the game, driving from house to house through the afternoon, watching it unfold. Like many Colts fans, she has still not completely recovered from the infamous business deal that packed up her team and shipped it off to Indianapolis in Mayflower moving vans. A certain generation of Baltimoreans never will.

"My father died during my senior year at Goucher," Betty Anne wrote me. "My mother stayed on in the house in Baltimore. . . . In 1991, I convinced my mother to move to a retirement community. I took charge of all the moving arrangements. After doing some comparison, I hired Mayflower to do the move. I had not discussed the details with my mother. On the morning of the move, a Mayflower van pulled up in front of the house. They were met by an irate ninety-one-year-old white-haired woman, who asked them why they had moved her Colts away in the middle of the night!"

I received many letters from fans who reminisced about their encounters with some of the game's great players. One of my favorites was from Jud DeLany, of Evans, Georgia, who recalled meeting the primary hero of this story, Raymond Berry, a few years after this game on the practice field at Vanderbilt

University, where DeLany played defensive back for the Commodores. The great receiver was participating in a Fellowship of Christian Athletes program that gave college teams a chance to learn from the pros.

"Berry took us on, came down the field and proceeded to give us an array of head fakes, shoulder fakes, double head fakes, stutter steps, hip fakes, change of pace, spins, etc., etc.," wrote Delany. ". . . No one could read Berry's moves and stay in cover position to knock down the passes, let alone the prospect of ever intercepting one. Berry used eye moves, shouts, hand waves, and other moves to distract us and destroy one's determination to stay close to him. After a while we started laughing and giggling. . . . As it turned out, this was actually a very useful practice session for many of us. Because it convinced us that we had no future in higher levels of football and had better get serious about our classwork and getting our diplomas. So many of us hit the books a lot harder, graduated, and went on to become successful doctors, lawyers, engineers, and such. And we must thank Raymond Berry for his career guidance."

One of my larger omissions in writing this book was to rely exclusively on the NBC radio broadcast of the game, expertly handled by Jim Bolen and Bill McColgan, and quoted throughout the text. The TV broadcast of the game was not saved, so I was delighted when I found a recording of the radio play-by-play. It turns out that NBC's was not the only one. Legendary broadcaster Bob Wolff also called the game, and might have been heard on the radio by more fans than those listening to Bolen and McColgan.

Alerted by his son Rick, I found the play-by-play man at his home in Tarrytown, New York, where, still in fine voice, he gave me a tutorial in the fine art of narrating a contest, and of the intricacies of radio and television broadcasting circa 1958.

"My job was not just to report the game, it was to *enhance* it," he said. "Good play-by-play is a *performance*. It is more like singing than talking, because there is a rhythm. Your voice rises and falls. I worked to capture the emotion of the contest; I always wanted listeners to feel the excitement."

He played for me portions of his own superb play-by play, including his call of the winning touchdown, which in the years after the game was wedded to Baltimore fans' memories by a popular 45 rpm recording of the winning play call: "And the Colts are the champions! Ameche scores!" Long before the age of video replay, the NFL Network, and ESPN Classic, listening to Wolff's emphatic call of the final play was the closest a Colts fan could get to reliving the moment.

Many regional radio stations functioned independently, purchasing broadcasts of sporting events from the national networks or from major advertisers, who employed their own broadcast teams. Wolff was hired to call the game for radio by the National Brewing Company, which offered its own feed of the game to radio stations around the country for free, provided that they aired the beer commercials. Wolff doesn't know how many markets carried his play-by-play, but suspects it may have been as many or more than those who took the NBC feed. Baltimoreans listening to the radio heard Wolff's description.

His memory of the 1958 game is that it was harsh. Because Yankee Stadium was designed for baseball, the radio broadcasting booths were on the mezzanine level behind home plate, far out of position for calling a football game. He was given a cramped spot on a mezzanine level ledge over the thirty-yard line, fully exposed to the elements, were he sat with his spotters—the eventual TV talk show host Maury Povitch, then a teenager, helped him with the Colts—and an audio engineer. There was no heat, and as the afternoon grew darker and more wintry, Wolff got colder and colder. He didn't even have binoculars to help sort out the action, and had no table or flat surface on which to spread his notes. There was no room to place a cup of water or coffee, which was just as well, because once he made his way to the ledge, there was no chance of climbing back through the stands to reach a toilet and return without missing some of the action. It was, essentially, a solo performance as bare as broadcasting gets, just an announcer's eyeballs and his voice. Wolff didn't hear his own call of the game until many years later. "I thought it sounded pretty good!" he said, less boastful than genuinely surprised.

Wolff was thrilled when ESPN used some of his play-by-play in a two-hour documentary reconstruction of the game last year. The sports channel collected excellent old black-and-white film footage of nearly every play, colorized it, and matched it with the radio broadcasts, both Wolff's and NBC's. Along with some of the surviving players, Wolff was interviewed for the program, which is one of the highlights of a long career that included calling Don Larsen's perfect game in the 1956 World Series.

The ESPN documentary was just one of several events that marked the half century anniversary of the game. The Baltimore Ravens and a group of local sports boosters in that city put together a whole weekend of commemorative events, one of which I attended at a hotel in Baltimore's Inner Harbor two days after Christmas. The Ravens and the NFL flew in many of the surviving players. The event I attended was a cocktail party, complete with two well-stocked open bars and sumptuous buffets, including sushi and other delicacies. NFL commissioner Roger Goodale was present, along with the Ravens owner, coaches, and many current players. Artie Donovan sat off to one side during this swank affair beside a bucket, thoughtfully stocked with ice and his favorite Schlitz beer. He was grinning from ear to ear, and ready with a story for anyone who came close.

This time the best story I heard was not from Artie, however. Raymond Berry, looking youthful and clearly enjoying a momentary return to the spotlight, told a group including Ravens head coach Jim Harbaugh and defensive coordinator Rex Ryan (who would, in a few weeks, be named the head coach of the New York Jets), about his favorite halftime speech of all time.

"It was at that game against the Redskins a few years earlier, the one where we came back to win on the last play (the final game of the 1956 season)," said Berry. "We were way behind at halftime. Weeb said a few things to us, and then announced that Gino, our team captain, had some remarks. I was toward the back of the room and started inching my way forward, eager to hear how an old pro like Gino would fire up his teammates. I braced myself for an inspirational oration, or at least an attempt at one. So Gino gets up, and he says something like this: 'The wife and I are having a party after the game. It will be ten bucks per person, fifteen if you're bringing a date. You can pay me after the game. And, oh yeah, let's win it, okay? The party will be more fun if we do."

Berry just shook his head.

"Pro football," he said. "It really hit me at that point. This was not the same old rah-rah college game. And you know what? We went out and won that game, and Gino and his wife, they threw a sweet party afterwards."

Distant Replay

In the spring of 2007, Mark Bowden sat down with Philadelphia Eagles head coach Andy Reid to review the original coaches' film of the 1958 NFL Championship game. This piece, which first appeared in the October 2008 issue of the Atlantic *magazine, has been reprinted with the author's permission.*

Watching game film with Andy Reid, head coach of the Philadelphia Eagles, can make you woozy. He lounges behind the wide desk in his office, feet up, using a wireless control to freeze the image of a play on a screen at the opposite end of the room, and then starts rolling it forward and backward, forward and back, first the whole play and then only portions of it, forward and back, forward and back, until he has pieced all the moving parts together.

Reid is a very big man, a former collegiate offensive lineman, and when I met him last spring, he was in full off-season mode: tan, relaxed, and draped in a colorful Hawaiian silk shirt large enough to display the entire Amazon rain forest. Reid was coming off another winning year—the Eagles had made it to the second round of the post-season playoffs just months earlier—and he was already well into his preparations for the next season. Pro football is a year-round occupation these days, so he was doing me a favor by agreeing to help me with research for my book, *The Best Game Ever*, an account of the celebrated 1958 NFL Championship game between the Baltimore Colts and the New York Giants.

I've written about football in the past, but I am by no means an expert, so I had gone looking for a pro coach to help me break down film of the famous game. I live just outside Philadelphia and once covered the Eagles for the local newspaper, so I phoned Derek Boyko, the team's affable public-relations director. Boyko warned me that the club's assistant coaches were probably too busy, but he nevertheless agreed to ask around. He called back to say that all of the coaches, curious about the way the game was played before most of them were born, had expressed an interest. "But they need permission from Andy," he said. "I'll ask him when he comes back from leave in a few weeks."

Boyko called me weeks later to say, "Andy wants to do it."

It seemed odd at first for a pro coach to have never seen film of this historic game—a little like finding a doctor of English literature who had never read *Macbeth*. But success in pro football, as in any intensely competitive, constantly evolving arena, depends primarily on current intelligence: What did my opponent last do against me? What did he do last week? A pro coach is not inclined to search for what he needs in old black-and-white film. History is . . . well, *history*.

But no craftsman or professional can be completely uninterested in seeing how he measures up against past standards of excellence. How good was the game then? How capable were the players? How clever were the coaches and schemes?

The game in question defined excellence for an era. It pitted the best defense in the NFL, the Giants, against the best offense, the Colts, playing for all the marbles. It featured seventeen future NFL Hall of Fame players, coaches, and owners. On the field were great athletes like Johnny Unitas, Raymond Berry, Lenny Moore, Gino Marchetti, Frank Gifford, Andy Robustelli, Emlen Tunnell, Rosey Grier, and Sam Huff. Coaching on the sidelines were Vince Lombardi and Tom Landry for the Giants, and for the Colts, Weeb Ewbank, the only pro coach who ever took teams from two different leagues (the NFL and the AFL) to national championships.

Reid was born in the year this game was played, and one reason he had never seen it is that the TV broadcast has been lost. But for serious study, I had wrested something even better from the archives of NFL Films: the grainy, monochrome "coaches' film" of the game, soundless footage shot from the sidelines high over midfield, with all the time-outs, huddles, and game breaks edited out.

Instant analysis envelops pro football like a cloud, but with most plays there is no way to tell what really happened and why without a careful, slow-motion dissection of the film. Reid is one of this craft's most successful practitioners. Even among pro coaches, he is notable for toting thick binders filled with notes and plans, and for fielding highly complex systems on both sides of the ball. Earlier in his career, he was quarterbacks coach for the Green Bay Packers, grooming Brett Favre and helping that team to a Super Bowl championship in 1997. His tenure in Philadelphia has been the most successful of any coach's in the team's long history: starting in 2001, he led the Eagles to four consecutive National Football Conference championship games and a Super Bowl—although, much to the consternation of long-suffering Eagles fans, he has yet to bring the Lombardi Trophy home to Philadelphia.

We watched the game in his office in the Eagles' training complex, just a few blocks from Lincoln Financial Field, where they play. When I covered the team in the early 1990s, the Eagles' offices, locker room, and workout facilities were housed in a few cramped, dark, damp rooms in the basement of the now-demolished Veterans Stadium. Today the team, whose worth is estimated at more than $1 billion, is housed at a state-of-the-art facility that sprawls over an area as large as a college campus.

"Okay," he'd say, when he had examined a play from snap to tackle, "here's what happened." Then out would pour a detailed explication: what the offense was trying to do, how the defense was trying to stop it, the techniques (good and bad) of the various key players, the historical roots of the formations and the play's design, and ultimately why it worked or failed, and who was responsible, either way. The wealth of information Reid gleaned from a single play reminded me of the way Patrick O'Brian's nineteenth-century naval hero, Jack Aubrey, eyeballing an enemy ship during a sea chase, could read from the play of its sails and the disposition of its crew the experience, intentions, strengths, and weaknesses of his opponent.

Reid's insight told on the first offensive play of the game. Colts coach Weeb Ewbank had designed a trick play, so secret that in his pregame meeting with his team in the visiting locker room at Yankee Stadium, he had *mouthed* the play call to them, fearful that the room was bugged. Observing the opening formation, Reid noted with surprise that all but one of the Colts linemen were positioned to the left of center Buzz Nutter. "This is a completely unbalanced formation," he told me. "You can't even do that today." The rules would no longer permit it: "You have to have *some* guys on the line of scrimmage." In the backfield, fullback Alan "The Horse" Ameche, a Heisman Trophy winner at the University of Wisconsin, was lined up behind quarterback Johnny Unitas; right halfback Lenny Moore was three steps to Ameche's right; and left halfback L. G. Dupre was split far out to the left side of the backfield.

Unitas didn't give the Giants a chance to set up in a recognizable defensive formation, even if they had one for such a bizarre look. He bent over, and Nutter immediately snapped the ball. Moore took the handoff—and was tackled for a loss.

"So they came out with a trick play in mind, and it really wasn't all that good," Reid said, chuckling. The main reason the play failed, he pointed out, was a missed block by Dupre, a speedy back whose initials, which stood for Louis George, had earned him the nickname "Long Gone." While Moore took the handoff from Unitas and followed Ameche around the left side of the Colts line, Dupre's job was to race forward and hit Harland Svare, the Giants' right-side linebacker, taking him out of the play. But the film tells the tale: "He didn't get the crack [block] right here," said Reid, using a red laser to point at Svare dodging Dupre, "and he kind of screws the play up." Svare races into the backfield, forcing Moore to step in front of Ameche, his blocker; the two briefly collide, and then as Moore tries to recover and race to the outside, he is pulled down for the loss.

"And then, the fullback forgot the snap count," Reid said, rolling the play back to the beginning again. Sure enough, on the snap of the ball, Ameche remains in a set position until Moore actually takes the ball from Unitas. "He forgot that it was a quick count . . . That's that Wisconsin education right there."

I told Reid that I had listened to the NBC radio broadcast, and had been struck by how much more quickly the game moved then than it does today. Breaks between plays and possessions are longer and more frequent now, to allow for more commercials, and the use of video replay to reexamine contested calls by the referees causes still more delays. Modern coaches use these gaps in the action for analysis, for sideline conferences and hand signals, or, in the case of the quarterback, for giving instructions over a direct radio link to his helmet. In 1958, the game, once started, was primarily in the hands of the players. Unitas called his own plays. Defensive field captains like the Giants' Sam Huff were on-field tacticians. The game was faster and simpler.

It also lacked many of the refined mechanical and tactical innovations that are commonplace in modern football. For instance, Reid was surprised to note that wide receivers assumed a three-point stance before the snap of the ball—today they stand upright, which allows them a broader view of the defensive backfield. The pass defenders, meanwhile, stood upright on the old film, with one foot forward, one back, and then just backpedaled to stay with the receivers. In the modern NFL, backfield defenders poise in a forward crouch with their weight evenly balanced on both legs, and retreat by taking short stutter-steps backward, ready to bolt in either direction and avoiding the crossover step, a potentially costly mistake that can offer a receiver the split-second advantage he needs to break away.

Basic positioning along the line of scrimmage has changed as well. A few plays in, Reid noted that the Giants' defensive tackles, Dick Modzelewski and Rosey Grier, were "flexed back off the ball"—that is, set up more than a yard away from the Colts' linemen. "That's probably for the run game," Reid said, explaining that by hanging back from the line of scrimmage, the defenders could get a better look at the direction of the play before attacking.

I asked, "Why wouldn't you do that today?"

"Well, you give those big guys a head start on you," Reid said. "At that time I would imagine that the linemen were fairly equal athletically, and now the offensive linemen are so big and the defensive linemen are relatively smaller." If you're a defender today, he went on, and you spot a three-hundred–plus-pound blocker a two-step running start, he'll knock you "right on your ass."

Reid surmised correctly. I checked the average weight of the starting offensive and defensive linemen in the '58 game: the Colts' offensive front five weighed an average of 243 pounds, and the Giants' defensive front five weighed an average of 244 pounds.

Today, offensive lines on average weigh nearly twenty-five pounds more than defensive fronts.

Not everything has changed as much. Reid recognized one Colts offensive formation as "the one we run the most—two receivers, two backs, and a tight end." And he even noticed some of his own plays in the mix. "Look, this is a rattler route," he said, watching Raymond Berry twist his way into the backfield, turning the Giants' cornerback completely around and gaining a step. "This is the one we ran in the Super Bowl that got picked by stinkin' Rodney Harrison." (Harrison's interception in the closing minutes of Super Bowl XXXIX clinched the New England Patriots' 24–21 win over the Eagles.)

After the Colts' opening boondoggle, the Giants settled into a 4–3 defense, which remains the pro standard. What we were watching on film was the original 4–3, contrived by New York defensive coach Tom Landry, years before he helped create a dynasty as head coach of the Dallas Cowboys. It features four players on the line of scrimmage backed by three linebackers; four pass defenders back up this formation: two cornerbacks split wide on either side, and two deep defenders, or safeties. The 4–3 was designed to counter the growing sophistication of passing offenses. Before the 1950s, football had primarily been a ground game, but after the invention of the wide receiver in 1949, defenses struggled to cover pass catchers without becoming too vulnerable to the run.

But while the 4–3 has survived to the present day, the simplicity of the old game often amazed Reid to the point of disbelief. The offensive formations were so basic that many of them are no longer even used in the pro game. The Giants frequently lined up in the T-formation—the quarterback behind the center, and the three running backs lined up horizontally about three yards behind him—and both teams employed the antiquated "single wing," where one halfback and the fullback line up beside each other, behind the quarterback, while the other halfback splits wide, sometimes all the way out to the flanker position.

The game as it was played in 1958 "is still an entertaining sport to watch, but it's just not near as complicated," Reid said. "If I'm calling the plays" on offense, he went on, "I get paid to get into a rhythm with the guy calling the defense" on the other side. When a coach achieves the right "rhythm," he can sense what his opponent is thinking—and for Reid, grasping the "rhythm" of the classic game was fairly easy. "I can see what the offense is doing," he said. "You can almost call it offensively and defensively."

For instance, he was struck, early in the game, by how close behind the line of scrimmage the Giants' safeties, Emlen Tunnell and Jimmy Patton, were setting up. Safeties ordinarily play five to ten yards back. Tunnell and Patton were just three or four yards back. "First time I saw those safeties that tight," said Reid, "I'd take the tight end up the seam," referring to the hash marks that line the field to the right and left of the center.

As if hearing Reid's advice, that's what Unitas did two plays later. First, he felt out the defense: facing second down and long, the quarterback handed the ball to Dupre, who plunged into the left side of the Giants' defense, where he was hit by Tunnell.

"'Okay,' the Colts are saying, 'this guy, number 45 [Tunnell], is getting tight, and he was very aggressive on the last play, so we'll sell a hard fake,'" Reid speculated. The Colts would set up as if they were going with another running play, he predicted, with the tight end, Jim Mutscheller, "coming up and out like he is going to crack" Tunnell with a block, but instead going past him up the field. "Then they should try and get [a pass] over the top to Mutscheller."

On third down, Mutscheller moved just as Reid had suggested, faking a block on Tunnell and racing up the hash marks. Unitas faked the handoff and dropped back, looking downfield toward his tight end.

"But this guy [Tunnell] sniffs it out!" Reid said, impressed, watching as the safety turned and matched the tight end stride for stride. Unitas, harried suddenly by the Giants' blitzing right cornerback, instead hurried a throw to Moore—"his safety valve," said Reid—that was almost intercepted.

Because the ploy failed, most spectators, myself included, would not have recognized Baltimore's intent, or understood why it failed. Reid saw the reason. He froze the play and noted the fullback, Ameche, missing his block on the Giants' cornerback, forcing the quarterback to hurry his throw. Players are forever screwing up the coach's perfect plans.

The Eagles coach saw another opportunity later in the game, when the Giants' safeties opted to line up farther downfield in a "cover four" defense, with the four players in the backfield—Patton, Tunnell, Carl Karilivacz, and Lindon Crow—divvying up the defensive secondary into four lanes, each covering one.

"The thing you'd tell Johnny [Unitas] right here," Reid said, "is to take your best mismatch. You put T.O. [former Eagle, now Cowboys receiver, Terrell Owens, a noted deep threat] here and just picture him running a post over the top of that guy [Crow]." Sure enough, several plays later, the Colts exploited the formation, zeroing in on the most obvious mismatch by sending the speedy Moore racing down the right side of the field one-on-one with Crow. Unitas heaved the ball for a sixty-yard gain.

Reid was impressed with Moore's speed and hands; less so with his blocking. On a later play, when Moore lined up in the backfield, Reid laughed and rolled the film back. "Watch this," he said. The ball is snapped and Unitas is eventually brought down by the Giants' defense, while Moore simply stays put in the same stance he was in before the snap of the ball. In slow motion, his statue-like pose is comical.

On a later play where Unitas was sacked, Reid again laughed and pointed to Moore missing an assignment. "Lenny didn't help, picking his nose right there, man. That's pissing me off." Then, on another play, "Lenny needs his ass whipped a little bit right here."

(In the Hall of Famer's defense, his back was injured early in the game when Huff picked him up and slammed him into the ground. Moore nearly came out after that, but Ewbank urged him to continue playing, if only as a decoy, because the Giants' defense was keying on him.)

Time after time, watching the vaunted Giants defense in action, Reid remarked how much he wished he could play against it. Landry's squad lined up in the same formation, with the same personnel, on almost every down.

"Very seldom do you see the same formation in a game anymore," he said. "That's just the way it is today. But this was just a part-time job for these guys. They didn't have the time to be in the building [for classroom study] all day."

Again, Reid was right. Most pro players in the 1950s held down full-time jobs off the field. Huff was a salesman for the textile company J. P. Stevens. Unitas and many of his teammates worked at Bethlehem Steel. Art Donovan, the Colts' hilarious defensive tackle known as Fatso, was a liquor salesman. Most of the men earned less than $10,000 a year playing football. The highest-paid stars made between $15,000 and $20,000— enough to support a middle-class lifestyle in 1958, but nothing like today's hefty paychecks. Players who took off from their full-time jobs to play were often expected to make up the time by working long hours in the off-season. This made them better prepared for life after football than many of their modern counterparts are, but it also meant that they were less prepared for Sunday's action.

Still, even if players had been able to devote time to perfecting more-complex schemes, Reid noted, there simply wouldn't have been enough time to implement them, because of the quicker, pre-television speed of the game. In today's NFL, coaches will often alter both the personnel and the formation of their teams between downs.

The biggest difference between the two eras—literally— is the size and speed of modern athletes. The average player on the 1958 Colts starting team weighed 222 pounds. The average weight of a 2007 Indianapolis Colts starter was 243 pounds. And there is ample reason to believe that today's pros are not just bigger, but faster. For one thing, the league draws on a talent pool far broader and deeper than in the past. It was widely believed (and the evidence on the field suggested) that in the 1950s the league limited the number of African American players, with an unwritten agreement restricting each team to seven. Today, merit is the only criterion, and in some parts of the country, prospects for the pro game are selected and groomed when they are still in grade school. Training methods, dietary habits, coaching, and the quality of competition at all levels have vastly improved. In most cases, the modern pro football player has been preparing to play the game for most of his young life.

Even the kickers have evolved. Few modern teams lack field-goal kickers who can readily boot the ball through the uprights from forty yards out, while the old toe-kickers, like Steve Myhra for the Colts and even Pat Summerall for the Giants, were shaky beyond twenty. The consistency of modern kickers has transformed offensive strategy. In the overtime period of the classic game, for instance, the Colts elected to run five plays from inside the Giants' twenty-yard line, because Ewbank did not trust Myhra enough to wager the game on his leg.

I asked Reid whether any of the legends on the field in 1958 might be able to keep up in today's game.

"I was looking to try to see players that I thought could play today," he said. "I think Moore probably could, and Raymond Berry would probably find a way to play. Gifford. Andy Nelson,

261

he looked pretty good on that one run. I don't know what kind of all-out speed he had, but it looked like he moved around pretty good. And Unitas. Unitas could play."

Reid noticed a similarity between the old Colts superstar and the future Hall of Fame quarterback he had coached in Green Bay.

"There are only two quarterbacks that finish their throw," he said. "You always teach chin-to-shoulder follow-through. Your head follows through to your chin when you throw . . . The ball is going to go where your head goes, and if you are consistent with your head placement . . . normally good things will happen. There are only two quarterbacks who do it. Unitas and Brett Favre. Watch: every time, they follow through. It's chin to shoulder. You won't find any other quarterbacks that do it, but both those guys do it naturally."

We were watching Unitas at his finest. With less than two minutes on the clock, down by three points and eighty-six yards from the goal line, he orchestrated a brilliant seven-play passing drive. Three completions in the middle of this march, all of them to Berry, set up a game-tying field goal. (Sam Huff says that he is still haunted, a half century later, by the Yankee Stadium loudspeaker barking "Unitas to Berry, Unitas to Berry.") With just seven seconds on the clock, Ewbank had no choice but to send in Myhra, who booted the game-tying nineteen-yard field goal to set up the first overtime in pro history. It remains the only overtime ever in an NFL Championship game.

At this point, Reid had become a rapt spectator.

"This is just simple football right now, man," he said.

The Giants won the toss and got the ball first in overtime, but they failed to make a first down. They punted, and Unitas did it again, this time without pressure from the clock, mixing runs and passes to move his team eighty yards in thirteen plays. Berry caught two more passes for twenty-one and twelve yards, and then Unitas, spotting Huff cheating to his right in an effort to stop Berry, sent Ameche up the center on a perfectly executed trap play. The Colts' right tackle, George Preas, raced across the defensive backfield to flatten the middle linebacker and clear a path for the fullback, who sprinted twenty-two yards up the middle of the field to the Giants' twenty-yard line.

It ended five plays later, when Ameche plunged over the goal line for the winning touchdown—with Moore, still playing hurt, throwing a perfect block to clear the way. Reid said, simply, "Awesome."

Source Notes

Interviews

Al Barry

Raymond Berry

Al Brennan

Lindon Crow

Milt Davis

Art Donovan

Rosey Grier

Marcia Hersch Haskin

Milt Horn

Sam Huff

Jack Kemp

Neil Leifer

Gino Marchetti

Don Maynard

Bob Mischak

Jim Mutscheller

Andy Nelson

Buzz Nutter

Andy Reid

Alex Sandusky

Pat Summerall

Charley Winner

Bibliography

Books

America's Game: The Epic Story of How Pro Football Captured a Nation, by Michael MacCambridge, Anchor Books, 2005.

Johnny Unitas: America's Quarterback, by Lou Sahadi, Triumph Books, 2004.

Johnny U: The Life and Times of Johnny Unitas, by Tom Callahan, Crown Publishers, 2006.

The Greatest Football Game Ever Played, by John Steadman, Press Box Inc., 1988.

Backseat Quarterback, by Perian Conerly, University Press of Mississippi, 2003.

Sundays at 2:00 with the Baltimore Colts, by Vince Bagli and Norman L. Macht, Tidewater Publishers, 1995.

Of Mikes and Men: From Ray Scott to Curt Gowdy, by Curt Smith, Diamond Communications, 1998.

Football in Baltimore: History and Memorabilia, by Ted Patterson, The Johns Hopkins University Press, 2000.

The Fifties, by David Halberstam, Fawcett, 1993.

Wellington: The Maras, the Giants, and the City of New York, by Carlo DeVito and Sam Huff, Triumph Books, 2006.

All Things Being Equal: The Autobiography of Lenny Moore, by Lenny Moore with Jeffrey Jay Ellish, Sports Publishing LLC, 2005.

Tales from the New York Giants Sidelines: A Collection of the Greatest Stories Ever Told, by Paul Schwartz, Sports Publishing LLC, 2004.

Always a Winner, by Don Shinnick as told to James C. Hefley, Zondervan Publishing House, 1969.

Tom Landry: An Autobiography, by Tom Landry with Gregg Lewis, Harper-Prism, 1991.

When the Colts Belonged to Baltimore: A Father and a Son, a Team and a Time, by William Gildea, Houghton Mifflin, 1994.

Tough Stuff, by Sam Huff with Leonard Shapiro, St. Martin's Press, 1988.

When Pride Still Mattered: A Life of Vince Lombardi, by David Maraniss, Simon and Schuster, 2000.

Pigskin: The Early Years of Pro Football, by Robert W. Peterson, Oxford University Press, 1997.

The Game of Their Lives, by Dave Klein, Random House, 1976.

The Football Encyclopedia: The Complete History of Professional NFL Football from 1892 to the Present, by David S. Neft, Richard M. Cohen, and Rick Korch, St. Martin's Press, 1991.

Pamphlets

"Here's Why It Was the Best Football Game Ever," by Tex Maule with illustrations by Robert Riger, William H. Shriver and Helicon Press (a reprint from the pages of *Sports Illustrated*), 1959.

Some Tips From Raymond Berry: Drills for Catching, by Raymond Berry, unpublished, 1972.

Recordings

The NBC Radio Broadcast, NBC News Archives. Announcers Joe
    Boland and Bill McColgan.
NFL Films *The Greatest Game*, 1998.
NFL Films *1958 Baltimore Colts Team Highlights (Season in Review)*.
NFL Films *1958 New York Giants Highlights (Season in Review)*.
NFL Films *1958 Championship (Coaches' Tape)*.

Chapter One
Football Noir

It was freezing . . . black and white. Field conditions are from press accounts,
the NBC radio broadcast, and interviews with players. Attendance from
The Football Encyclopedia, press accounts. Although many subsequent
accounts of the game have said that it was a full house, including
Wellington, the fact that the stadium was not full was noted in John
Steadman's *The Greatest Football Game Ever Played,* along with many press
accounts at the time. Steadman wrote: "Six thousand less than had
watched them on the same field Nov. 9 [which] set what became . . . an
all-time New York pro football crowd, 71,163. Why was this one not
a sellout? It couldn't be blamed on television because the New York
metropolitan area was blacked out. Numerous other factors were responsible. It was the Sunday after Christmas, the end of the holiday
weekend, when a segment of the population had traveled home for
family visits. There also were airline strikes in some parts of the country
—plus the New York daily newspapers were shut down for seventeen
days" (p. 29) . . . Images from NFL Films. *Spooky black and white . . . black
backdrop.* The number of TV viewers varies from account to account. I

have gone with MacCambridge's number, which is the most conservative. *Entertainment Weekly* in 2008 ranked the game as number 14 on a list of "the greatest moments in the history of television," right behind the Watergate hearings and just ahead of Oprah Winfrey's first national telecast. *National Football League . . . in Philadelphia.* NY Times, 12/29/58, Jack Gould, "Football Blackout Pierced." Gould wrote: "The picture was badly speckled and streaked but even with the visual handicaps the game was the sports spectacle of the year." *President Eisenhower . . . Coca-Cola.* NY Times, 12/29/58, (UPI) "President Passes Leisurely Sunday." *Brooks Robinson . . . game live.* Steadman, *The Greatest Football Game Ever Played. Auto mechanic . . . for the game.* Ed Chaney, Jr, letter to *The Baltimore Sun,* 12/28/83. *At the home . . . against listening.* Gildea, *When the Colts Belong to Baltimore. Many of the viewers . . . struck match.* NFL Films documentary, game day photos in *The Baltimore Sun* library. Some of the ambience of the grandstands in the period is from my memory of attending games with my father and brothers at Wrigley Field, Shea Stadium, and Memorial Stadium during the same period. *Nineteen-year-old . . . the day before.* Gildea. *Behind the end zone . . . on his birthday.* Leifer. *Joanne Kemp . . . NFL quarterback.* Jack Kemp. I covered some of the games Jeff Kemp ably quarterbacked for the Philadelphia Eagles in 1991. *Marcia Hersh . . . is being made!"* Marcia Hersh Haskin. *Consider the men . . . Hall of Fame.* The NFL Hall of Fame. *In 1958 . . . provide the Spark.* David Halberstam, *The Fifties.*

Early in the third quarter . . . room to maneuver. Background about the team comes from having grown up partly in New York and Baltimore during this period, general reading, and press accounts of the 1958 seasons in the *NY Times* and *The Baltimore Sun,* and NFL Films' excellent documentaries about the 1958 season of both teams. Details of the game are from the NFL Films documentary, the coaches' film (supplied to me by NFL Films). Andy Reid, the head coach of The Philadelphia Eagles, who kindly spent hours reviewing this film with me, breaking

the game down play-by-play and giving me invaluable insight and analysis. The NBC radio broadcast of the game was provided by NBC. I
also referred to the detailed play-by-play account of the game by Steadman. *Lindon Crow . . . anything fancy.* Crow. *The play called . . . five-yard line.*
Mutscheller, NFL Films *The Greatest Game* (interview with Cliff Livingston). Tom Callahan described the mix-up on this play in his book *Unitas,*
through the eyes of both Ameche and Mutscheller, who told the author, "He [Ameche] threw like a girl. But even Alan could have completed that one." *It set up . . . much give.* NBC radio broadcast, NFL Films
The Greatest Game. Looking on . . . a healthy sign. Background about Bell is
from MacCambridge, pp. 41–42, Steadman, and a marvelous profile
of Bell by Al Hirschberg in the *NY Times,* "He Calls the Signals for Pro
Football," 11/23/58. *Still, there was TV . . . suspense of live action.* Halberstam,
pp. 185–186. *That's how it had . . . right in the game. . . ."* "Television Forward Passes Football to the Home: A Kick-Off on the Air" *NY Times,*
10/15/39. *Baseball seemed made . . . Red Barber.* George Vecsey, "Voices
From the Past Are Echoing Today" *NY Times* 1/13/08, *In the full-throated
din . . .* Crowd noise from the NBC radio broadcast. *Milt Davis . . . like a
wooden peg.* Davis. *Alex Webster . . . awarded the touchdown.* NFL Films *The
Greatest Game,* Nelson, Davis.

Chapter Two
Raymond

The tall, skinny young man . . . same routine. Brennan, Berry. *Brennan had only
. . . was desperate.* Berry. *His name was Raymond . . . he told Winner.* Winner.
At a time when . . . locker to dry Berry, Winner. *Imagine how . . . little more room.*
Donovan, Sandusky, Marchetti, Winner. *Raymond had been drafted . . . lists
of reminders and observations.* Berry, Winner. *Football was a game . . . you were
dead.* This is my observation after interviewing pro football players for

three years after games; I covered the Philadelphia Eagles for *The Phila-delphia Inquirer* from 1990 through 1992. *Not Raymond . . . wide receiver.* Berry. *The idea of splitting . . . size and speed.* Most of this history was drawn from MacCambridge, but also from *The Football Encyclopedia,* and from Peterson, *Pigskin: The Early Years of Pro Football. When the position . . . rela-tively new, too.* Berry, http://smumustangs.cstv.com, "90 Greatest Mo-ments in SMU Football History." *The record didn't show . . . getting good.* Winner, Berry, Mutcheller, Donovan, Marchetti, Shinnick, *Always a Winner,* Callahan, *Johnny U,* Sahadi *Johnny Unitas: America's Quarterback,* Bal-timore Colts Press, Radio, TV Guide, 1959–1960," NFL Films docu-mentary *The Greatest Game,* and *1958 Colts Team Highlights (Season in Review), The Football Encyclopedia. But no one was more aware . . . terrific shape.* Berry. *At the time . . . boring routines.* Berry, Donovan, Nutter, Marchetti, Sandusky, Davis, Winner. *Raymond was one . . . "Johnny."* Berry, Winner.

Chapter Three
Johnny U

Raymond got . . . "Unitas." Berry. *He had grown up . . . ". . . professional foot-ball."* Sahadi pp. 27–31, Callahan pp. 16–17. *At the time . . . love of the game.* MacCambridge, Peterson, *NFL Encyclopedia,* DeVito, *Wellington. John would go on . . . first-string quarterback.* Callahan p. 21, Sahadi p. 32, Berry, Winner.

    As John was maturing . . . Paul Brown. Halberstam, Peterson, MacCam-bridge, Winner. *In the words . . . inquiry."* MacCambridge, p. 23. *As a high school coach . . . they knew it."* MacCambridge, Winner. *Before Brown . . . Sun-day afternoon.* Berry, Winner, Donovan, and my observations of modern football practices under Buddy Ryan, a disciple of Weeb Ewbank, dis-ciple of Brown. *Led by Otto . . . Weeb Ewbank.* MacCambridge, *The Football Encyclopedia. Weeb was . . . to do so.* Winner, Berry, Mutscheller and Donovan (on Weeb's handling of Ameche) Sahadi quotes Unitas about in, pp. 276–277, "Weeb was on him constantly. He would just berate Ameche constantly. Weeb felt he had to do that, to get after Ameche to make him play. And you really didn't have to." The Renfro anecdote is from Berry. *Despite this tendency . . . that he did.* Mutscheller, Nutter, Donovan, Sandusky, Winner.

In the years . . . build a winner. Jesse Linthicum, "Rosenbloom, Head of Colts, Has Fine Football Background," *The Baltimore Sun* 9/30/56, MacCambridge pp. 78–79, Ted Patterson, "Football in Baltimore" p. 97, *The Football Encyclopedia. Weeb got the job . . . six points!* Winner, Berry, Donovan. The Finnin anecdote is from Donovan. The Womble story is from Winner.

John Unitas . . . had left the field. Callahan, Sahadi, Berry, Winner, Donovan. *Staying after . . . the torture of training camp.* Donovan. Nutter, Winner. *The brutal summer practices . . . every penny.* Parker interview in Bagli & Macht, *Sundays at 2:00 with the Baltimore Colts* p. 23. *Competition was fierce . . . out of his job.* Nutter, Sandusky. Jack Bighead, an all-American at Pepperdine University, played two years in the NFL, one with the Colts and the other with the Rams. He caught just six passes. He had played himself in the movie *Jim Thorpe—All-American,* and went on to a long career playing bit Indian roles in television and film. *Raymond found . . . from a distance.* Berry, Winner. The description of Unitas's exaggerated throwing motion comes from Andy Reid, who noted that Brett Favre, whom he coached as an assistant at Green Bay, was the only other quarterback he had ever seen who threw that way. "It's perfect mechanics," Reid said. "It makes for consistent accuracy." *The coaches were all amazed . . . ungainly stoop.* Winner, Ewbank in Bagli & Macht, p. 47. *The first few times . . . get in his way?"* Callahan, p. 80. *Unlike Shaw . . . receivers' hands.* Reid, Berry. *"I can work with . . . passing game.* Berry. *Don Shula . . . two touchdowns.* Callahan, p. 69. *Lenny Moore . . . cover, too.* Callahan, p. 96. Moore, "All Things Created Equal." *Both Raymond and John . . . resident nut.* Winner,

Berry. *For all his intensity . . . to his players.* Winner, Marchetti. *When Gene . . . handed it over.* Donovan, Sandusky. *At the beginning . . . league championship.* Nutter. *So Rosembloom was . . . scouting trips.* Winner. *Weeb already had . . . Andy Nelson.* Winner, Berry, Donovan, Mutscheller. *His offense . . . this guy?* Mutscheller. *From that first day . . . would need.* Winner, Berry, *The Football Encyclopedia.* "*I always figured . . . Cameron Snyder.*" Callahan p. 3. *He was the opposite . . . trusted him completely.* These are impressions formed in part by my own memory of Unitas, but also from interviews with his teammates, and by Callahan and Sahadi. *According to Callahan . . .* "*Shaw ain't coming back.*" Callahan p. 81. *Throughout the game . . . all that would follow.* Mutscheller, Berry, Nutter, Callahan p. 81.

Chapter Four
Huff

The Colts team . . . in NFL history. The Football Encyclopedia. There was more to it . . . elected All-Pro. Berry, Winner, Huff, Reid, *The Football Encyclopedia. Success not only . . . he missed.* Winner, Berry. Raymond wrote and self-published a handbook in 1972 entitled, *Some Tips from Raymond Berry: Drills for Catching,* which breaks down his methodology in great detail. The terminology quoted here is from this handbook. *Weeb sometimes worried . . . pointing at the receiver.* Gildea p. 125. *Weeb had such respect . . .* "*Why didn't you say so?*" Winner, Berry. *During the season . . . and play action.* Berry, Sahadi's interview with Unitas at the end of his biography p. 273, Bagli & Macht p. 72. *He got better every year . . . John didn't play. The Football Encyclopedia. He watched it on television . . . the New York bench.* Donovan, Callahan pp. 135–137, Sahadi (Unitas interview) pp. 258–259. *The franchise . . . point spreads.* Callahan, Sahadi, Donovan, Winner, Berry, Nutter, Marchetti. *The Giants were one of the . . . a professional triumph.* This thumbnail sketch of the Maras is from Carol DeVito's *Wellington: The Maras, the Giants, and the City of New York. More than most . . . the NFL championship.* Huff, Grier, Huff in Dave Klein's, *The Game of Their Lives,* David Maraniss's *When Pride Still Mattered,* p. 160, Huff & Shapiro's *Tough Stuff,* Tom Landry & Gregg Lewis, *Tom Landry: An Autobiography. A squat, dark, driven man . . . Book of Revelation."* Maraniss, p. 155. Impressions of Lombardi are mostly from Maraniss's superb biography. The connection, or lack of it, with Wellington Mara is on p. 153. "rough soul" is on pp. 98–99. *But Lombardi . . . split him wide.* Maraniss, Reid, who in watching the championship game film noted with admiration as the Giants' offensive line executed a perfect "Packers" sweep months before Lombardi began coaching in Green Bay. *The new offensive coach's . . . the team's history.* Maraniss p. 158, Gay Talese, "Of Pigskins and Hams," *NY Times,* 6/26/58. *As important . . . was required.* Landry & Lewis, The split lip story is on p. 93. Huff. *In his first game . . . team in the league.* Landry & Lewis, the Mac Speedie story is on p. 87. *As talent scouts . . . best defensive backs in league history.* Neil Amdur, *NY Times,* "Emlen Tunnell, 50, Dies, Star of Football Giants," 7/24/75. *The Maras had signed Rote . . . first pick.* DeVito p. 121. *The Maras tracked down . . . season started.* Klein pp. 63–78, Arthur Daley, "Clutch Hitter," *NY Times* 11/24/57. *Andy Robustelli . . . Los Angeles Rams 1956.* DeVito p. 135. *The Rams threw in . . . "The great negotiator."* Grier. *The Maras traded for . . . Carl Karilivacz.* Louis Effrat, "Giants Hope to Draft 1959 Quarterback Before Supply Runs Out," *NY Times,* 11/25/58. *They used their first . . . their running game.* Arthur Daley, "The Eager Beaver," *NY Times* 9/18/58. *Of all the players . . . him as Sam.* Huff, *The Football Encyclopedia.*

Sam Huff had been . . . cut the next day. Huff, Huff & Shapiro, Maraniss. Huff has been telling these stories for many years, and there tend to be slight variations, but I went with my interview.

Just as he had . . . even his name seemed perfect. Huff, Landry & Lewis, "Tex Maule "Giants' Killer," *Sports Illustrated,* 11/24/58. Time "A Man's Game" 11/30/59. The sleeping Grier anecdote is from Dave Anderson, "For Mara, Memories Are Framed Forever," *NY Times,* 1/7/01.

Chapter Five
Getting There

When the Giants . . . paid less than $10,000 a year. Perian Conerly, "Backseat Quarterback," Huff, UPI "Gifford, Star Halfback of Giants, Signs Seven-Year Film Contract," *NY Times* 2/18/58, Gay Talese, "Gifford, Ace Halfback of Giants, Is Ready to become Actor," *NY Times*, 6/26/58. Gifford on dining with Hemingway in Paul Schwartz, *Tales from the New York Sidelines*, pp. 24–25. *The extra money . . . another sterling season in 1957.* Huff, Huff & Shapiro. *Many of the Giants . . . playing cards and talking.* Perian Conerly, Klein p. 212. Arthur Daley, "The Old Pro," *NY Times* 11/4/58. *This life was a far cry . . . made playing in the city a pleasure.* Mutscheller, Marchetti, Donovan, Sandusky, Berry, Winner, Gildea (the Ogden Nash poem is from p. 11), Steadman, Tex Maule, "Love Affair in Baltimore," *Sports Illustrated*, 12/1/58, Bagli & Macht, Callahan.

    That pleasure . . . "Big Daddy" Lipscomb. Davis, Marchetti, Winner, Grier, Moore's "All Things Being Equal," Klein, Bagli & Macht (particularly Parker's comments pp. 17–30). *Lipscomb, a giant . . . to disappear in his grasp.* Winner. The "North College" anecdote is from Bob Wolff, "There Are No Great Teams Anymore . . ." *NY Times*, 12/25/88, and from Curt Smith *Of Mikes and Men*, quoting Wolff, p. 59. *He was a pro wrestler . . . dangerous scowl.* Donovan, Marchetti, Winner. Moore p. 73 (on how fighting led to Lipscomb's release from the Rams). *At one training camp . . . I change seats."* Winner. *On the practice field . . . in the shade!"* Winner. *Blacks were considered . . . as his white teammates.* Davis, Moore. *Moore, who was a jazz . . . we never mingled."* Moore p. 75. *White teammates . . . kill his business.* Moore writes movingly about this experience. He described attending a banquet honoring a prize fighter in Baltimore that attracted many of the city's pro athletes, including many of his teammates. They had just won the '58 championship game, and Moore found he was the only black person to show up for the event at a white country club. He was admitted only after a long and embarrassing delay, and felt shunned. "I saw my teammates, Art Donovan and Jim Mutscheller; but they didn't seem too eager to speak to me." He ended up leaving the banquet feeling disappointed and insulted. (pp. 93–94). Davis described being refused admittance to the movie theater, and Ameche's response, and was shocked when I told him later about Parker's experience at Ameche's restaurant in Reisterstown, which was related to me by Marchetti. *There was a kinship . . . "Big Daddy."* Davis. *Rosenbloom may have . . . several Colts ones.* Parker in Bagli & Macht. *Weeb wanted to convert . . . I'd just applaud."* Donovan. *Parker learned . . . several times a week.* Parker in Bagli & Macht pp. 20–21.

 The owner didn't just . . . their homes. Marchetti, Berry. *The highest-paid player . . . $11,250.* Marchetti. *Buzz Nutter . . . $6,500.* Nutter. *Davis made . . . previous season.* Davis. *Moore was earning . . . $12,000.* Moore, "All Things Being Equal," p. 81. Moore started the 1957 season earning $11,500, and annual raises tended to be in the $500 to $1,000 range. *Raymond was . . . at that point.* Berry. *John Unitas . . . by 1958.* Callahan p. 172. *Even the lowest of these . . . $20,000.* Income figure is from the U.S. Census, "Current Population Reports, Consumer Income," 2/28/63. Car prices from www.thepeoplehistory.com/50scars.html. My parents bought our house in Timonium, Maryland, a Baltimore suburb six years later for $25,000. *Despite their contract battles . . . quite lucrative.* Steadman p. 78, Nutter, Berry, Donovan, Sandusky, Marchetti, Davis. *Just weeks before . . . hamburger chain called Gino's.* Marchetti. *There were chances . . . double their salary.* Steadman p. 77. The winnings were widely reported in the days after the game.

 Frank Gifford . . . wouldn't blame him." UPI "Gifford, Star Halfback of Giants, Signs Seven-Year Film Contract," *NY Times* 2/18/58, Gay Talese, "Gifford, Ace Halfback of Giants, Is Ready to become Actor," *NY Times,* 6/26/58. *Gifford may just . . . pilot episode.* AP, "Gifford Joins Football Giants," *NY Times* 8/7/58. http://www.filmreference.com/film/41/Frank-Gifford.html. *The team dropped . . . two more.* Barry, Louis

Effrat, "Football Giants Open League Season by Overpowering Cardinals . . .," *NY Times*, 9/29/58. *They lost . . . Unitas-less Colts. The Football Encyclopedia. In that Colts victory . . . pelting them with stones.* Louis Effrat, "Summerall's Kick Wins 24-21 Game," *NY Times*, 10/10/58. Arthur Daley, "The Tightrope Walkers," *NY Times*, 11/16/58. *It was during halftime . . . trade for him."* Nutter. *The win tied . . . championship game. The Football Encyclopedia. New York played . . . Giants won 13-10.* Summerall, Huff, Tex Maule, "49 Yards and One Foot," *Sports Illustrated*, 12/22/58. *The victory set up . . . play the Colts.* Huff. *The Football Encyclopedia.*

Chapter Six
Fumble-it is

The Colts flew . . . free sandwiches and beer. Donovan, Berry, Steadman pp. 24–25. *The team offered . . . at eleven.* Donovan. *Just before curfew . . . one shouted.* Marchetti. *Weeb liked . . . you could find.* Donovan, Nutter, Winner. *Any edge . . . his team, too.* Winner, Steadman pp. 20–21. *Mornings in the hotel . . . who they were playing.* Steadman pp. 26–28. *They took a bus . . . the locker room.* Donovan, Berry, Steadman pp. 28–29.

    To Raymond . . . the big game. Berry. *With them were . . . up to the Bronx.* Albert Sehlstedt, Jr. "Looking Back, It's still 'The Greatest,'" *The Baltimore Sun*, 12/18/83. Steve O'Neill, "Strain of Battle Tired Fans, Too," Baltimore News-Post, 12/29/58.

    Both teams . . . fill the seats. Coaches' game film, NFL Films. *Teenage photographer . . . left field wall.* Leifer. *In the radio broadcast booth . . . share of enthusiasm.* NBC radio game broadcast. *In the press box . . . contradicted the label."* Red Smith, "Colts Had Horses for Stretch Run," *The Philadelphia Inquirer*, 12/30/58. *Down on the field . . . before they do."* Donovan. *Back in the locker room . . . mattered that season.* Winner, Donovan, Berry, Marchetti, Davis, Sandusky, Steadman pp. 30–31, Sahadi, pp. 6–7. *In a ghostwrit-*

ten . . . all week. Cameron Snyder, "Charley's Words Put on Wall," *The Baltimore Sun,* 12/27/58. Shinnick "Always a Winner," p. 88. *Linebacker Don . . . with the world.* Steadman, Shinnick, p. 89.

In 1958 . . . in the grandstand. John P. Shanley, "Football on Camera," *NY Times,* 10/26/58. *New York won . . . on its own twenty.* Game film and the radio broadcast. *Early in the season . . . run the offense.* Klein pp. 220–221, Maraniss, p. 171. *His first attempted pass . . . could not move it.* Game film and radio broadcast. *Al Barry . . . evil grin.* Barry. *Lombardi's offense . . . Lindon Crow.* Game film and radio broadcast. *Crow was from . . . sprinted downfield.* Crow. *Crow recovered . . . field goal.* Game film and radio broadcast. *It was on . . . Dick Syzmanski.* Mutscheller, Donovan, Winner, Bagli & Macht pp. 43–44. *His uniform . . . could score.* Game film, radio broadcast, Donovan. *Lombardi chose . . . would be.* Game film and radio broadcast.

The Giants opened . . . on his back. Game film and radio broadcast. *The running back . . . told Moore.* Moore, p. 91, and in NFL Films' *The Greatest Game,* 1998. *The touchdown had come . . . of accomplishment.* Game film, Berry. *In fact, Grier . . . long blue cape.* Grier, game film. *Sloppy play . . . the goal line.* Game film, radio broadcast. *When the Colts . . . softly thrown pass.* Berry, game film. *The Baltimore Colts . . . Alex Webster fumbled.* Game film, radio broadcast.

Chapter Seven
Three Plays

In their locker room . . . "We'll win." Huff. *Up in the NBC . . . stay alive.* Radio broadcast. *At one end . . . waved him back.* Leifer. *Emotions on both sides . . . were following him."* Game film, radio broadcast, Huff, Donovan, Marchetti, Winner. Gordon S. White, Jr. "Baltimore Coach Nettled by Huff," *NY Times,* 12/29/58. In a 12/28/59 *NY Times* article, "Football in His Eyes," Weeb acknowledged attacking Huff. "I'm not proud of what

I did," he said. *Watching from his own . . . strong wind.* Klein. *His teammates . . . Landry's defense.* Game film, radio broadcast. *Huff would goad . . . in the first half.* Huff, Klein, pp. 222–223 (Conerly on the rivalry), p. 32 (Huff on Gifford). *But the magic . . . smell another championship.* Game film, radio broadcast, (on Schnelker) Huff, Crow, Mishak, Barry, *Football Encyclopedia*), Davis. *Up in the press box . . . new Corvette.* Steadman p. 37, Perian Conerly p. 229. *Baltimore was not about . . . said Marchetti.* Donovan in NFL Films' *The Greatest Game.*

Time was running out . . . hopes fading. Game film, radio broadcast. *New York coach . . . half century later.* Game film, radio broadcast, Donovan, Marchetti, Klein (Stroud on pp. 116–117), Steadman pp. 38–39. In Michael Eisen's *Stadium Stories: The New York Giants*, published in 2005, Gifford says, "There's no question in my mind, even this far removed from it," that he made the first down. Gifford and most of the principles discuss the play on camera in the NFL Films' *The Greatest Game.* In that documentary, it is interesting to note that the New York writers claim that Gifford made it, while the Baltimore writers all insist that is was clear that he did not. The angle of the game film is inconclusive, the camera is at such a distance and the pile of bodies too thick, but I find it significant that the NBC announcers calling the game on radio never wavered in their view that Gifford failed to make the first down. I found a curious account of this play that stands as a testament to the fallibility of human memory: In Bagli & Macht, p. 83, Ordell Braase insists that Marchetti was not playing on this down; that he had already been injured and "was sixty yards downfield lying on a stretcher." Braase goes on to describe his part in the play in great detail, placing himself in on the tackle with Donovan. "This was one of the biggest plays of my career . . . but the play-by-play accounts have Marchetti making that tackle on Gifford, and he was in the locker room on a stretcher." The game film shows that Marchetti was on neither the sideline nor in the locker room; he made the tackle, saved the first down, and broke his ankle on that play. *But the ruling . . . loneliness at the top.* Kemp, Huff, Maraniss p. 187, Red Smith, "Colts Had Horses," *The Philadelphia Inquirer* 12/30/58, Steadman p. 48 and p. 75. Louis Effrat, "Football Game in His Bedroom Keeps Giant Coach From Sleep," *NY Times* 12/30/58. *And we see . . . had decided the other way.* Radio broadcast, Huff.

Exuding the calm . . . get to work." Berry, Mutscheller, Nutter. *He led off . . . three men's heads.* Game film, radio broadcast. *Marchetti was watching . . . study in intensity.* Marchetti and the famous photo, which can be viewed at the Web site for the Pro Football Hall of Fame: www.profootballhof .com. *John's deliberate . . . just three yards deep.* Berry, Huff, game film, radio broadcast. I am indebted for help in analyzing these critical plays to Berry and to Andy Reid, and also to a terrific and very detailed illustrated account of the game's crucial plays, later published as a pamphlet, by *Sports Illustrated*'s Tex Maule and Robert Riger, "Here's Why It Was the Best Football Game Ever." *Here's Berry . . . five-yard gain.* Berry, Callahan pp. 163–164. *Huff was so . . . inside their heads.* Huff. *Upstairs in the . . . play again.* Radio broadcast. *The Colts could not . . . another gain of fifteen.* Game film, radio broadcast. *With less than a minute . . . first two targets.* Game film Berry. *Before the game . . . from behind.* Berry, game film, radio broadcast. *Three plays . . . sprinted on.* Huff, game film. *Back in Baltimore . . . on the top step.* *The Baltimore Sun,* 12/29/58/. *George Shaw . . . crossbar.* Edwin H. Brandt, "Myhra thought his kick would be good for tie," *The Baltimore Sun,* 12/29/58. *In Baltimore . . . ceiling fixture.* Gildea p. 239.

Chapter Eight
Living to See Sudden Death

Sam Huff . . . a little happy. Huff. *With seven seconds left . . . talking about?"* Game film, radio broadcast, Huff. *Few of his teammates . . . asked Barry.* Barry. *"What happens now? . . . the receiver.* Summerall, NFL Films' *The Greatest Game.* "Shit, *man . . . said Huff.* Huff. *Gifford was . . . I just can't."* Klein p. 22. *Colts safety . . . wanted to win.* Nelson. *Raymond had . . . of the field.* Berry. *Bert Bell had fought . . . proved his point.* MacCambridge x-xi, xvi, Hirschberg, *NY Times* 11/23/58. *At midfield . . . hands on his hips.* Game film, radio broadcast, Steadman p. 41. *At Henry Mack's . . . another beer.* Ed Chaney, Jr, letter to *The Baltimore Sun,* 12/28/83. *A most historic moment . . . set for the kickoff.* Radio broadcast.

It was now . . . was heading. Radio broadcast. MacCambridge p. xi. *At ground zero . . . to ice.* Berry. *Weeb stood . . . for Gino."* Steadman p. 41. *Colts kickoff man . . . to a score."* Game film, radio broadcast, Steadman p. 42. *Indeed, Howell once again . . . dramatic performance ever.* Game film, radio broadcast, Effrat, "Football Game in His Bedroom," *NY Times* 12/30/58. *The first play . . . knocked the football away.* Game film, radio broadcast, Crow. *Sensing triumph . . . thousands sitting overhead.* Game film, radio broadcast, Leifer, Marchetti. *On second and ten . . . hauled in the pass.* Berry, game film, radio broadcast. *"Unitas to Berry . . . that way again.* Huff, Berry, game film, radio broadcast. *Crouched behind center . . . he's been had.* Sahadi (Unitas interview) p. 271, Huff, Berry, game film. *And the trap . . . forty-four-yard line.* Huff, Klien (Unitas interview) p. 202, game film, radio broadcast. This is the play that haunts Huff, the play-calling trump that he recalls as the game's turning point. *It was the knockout punch . . . one minute earlier.* Huff. *But Weeb . . . unless he had to.* Bagli & Macht (Weeb interview) p. 44.

It wouldn't come . . . NBC had lost its connection. Game film, radio broadcast, Berry, Huff. *Nowhere was this taken harder . . . the screen.* Ed Chaney, Jr, letter to *The Baltimore Sun,* 12/28/83. *Joey Radomski . . . absolutely appalling."* Gildea, pp. 240–241. *Someone in the crowd . . . remarkably, prepared.* Smith, *Of Mikes and Men* (interviews with Chris Schenkel, Chuck Thompson, and Lindsey Nelson) pp. 62–64. *In years to come . . . eight-yard line.* Shanley, "Football on Camera" *NY Times,* 10/26/58, radio broadcast, NFL Films' *The Greatest Game,* Smith pp. 62–64, Klein, p. 203. *On a play called . . . two-yard line.* Mutscheller, Steadman pp. 65–66, Callahan

p. 169, game film, radio broadcast, Paul Zimmerman, *Sports Illustrated*, 9/23/02. Zimmerman wrote, "Almost forty years later it still bothered John Unitas, the idea that people accused him of gambling at the end of the overtime drive . . . "It wasn't a gamble," said Unitas. "They didn't see what I saw . . . It was not a gamble, it was an educated move." *So it was third down . . . New York Giants seventeen.* Sahadi (Unitas interview) p. 272, Callahan p. 170, NFL Films' *The Greatest Game*, game film, radio broadcast. *Neil Leifer . . . famous photo of the game.* Leifer. *Up in the owner's box . . . I have ever seen."* Louis Effrat, "Colts Beat Giants, Win in Overtime," *NY Times*, 12/29/58, Steadman, p. 45. *Ameche was . . . locker room.* Nutter. *Their quarterback wasn't watching . . . from work.* Game film, Gildea noticed the same thing about Unitas's demeanor on that final play, pp. 8-9.

Chapter Nine
Epilogue

Alone in the locker room . . . quick flight home. Marchetti, Donovan, Steadman p. 47. *Once Raymond saw . . . it shook him.* Berry. *"WHO OUGUTTED WHO . . . happy din.* Steadman p. 45. *Raymond retreated . . . how he felt.* Berry, Tex Maule, "The Best Football Game Ever Played," *Sports Illustrated*, 1/5/59. *Out on the field . . . can you do?"* Steadman pp. 44–45, 47–65. Schwartz p. 158. *The gloom in their locker room . . . are the greatest."* NFL Films' *The Greatest Game*. *"We are the best . . . in the world!"* Steadman p. 47. *It went on . . . disappointed Giants fans.* Donovan. *Raymond also . . . game film.* Berry. *Ameche also stayed . . . made the big time.* Steadman p. 67, the clip of Ameche's *Ed Sullivan Show* appearance is in the NFL Films' *The Greatest Game*. *John had turned down . . . family-sized vehicle.* Steadman p. 67, Callahan pp. 174–75. *He went right back . . . it was Unitas."* Sahadi p. 56. *The team rode the bus . . . world champions escaped.* "30,000 Fans Greet Colts in Rowdy Airport Party," *The Baltimore Sun*, 12/29/58.

Carroll Rosenbloom . . . for $3,111. "Colts Team to Divide $50,000 Gift Purse," *NY Times,* 12/31/58, Steadman pp. 77–78. *The day after the game . . . fourth-quarter play.* Joe Trimble, *New York Daily News,* 12/30.58. *In the* New York Times *. . . is a football."* Arthur Daley, "One for the Books," *NY Times,* 12/29/58. *"The Best Game Ever . . . well into the billions.* NFL News, 12/12/06. *Franchises grew . . . to the championship. Bringing the Heat,* p. 57, p. 477. Forbes figures reported by AP, 7/31/06. Namath's contract from MacCambridge p. 407. *The Colts and Giants . . . with the game.* Robert McG. Thomas Jr., "Jim Lee Howell, Ex-Giants Coach, Dies at 80," *NY Times,* 1/6/1995. MacCambridge p. 126. *Vince Lombardi . . . first two Super Bowls,* Maraniss. *Tom Landry left New York . . . and winning two.* Landry & Lewis. *The great Giants teams . . . traded to Washington. The Football Encyclopedia. Frank Gifford remained . . . Monday Night Football broadcast.* NFL Hall of Fame bio. *His teammate . . . kicker in football.* Summerall. *The great Baltimore Colts . . . mixed feelings.* Memories of a former Baltimorean. William N. Wallace, "Carroll Rosenbloom, 72, Drowns in Miami . . ." *NY Times,* 4/3/79.

Acknowledgments

I would like to thank Morgan Entrekin, my editor and publisher, who had the idea for this book. In the summer of 2006, soon after the publication of my book *Guests of the Ayatollah*, we were discussing future projects, and Morgan suggested that I might consider supplementing my longer books, which usually took three to five years to research and write, with shorter ones that would not require such extensive legwork. As an example he cited David Halberstam, the great former *New York Times* reporter and author of such books as *The Best and the Brightest* and *The Powers That Be*, who in recent years had adopted just such a pace, writing smaller books on subjects he enjoyed, often concerning sports, beyond the weighty matters of war, history, and state that formed the bulk of his life's work. I had met David, had long admired him, and had read many of his books, both the short ones and the long ones.

"Why don't you consider a book about the 1958 NFL championship game?" Morgan suggested. "The fiftieth anniversary is coming up in two years, and I would love to publish a book to coincide with it."

As those who have read the book now know, I had grown up for the latter part of my childhood in Baltimore, and remembered the great Colts teams and players. I am a lifelong football fan, and played the game as a boy. Football was a part of my writing past, too. For three years at *The Philadelphia Inquirer* I had been the paper's football reporter, and the second of my books, *Bringing the Heat,* was about the 1992 Philadelphia Eagles. The idea immediately appealed to me.

It wasn't until I was months into the project that I heard about David's tragic death in a car accident on April 23, 2007 in Menlo Park, California. I was shocked to read that he had been killed researching a book on the same topic, not the least of which because Morgan and I had him so much in mind when we decided to undertake it. None of the players I had interviewed had been contacted by David, so I assumed that he must have just begun. I had been inspired by him from the days when he exposed the lies of American officials in Vietnam to his work as one of the great synthesizers of modern history. I had favorably reviewed his book *War in a Time of Peace* for *The Washington Post,* and he had very generously praised my book *Black Hawk Down* on numerous occasions. Indeed, after that book was published, he had sought me out to congratulate me personally, and we became friends. I had found him to be a warm and dynamic intellect, someone who embodied the highest values and traditions of journalism, and someone who fully understood the sheer *fun* of this kind of work. He would have done a great job with this story, and as much as I enjoyed working and writing it myself, I would like to have read his version. Indeed, if I had discovered that he was at work on the same story, I would have stopped. I discovered it only after he was killed. So, in a sense, I completed this book only because David could not, and have presumptuously dedicated it to him.

I was greatly assisted by Terrence Henry of *The Atlantic,* who helped find old newspaper stories, locate the players, and who even conducted several of the interviews for me. I would like to thank all of the players who consented to be interviewed for the millionth time about a game most of them only dimly remember, but most particularly Raymond Berry, whose memory of the game is as complete and precise as it was the week after it was played. Indeed, Raymond's insights shaped this book, and it is, in large part, about him. Few people can be said to have left such an impact on their chosen field. His just happened to have goal posts at either end.

Andy Reid, head coach of the Philadelphia Eagles, sat with me for hours reviewing the coaches' film of this game. I approached the Eagles' public relations chief, Derek Boyko, for help in finding a coach familiar with the pro game to help me analyze the film of the game. Initially Derek said he thought the team's coaches would all be too busy to help me, but they might be able to recommend someone who could. When he called me back, he said that all of the team's assistant coaches were eager to review the film with me themselves, but they would have to first get permission from Reid. Then Boyko called to say that Andy wanted to do it himself. I was originally scheduled to spend an hour with the head coach, but Andy asked his video staff to convert the DVD I brought with the old game film into a format that he could use on his own computer system, and then spent four or five hours with me breaking down the game play by play. It was tremendous fun, a fantasy for any lifelong football fan like myself, and his insights informed much of my understanding of what was happening on the field. I remain grateful.

I would also like to thank Meg Nakahara of the NBC News archives for providing me with a copy of the complete radio broadcast of the game, and my thanks go out to the late Joe Boland and Bill McColgan for their exciting, superb commentary, which spices my narrative throughout. I am grateful to Chris Willis of NFL Films, who dug out for me the old coaches' film of the game, along with the excellent documentaries prepared by that organization. My brother-in-law, Milt Horn, put me in touch with some fans who attended the game. Al Brennan helped set up a delightful lunch with Art Donovan and Alex Sandusky. The memoir written of this game by my late friend and colleague John Steadman, from the *Baltimore News-American*, was an invaluable source. John was a dogged and careful reporter, and he not only provided his own thorough account of the day, but with characteristic professional generosity included verbatim the stories of nearly every reporter in the press box. Paul McCartle at *The Baltimore Sun*'s library pulled together a rich trove of that newspaper's reporting and clips. I found William Gildea's delightful *When the Colts Belonged to Baltimore*, a very rich source of insight and anecdote, and I recommend his book to anyone curious about the special relationship between the city and the team broken by Robert Irsay's unforgivable decision to ship the franchise to Indianapolis.

Many thanks to all of the folks at Grove/Atlantic, particularly Michael Hornburg and Andrew Robinton, for their help in shepherding this book into print.

Index